The Modern
Social Conflict

The Modern Social Conflict

AN ESSAY ON THE POLITICS OF LIBERTY

Ralf Dahrendorf

Yea but I vilifie the present times, you say, whiles I expect a more flourishing state to succeed; bee it so, yet this is not to vilifie modernitie, as you pretend.

G. Hakewill, *Apologie* (1635)

Weidenfeld and Nicolson
London

First published in Great Britain in 1988 by
George Weidenfeld and Nicolson Limited
91 Clapham High Street, London SW4 7TA

Copyright © Ralf Dahrendorf 1988

British Library Cataloguing in Publication Data

Dahrendorf, Ralf, *1929–*
  The modern social conflict: an essay on
  the politics of liberty.
  1. Western world. Liberty
  I. Title
  323.44′09182′1

  ISBN 0 297 79357 8

Photoset by Deltatype, Ellesmere Port

Printed and bound in Great Britain
by Butler and Tanner Ltd,
Frome and London

Other books by Ralf Dahrendorf

Class and Class Conflict in Industrial Society
Essays in the Theory of Society
Society and Democracy in Germany
The New Liberty
On Britain
Life Chances
Law and Order

Contents

Preface

This is a book of ideas and analysis. It is an attempt to make sense of modern society in the light of the experience of an author whose social science has long been tempered by more practical concerns, such as winning elections and running institutions. When I called the book an essay, I had in mind the enlightened spirit in which 'An Essay Concerning Toleration' or 'An Essay on the History of Civil Society' were written more than two centuries ago. Both toleration and civil society play a part in my argument, though this is, as the title says, an essay concerning the modern social conflict and the politics of liberty.

In the last quarter of the twentieth century the tone of public debate is set by those who worry about innovation. 'How can we stimulate economic growth?' is the question uppermost in the minds of leaders. Great hopes are placed on new technologies, the information society, but also on entrepreneurs and the pulling force of incentives. This is Schumpeter's time, not that of Keynes. Increased flexibility, reduced social services, tax cuts are the order of the day. Even in the vast socialist empires of China and the Soviet Union, restructuring means the encouragement of initiative, of markets rather than plans. For friends of liberty, this is fine. Liberty needs change, innovation and a sense of enterprise; rigidity, stagnation, sclerosis are enemies of freedom.

Yet this is only one half of the story of human life chances. Leaving on one side the question of whether the great restructuring of the 1980s has actually worked, there are issues which it has left untouched. Worse still, some questions have become less tractable as a result of the new emphasis on growth and enterprise. In many European countries, unemployment has first grown in size and then hardened in kind; of the 10 per cent or more unemployed, about half have been in that position for more than a year. In the United States, the apparent miracle of the creation of millions of new jobs has to some extent detracted from an increase in the number of people below the official poverty line. A portion of these now find themselves in persistent poverty; they have become an underclass. Moreover, in both Europe and the United States, those who are most at risk seem to have a fatal fascination for the rest. There are many who fear that they too may one day be left out. A sense of decline has set in even where it is not based on the actual reduction of real incomes. Beyond economics, those at the margin of society have developed a curious magnetism, especially for the young. Their culture, if that is what it is, begins to envelop the rest like the sound of disco music.

If we look further afield, these may seem minor problems. As the developed world seeks new springs of growth, the less developed world sinks deeper into the quagmire of hunger, illness and tyranny. Of the five billion humans on our globe at the end of the 1980s, about one billion are in one way or another a part of the world of increasing life chances. At the other end, however, one billion find themselves at the very margin of existence. Most of them have little chance of surviving the next decade. The majority of those in between – three billion human beings – can at best hope to survive in their traditional cycle of poverty. There is no sign whatever of the wealth of the First World, or even the modest prosperity of the Second, let alone the dynamism of the *nics*, the newly industrializing countries, spilling over to the rest. For friends of liberty, this is unbearable.

Thus there is growth and there is poverty. Requirements of innovation compete with demands for justice. Such antinomies offer a first glimpse of the modern social conflict. I shall give them rather more technical names, but these do not detract from the fact that some people devote their energies to wealth creation, others to the extension of civil rights, and more often than not the two parties are at odds with each other. This is strange, because it is not inevitable. Liberty needs both, prosperity and citizenship, though perhaps citizenship rights for all are a condition of the enduring wealth of nations. But the moments of history when both were advanced by one set of policies, or even by one group, have remained rare. Most of the time, advocates of more choice and advocates of more rights for all have fought each other.

Many people believe that they have to take sides in this conflict. At any given moment, they may be right. In view of the dominant growth mood of the times, this essay is a plea for a new emphasis on citizenship. There is no better way of achieving this objective than by strategic changes which extend people's choices by enabling more people to choose. But in seeking such changes we must beware of one misunderstanding. Improved human life chances are not to be found in a synthetic 'third way' somewhere between the great forces of history. The halfway house of compromise is as great a risk to freedom as the dogmatism of extremes. While the latter means autocracy, the former leads to bureaucracy, and both are informed by the mistaken view that there is one valid answer to problems. My view is emphatically different. The politics of liberty is the politics of living with conflict. Diversity and equality each have their place in a constitution which seeks the greatest life chances for all.

Before I go on to indicate how this book tackles the subject, let me say a few words about those to whom it is addressed. Authors can of course be terribly wrong when they try to visualize their readers, but the risk does not deter them from having a view. At one stage I thought of George Bernard Shaw who sixty years ago wrote *The Intelligent Woman's Guide to Socialism and Capitalism*. The present essay is only in part about socialism and capitalism, but more importantly, intelligent women today would not appreciate being singled out in that way. Yet as a matter of fact, I did have certain women in mind as I was writing. When I lectured on the subject at the University of Basel in 1986, I found in my audience a number of attentive and critical wives of distinguished citizens of that city who wanted to transcend their husbands' interest-led views and make up their own minds. As a Visiting Scholar at the Russell Sage Foundation, I benefited from many a conversation with women fellows about comparable worth and women's rights, and also about effective ways of shifting entrenched structures and attitudes without leaving a trail of disaster. My wife, Ellen, and I share a need to place events of the day in context. Then I thought of my daughters Nicola, Alexandra and Daphne who have not found the world of the 1980s easy to cope with, but have not given up the search for meaning in what they are doing.

In the University of Oxford where I have taken up the post of Warden of St Antony's College as this book was completed, there is the expression 'town and gown'. I suppose this essay is addressed to those in gowns who like to look beyond the boundaries of their subject, be it economics, history or almost any other discipline of scholarship, as well as to those in town who share the concerns of 'intelligent women'. I hope that my professional colleagues in sociology will not be unduly disappointed. They may find too much politics on the one hand, and too much personal experience on the other. But then this book is not intended to be an original contribution to scholarship. It is an attempt to understand the forces at work in modern societies and to define the hopes for the future.

The book has several layers which I have tried to combine to form a viable whole. One of these layers is historical, if the social scientist can ever make such a claim. I am tracing the modern social conflict through the two centuries since the great revolutions. This inevitably leads to excursions and byways, such as the chapter on totalitarianism, which also explains the sources of my own liberal convictions. The 1960s, 1970s and the 1980s each deserve their own chapters. The contemporary bias of historical analysis remains evident throughout. Another layer of the whole is of course the subject of social conflict in the narrower sense, and more particularly of class conflict and what happened to it. I say 'of course' because some readers may have heard of my *Class and Class Conflict in Industrial Society* which was written thirty years ago. At the time, I propounded a view of conflict as a potential for progress which has remained with me to the present day. But to be fruitful conflict has to be domesticated by institutions. Yet another layer of this book has to do with the deceptions of revolution, and with the need for strategic changes instead.

Perhaps the word 'modern' in the title of this book will raise the eyebrows of those who share my dislike of labels. Its intention is largely practical. This essay is about the moderns, not the ancients. It is actually only about some moderns during a portion of the modern times, since it begins in the eighteenth century and makes but scant reference either to the developing countries (which I regret and hope to remedy at a later date) or to the countries of really existing socialism. I am writing about what I shall call the OECD world – the members of the 'club of the rich', the Organization for Economic Co-operation and Development – and above all about the three countries which have engaged my heart as well as my head, Germany, England and the United States of America.

But it is not as easy as that to get away with the moderns and their age. (Actually, the subject will be treated properly in the first chapter.) The word 'modern' itself is peculiar. Can it possibly mean more than that certain styles of dress and perhaps of thought are *à la mode*, in fashion? Several authors have recently traced the history of the word, to Baudelaire who indeed saw it this way ('modernity, that is the transitory, the fleeting, the contingent . . .'), to the debate about the ancients and the moderns which culminated in the Académie Française in 1687 (were the ancients perfect or can the moderns equal them?), and further to the time of the Archdeacon of Surrey, George Hakewill, from whom I have borrowed the motto of this book.[1] He would have remained one of those names in capital letters which follow quotations in the *Oxford Dictionary*, were it not for Robert Merton's brilliantly amusing discussion of Hakewill's contribution to the highly relevant debate about whether we stand *On the Shoulders of Giants*. Merton even quotes the full title of the book, *Apologie or Declaration of the Power and Providence of God in the Government of the World . . .* which was first published in 1627, and last in the third and enlarged edition of 1635.

Hakewill argues against 'pretended decay' and makes it clear that modernity is a phenomenon which calls for views and values; one can be for it and one can be against it. I quoted Hakewill because, like him, I am for it. While I shall 'vilifie the present times' often and harshly, 'this is not to vilifie modernitie'. This means above all that the present essay is not an exercise in postmodernity. On the contrary, it can be seen as a sustained argument against the postmoderns.[2] There is no need for such language. The forces of modernity are as strong as ever. Moreover, it is only a step from postmodern to antimodern sentiments. Of these, we see more than enough. A new fundamentalism is but the extreme version of the politics of cultural despair, and that has always been incompatible with the politics of liberty. We still have a long way to go to the realization of a world civil society, and we had better get on with it.

'Postism' has of course become a veritable author's disease: more and more writers want to impress on us that unheard-of things have happened in recent times, but since they cannot put their fingers on them, they settle for the claim that we are therefore living post-some-other-time. Perhaps I should not be too hard on them. For one thing, some of these authors are very good. Daniel Bell's *Coming of Post-Industrial Society* remains an important book, although Bell has moved on to other and perhaps pro-founder things. I myself spoke of 'post-capitalist society' in my book on *Class*. And under the influence of the excitable 1970s, I began a long manuscript entitled 'Modernity in Eclipse', which fortunately I did not publish.[3] The redeeming feature of its title is that it avoids 'postism', though only just; an eclipse passes and through a glass darkly one can see the sun return unscathed. For me at any rate, the sun of modernity has returned.

This is an essay in the politics of liberty. Its political bent is evident throughout; the analysis is content neither with describing the equilibria of markets nor with invoking amorphous social forces. The liberal predilection will become apparent. I am advocating a constitutional liberalism here which is as interested in the method of progress as in the next steps on the way. The main title of the essay, *The Modern Social Conflict*, speaks for itself. Much thought has gone into it. For some time, my working title was 'Citizenship, Life Chances and Liberty', and in fact these three concepts, and notably the first two, will figure prominently throughout the analysis. The claim implied by the definite article in the title, '*the* modern social conflict', is deliberate. Many kinds of conflict will be discussed as we go along, but I believe that one antagonism opens our eyes to core processes of modern society and politics. It is that between wealth and citizenship, or, as I shall call it, between provisions and entitlements.

While I have written a few books, I have never before had the benefit of as much friendly assistance as with this one. In part, such help was institutional. I have mentioned the University of Basel in Switzerland already, where I held a Visiting Professorship in the summer of 1986 (endowed by the Society of Friends of the University in the city, the Freiwillige Akademische Gesellschaft) which enabled or perhaps forced me to think through the entire argument of this book. Another set of lectures, at the invitation of the Fondazione Giovanni Agnelli in Turin in Italy, added further stimulus. Giovanna Zincone of the Centro Luigi Einaudi in Turin, who has herself written a long dictionary article on citizenship (*cittadinanza*), made valuable suggestions about Chapter 2.[4] The University of Konstanz in Germany, with which I have been associated since its inception in 1962, has once again shown understanding for the needs of a vagabond professor. In 1986–7, the Russell Sage Foundation in New York actually gave the vagabond professor a title, Visiting Scholar.

My debt to the Russell Sage Foundation is great. The place on East 64th Street provided that mixture of comfort and stimulation which an author needs. Both the officers of the Foundation and my fellow scholars have supported me in innumerable ways, and sometimes without realizing that they were in fact extending a helping hand or saying a helping word. The Foundation's President, Eric Wanner, and Vice-President, Peter de Janosi, have gone much further. They have read the entire manuscript and offered thoughtful comments, encouraging me to reinforce the central points that the modern social conflict has to do with a clash between economic and political forces, and that living with conflict is a prescription as well as a description.

At the Russell Sage Foundation, I had the good fortune to be once again close to the great sociologist Robert K. Merton. In the last forty years, he has done more than anyone else to realize the hopes of the eighteenth-century thinkers in a new science of society. Structural analysis (as I would call it) is above all associated with the name of Merton. He helped get many of my generation launched, including those who, like myself, initially used his approach to different ends from his. Merton sets standards. In his subtle and kind manner, he is also a severe taskmaster. He read the manuscript of this book from beginning to end. His literally hundreds of suggestions for improvements, clarifications and, most frequently, the explication of overly allusive statements have changed this text. For some time, I was not altogether sure whether he actually likes it, but in the end his comments were generous and appreciative. My respect and admiration for Robert Merton is coupled with deep gratitude.

My friend the historian Fritz Stern has been even more closely involved with the process of writing this book than he was with earlier ones. His presence was already ubiquitous in the manuscript when he made his comments on it. He thinks that this is an austere book, which I do not mind because I prefer the discipline of the mind to evidence of emotion. Nevertheless, our common passions should be apparent here and there. One of them is to understand what he has called the second Thirty Years' War from 1914 to 1945, and to make sure that its murderous course is never repeated.[5] Another is the uneasy relationship between Germany and the West which has much to do with the politics of cultural despair on the one hand and that of liberty on the other. Fritz Stern and I have now gone a long way together. Our styles are different, but our concerns are similar, and our friendship warms the soul while it stimulates the mind.

My wife Ellen is the only person who has seen all versions of this manuscript, beginning with 'Modernity in Eclipse' a decade ago. She has encouraged me when I felt low and insisted that I continue when I felt weak. She has also made me appreciate that, while analysis is fine, I should not put pen to paper unless I had some contribution to make to improving the human condition. Ellen has given much critical advice both on the text in general and on specific matters in her own areas of expertise, which are Russian history and Soviet studies as well as contemporary issues of human rights. We share the hope that civil and civilized societies will spread, and we both know that this does not simply happen but demands our active commitment.

August 1987   R.D.

1 · Revolutions of Modernity

A Tale of Two Cities

Revolutions are melancholy moments of history. The brief gasp of hope remains submerged in misery and disillusionment. This is true for the great revolutions, like 1789 in France or 1917 in Russia, but applies to some lesser political upheavals as well. Before they occur, there are many years of repression, of arrogant power and malign neglect of people's needs. A stubborn old regime clings to privilege, and by the time it begins to reform its ways it lacks both credibility and effectiveness. People do not like it. Energies of conflict build up into a state of tense confrontation. It is a powder keg. When a spark is thrown into it – a spark of hope, as by grudging political reform, a spark of anger, as by a shot fired at the wrong time – an explosion takes place and the old edifice begins to crumble. Suddenly everything seems to give. Yesterday's high treason becomes today's law of the land, and yesterday's law today's treason. To the more excitable, vistas of unheard-of opportunities open up, 'people power', the liquefaction of everything hard and fast, utopia. Many are caught by a mood of elation. Not just the abuses of the old regime, but the constraints of society itself seem suspended. However, the honeymoon does not last. Normality catches up with people. After all, they cannot go on demonstrating every day, or even fighting a civil war. Individual circumstances are reflected in social conditions. Turmoil does not help economic development, and political instability raises fears. Suddenly the mood changes. Sometimes, a foreign power intervenes and thereby leaves utopia intact, though not the revolution. Sometimes, a Jacobin faction

1

within takes over from the impotent majority. Is not 'people power' a contradiction in terms? Quickly, the slogans of better days are perverted to justify a new regime of terror. This may be a 'temporary' dictatorship, a state of emergency in the face of outside pressure, or simply charisma in the midst of anomy; in any case, it leads to another period of repression. Many years later, people realize that there have after all been lasting changes. The first day of the revolution is celebrated as a public holiday. But in the meantime a generation of disillusioned men and women have vacillated between sullen submission and vain protest.

If this is so, why does anyone want revolutions? It is not certain that many people do; for most, the welcome interruption of daily routines is more than balanced by suspicion and fear. When the thunderstorm breaks a long period of heat and drought, people like the rain, but they would have preferred a little of it each day to the tumultuous opening of the skies. To be sure, not all people are alike. There are always free-floating groups whose members are more likely to enjoy the suspension of society than those who are anchored quite firmly. Also, the frisson of revolution contains a general appeal. At times, revolution seems another word for hope, that indispensable principle of life. After all, the real revolution may yet happen. Was not the American Revolution on balance a story of success? And what about the Chinese Revolution? But none of this really matters. People are not asked whether they want revolutions or not. Revolutions happen when there is no other way out. They are indeed like thunderstorms, or like earthquakes. To be sure, they are man-made, but men and women act under conditions which they do not wholly control. 'Mankind inevitably sets itself only such tasks as it is able to solve.'

The man who made this statement is also the author of a brilliant, if flawed, explanation of revolutions, Karl Marx. Fortunately, the flaws are sufficiently interesting to make their discussion worthwhile. Marx's theory has two parts, one sociopolitical, the other socioeconomic. The parts remain a key to understanding the modern social conflict, although the way in which Marx has linked them raises serious doubts. These elements of a theory of change by revolution have to do with the inhabitants of the two 'cities' of modernity, with the *burghers*, or bourgeois, and the *citoyens*, or citizens. The two will accompany us throughout this book, one being the herald of economic growth, the other of social equality. It is perhaps a pity that the

German term *bürgerliche Gesellschaft* confounds the two, though it is merely a rendering of the old notion of the *societas civilis*, civil society.

Let us consider then Marx's theory of revolution.[1] Its first part has to do with class. In every historical epoch two social classes are set against each other. The ruling class is ready for the battle from the outset; it has emerged from the previous epoch. The oppressed class on the other hand has to go through several phases of formation before it can engage in battle. Sporadic outbreaks of violence accelerate the process of organization; latent interests become manifest; the 'class in itself' turns into a 'class for itself'. As this happens, the conflict between the ruling and the oppressed class becomes more vicious. For a while, it is in the balance, but then the balance begins to tip. The oppressed class continues to grow in strength; some elements of the ruling class even come to have doubts and join the enemy. ('In particular,' Marx says in the *Communist Manifesto*, 'a portion of the bourgeois ideologues': all social scientists have had trouble defining their own role in their theories, and Marx was no exception.) Then the final battle commences, and a revolutionary upheaval puts an end to the epoch. The old ruling class disappears on the rubbish heap of history; the old oppressed class sets itself up as a new ruling class.

But the struggle of classes is not suspended in mid-air; the soldiers of the class war are in a sense puppets held by invisible social forces. This is the second part of Marx's theory. Ruling classes represent the 'relations of production' characteristic of an epoch. What is meant here is that they have an interest in keeping things as they are, 'things' being above all existing patterns of wealth creation, the laws which give them stability, and the distribution of power which backs them up. Oppressed classes on the other hand draw their strength from new 'forces of production'. These include all that makes for change, such as new technologies, new forms of organization, new rules of the game, and new gamekeepers. For a while, forces of production find adequate expression in prevailing legal and social conditions; but before long, the potential begins to outgrow the actual. Worse, actual relations of property and power hold down the development of the social potential of satisfying human desires. As the compatibility of the two declines, the intensity of the class struggle increases. Revolutions are not just extreme expressions

3

of protest, but assertions of new modes of social organization. They provide a passageway for opportunities which were held down by an old regime.

In the aesthetic terms of scientific method, this is a beautiful theory. One might call it one of the few theories which live up to the old dream of a social science that emulates the natural sciences in its power of explanation. But alas! the events which the theory is meant to explain resist its sweep, and the predictions which followed from it did not come true.

One can start unravelling the tapestry from one little corner. It is a part of Marx's theory that the revolutionary explosion occurs when conditions are worst for the oppressed. He even plays on words to this effect; the moment of greatest 'neediness' (of the poor) is also the moment of greatest 'necessity' (of change).[2] In fact, this is never the case. The most needy are more likely to be lethargic than active, and hopeless oppression creates the great silence of tyrannical rule. Explosions occur when there is some slight change – a spark of hope, a spark of anger – and often a sign of weakness on the part of those in power, a signal of political reform.

The mistake is no accident. It has to do with the fundamental weakness of a theory which cannot break out of the assumption of 'epochs' or systems. Of course, Marx knew that changes go on all the time. He even described the ruling class of capitalist society, the bourgeoisie, as one which 'cannot exist without constantly revolutionizing . . . the relations of production'. But this merely means that adjustments of practice and operation are part and parcel of the capitalist system. The system itself will disappear only when the great revolution comes. Until then, 'early capitalism' may become 'high capitalism', even 'late capitalism', or perhaps 'state capitalism', indeed 'state monopoly capitalism', but capitalism it remains. As long as there is no revolution, it cannot have disappeared. 'Real' change must be revolutionary change, and until it happens, the old categories of analysis apply.

This is what Karl Popper has called historicism.[3] Concepts of analysis are hypostasized. Instead of using them to identify aspects and elements of real societies, they are confused with reality itself. In fact, of course, there never was such a thing as a capitalist society or economy, but only societies and economies which displayed traits defined as capitalist to a greater or lesser extent. The poverty of historicism is that it blinds the user to the real world. In theory, it makes one search endlessly for ways to save explanations which have lost their grip. Marxists have had a terrible time coming to terms with the disappearance of the revolutionary proletariat. In practice, historicism makes one stare at revolutions as the only mode of 'real change' and thus miss the continuous changes of the reality of ordinary people. Marx's theory is too neat to be useful; it is a model which has little to do with the experience of history.

Where then did its author get it from? Partly of course from his master Hegel, whose dialectics overshadowed German thought both in the progressive years before 1848 and in the reactionary ones after. Hegel epitomized the illiberalism of dogmatic thinking, and those who tried to turn him upside down failed to break out of this straitjacket. But partly Marx was influenced by indirect experience. Born in 1818, he grew into a restless time. The rumblings of the French Revolution continued. As he turned from philosophy to political economy, Marx soon discovered that other dramatic transformation of the eighteenth century, the Industrial Revolution. One can almost see how the two events began to be superimposed on each other in Marx's mind. In Paris, the crowds had played a part in making history, and somewhere behind the demands of the Third Estate for more adequate representation in the Estates General there was a kind of class struggle. In Lancashire and Yorkshire on the other hand, new methods of production had allowed a new dynamic to unfold. The limitations of feudal bonds, and also of guilds and corporations, were broken by the new division of labour, new forms of contract, a new tone-setting group. So there were the twin elements of a theory of change, revolution or not.

The word 'revolution' has long been used for two quite different versions of dramatic change. One is deep change, the transformation of core structures of a society which in the nature of the case takes some time; the other is quick change, notably the circulation of those at the top within days or months by highly visible, often violent action. The first might be called social revolution, the second political revolution. The Industrial Revolution was in this sense social, the French Revolution political. But the two did not happen at the same time and in the same place. Clearly, some of the many changes brought about by the Industrial Revolution in Britain and elsewhere were political. These included the desire of the promoters of the new form of production to take part in the process of making laws which apply to all. Equally, some of the issues of the French Revolution were social and economic. The financing of public expenditure was such an issue, which in turn raised the question of the role of the King (whose expenditure it was) as well as the property of the Church and the aristocracy. Drastic changes happened with respect to all of them. Yet the Industrial Revolution in Britain occurred long after the civic revolution of 1688, and spilled over to pre-revolutionary France and other countries, whereas the political revolution of France did not in any sense unleash great economic forces. On the contrary, it may be said to have stalled the process of modern economic development in France. Some people have double vision and see the same thing twice; Marx's ailment was the reverse. His Hegelian eyesight merged two different things into one. Reality was the victim.

Marx of course was as much concerned about the one and only revolution of the future as he was about those of the past. In his predictions the flaws of his theory are also most apparent. Bourgeoisie and proletariat are the combatants of capitalist society. That much is a plausible description of some countries at certain times in the nineteenth century. Organized workers demand from those in power more rights and benefits. Marx would not have used this language, but it is not totally alien to his thinking either. The problem begins with the next step in his argument, which is that trade unions and socialist parties make their demands in the name of new forces of production. This, I suggest, is a meaningless statement. It always has been meaningless, despite numerous attempts by Marx and Marxians to define these new forces in terms of the 'associated producers', 'social ownership' or even the unconstrained discourse of autonomous individuals. There are political struggles, and there are tectonic changes of social and economic structure. They are undoubtedly related. But their relationship is not given once and for all. It varies from time to time and from place to place, and the moments at which the two coincided have been rare.

Actually, in some ways the eighteenth century was such a 'moment'. It was however a long moment. One is not talking of the day on which the Spinning Jenny was invented or the Bastille was stormed. The point is rather that one can after all tell one tale about the two cities. It is the tale of the bourgeoisie and its – if the word has to be – revolutionary role in the history of liberty. In order to make use of new opportunities of technology and the division of labour, the early entrepreneurs needed a form of labour which was unlike traditional patterns of bondage. They needed wage labour which involves contracts between parties which in formal terms were assumed to be equals. This in turn presupposed elementary civil rights for all. At the same time, these very entrepreneurs and those around them demanded for themselves a place in the sun, or more prosaically, social recognition and political participation. They were not going to be kept either in the *burghs*, the islands of liberty in an ocean of feudal dependence, or in second-class positions. Thus, the economic and the political interests of the early bourgeoisie converged in the demand for one great innovation, citizenship. It was, to be sure, a limited citizenship coupled with almost cynical new privilege; the new labour contract barely camouflaged deep asymmetries of power, and the Third Estate did not care for the Fourth once it had defined its own interest as the general will. But the seed was sown. The twin revolution of the eighteenth-century bourgeoisie was one of those rare moments of history for which Marx made a certain amount of sense, though by coincidence rather than design; the twins were fraternal, not identical, and the transformation occurred by strategic changes, not by revolution.

The Martinez Paradox

To speak of 'two cities' is metaphorical language for notions which must be defined more clearly since they are central to the argument of this book. I can think of no better way of approaching this definition than by telling a story. In March 1986 I visited Nicaragua. Even then, it did not take long to discover that the shelves in the supermarkets carried little, and what there was by way of foodstuffs or clothes looked drab and rather elementary. In a conversation with the Minister of Foreign Trade, Martinez, I brought up this observation and received a striking answer: 'You seem to be critical of the fact that there is not much to buy on the shelves of our shops. This may be true, but let me tell you something. Before the revolution, our supermarkets were full. Everything you could find in Miami was on the shelves in Managua as well. But the majority could not afford any of it. People pressed their noses against shop windows to admire the goods, but they were not for them. We have changed all that.

7

Today everyone in the country can afford what is there. And a bit of luck and America permitting, there will soon be more for all as well.'

Many people laugh when they hear the story. Paradoxes make people laugh, and I have come to call this the Martinez Paradox: the revolution has transformed a world of plenty for the few into one of little for all. On inspection, the story is not so funny. First there are the facts. The per capita gross domestic product of Nicaragua doubled between 1950 and 1976. This development was not linear; there were pauses in the late 1950s, and again at the time of the earthquake of 1972. After 1976, a downward trend began. It took the country back to the level of the early 1950s by the time of the revolution in 1979. After the revolution and until 1981 there was a slight improvement which soon gave way to further decline. In 1985, per capita gdp in Nicaragua was roughly what it had been in 1951. In part, this is a story of revolution, in part it is one of war and pressure from the United States. Figures of income distribution are harder to come by. It seems clear that real wages also declined, though by less than per capita gdp; by 1984 they were about one-third lower than in their heyday in the late 1960s. Urban incomes have held up better than rural ones; and in the country, the poor have done relatively better. The role of the state as an economic actor has increased significantly. Transfer incomes have grown. The blights of illiteracy, epidemics, unemployment have been fought with some success. One economist has summed up the net result in terms which are not dissimilar from the Martinez Paradox: 'from growth without redistribution to redistribution without growth'.[4]

There is another, more theoretical reason why the Martinez Paradox warrants more than a laugh. The minister introduced an important distinction which has a lot to do with the 'two cities'. It is the distinction between people's access to things and the things which are actually there for them to desire. It is entirely possible that large quantities and varieties of goods are available in the sense of being physically present where one would expect to find them, as in shops, but that many are unable to put their hands on them in a legal manner. In some cases, they lack the money; in others, they are not allowed to go and buy things. This is the case with the special shops of East European countries ('Intershops', 'Intourist') in which one must have either a permit or foreign currency to buy anything. It is equally possible that there are no barriers to prevent people from getting to the goods and services which they want, but that there are simply not enough of them. One method frequently employed in such cases is rationing. Everyone gets a ration book for 2000 calories' worth of food a day, and sixty cigarettes a week, so that there are no special restrictions on the access side, but there are limitations on the availability side. (In reality, it is likely that rationing would be coupled with privileges for the few and a black market for the many on which non-smokers trade their right to buy cigarettes.) In extreme cases, the situation can become more eerie. Everyone is allowed to go to places where there is nothing at all to get. The station is open, but there are no trains. Berlin was like that in 1945 during the days when the Nazis had left and the Russians had not yet taken control. Alternatively, one family or clan monopolizes virtually everything that there is, and doles out bits to allow at least the immediate servants to survive. 'Papa Doc' Duvalier in Haiti may have been an example.

The distinction hidden in the Martinez Paradox calls to mind the striking theory advanced by Amartya Sen in his book on *Poverty and Famines*.[5] In looking at historical famines, Sen discovered clear evidence showing that explanations in terms of what he sarcastically called 'fad', that is 'food availability decline', were false. Food in areas of starvation, including Bengal at the time of the great famine of 1943, may not have been plentiful, but there is evidence that there was no less of it than in previous and subsequent years. Nor was physical accessibility a problem; in some cases, food was actually exported from areas in which people were dying of hunger and hunger-related diseases. What then was the problem? Why did people starve? Here, Sen introduces his own concept of 'entitlement' (which I shall develop for purposes of this analysis). For Sen, entitlements describe a relationship of persons to commodities by which their access to and control over them is 'legitimized'. Entitlements give people a rightful claim to things. Thus it is not food availability, but the combination of modes of access (what Sen calls the 'entitlement set') of entire social groups, or rather its decline and eventual disappearance, which explains the great catastrophes of Asia and Africa.

Amartya Sen is a matter-of-fact political economist who likes to wrap his emotions in layers of rational argument, but his theory could hardly be more dramatic. In language which is certainly

9

not his, it means that in certain extreme cases it is not lack of goods but the presence of social barriers which accounts for the death of thousands, perhaps hundreds of thousands. Even when needs are uniquely urgent, most people do not transgress norms in order to survive but suffer the ultimate deprivation. 'The law stands between food availability and food entitlement.' This is not exactly a comforting idea. Sen himself has been worried that it may discourage food aid, and in a later paper has made a case for pragmatic relief measures. (He might have pointed out that emergency relief tends to cut through prevailing entitlement structures, but does not threaten them because it is by definition temporary, even one-off.) The theory is least comforting to those who have an interest in the maintenance of existing entitlements. If it is not more food but less privilege that is needed, nothing short of drastic social change will help. This is only one hint of the ramifications of a theory which at first sight seems technical.

Sen's concept of entitlements certainly is technical. In essence, it 'concentrates on the ability of people to command [things] through the legal means available in the society'. This is not a mere personal ability, but is itself socially structured, which is why Sen has later preferred to speak of 'acquirement': 'The entitlement of a person stands for the set of different alternative commodity bundles that the person can acquire through the use of the various legal channels of acquirement open to someone in his position.' It is worth noting the use of 'legal' means or channels in both definitions; entitlements are always in the nature of rights. However, this legal claim can be based on a number of qualities ('endowments') or activities ('exchanges'). Sen lists, apart from historical ownership, 'trade-based entitlements', 'production-based entitlements', 'own-labour entitlements', 'transfer entitlements'. They constitute what he calls the 'entitlement set' of a person. Sen proceeds to ask why and when there are 'entitlement failures', that is to say when and where access to the command over commodity bundles breaks down. His examples lead him above all to factors like rising prices and declining wages, but also to more direct forms of access blockage. Either way, he concludes, 'famines can be usefully analyzed in terms of failures of entitlement relations'.

Entitlement is a much used term in social science and social theory. Some have tried to capture the peculiar quality of private ownership with it, many others use the plural, entitlements, for the benefactions of the welfare state. The term seems to invite value judgements. Robert Nozick's 'entitlement theory' is the personal side of the 'minimal state' in that it defines the rights of individuals. Lawrence Mead pleads for a world 'beyond entitlements' in which obligations receive appropriate emphasis.[6] Sen by contrast uses the term in what he calls a 'descriptive rather than prescriptive' way. In that I shall follow him. Entitlements are in themselves neither good nor bad; they are socially defined means of access. One might call them entry tickets.

The other important aspect of Sen's definition is that entitlements have a normative quality. Like social norms, they have a degree of fixity, which means that they cannot be taken away without cost. The notion of norms is more general than that of rights, and indeed the fixity of entitlements can vary. At one end, basic rights are entitlements. They include constitutionally guaranteed rights associated with membership of a society. Citizenship rights have their place in this context. Other means of access are not as hard, yet also fairly firm once they are given. Access to markets falls into this category. It is anything but a matter of course. To all intents and purposes, China is not 'a market of one billion people' (as is sometimes loosely claimed) because for the overwhelming majority of Chinese the world of economic exchange or even the consumption of more-than-elementary goods is all but inaccessible. At the other end of fixity, real wages constitute entitlements (as does money more generally). Incomes can vary of course. One of the important changes of entitlements which Sen has observed with respect to poverty and famines has to do with declining incomes. This applies not only to developing countries. In some countries, real wages are more 'sticky', more fixed, than in others, at least in so far as downward movements are concerned. Perhaps it can be said that their entitlement character comes out even more clearly where this is the case.

One other aspect of entitlements deserves emphasis. Entry tickets open doors, but for those who do not have them these doors remain closed. In that sense, entitlements draw lines and constitute barriers. This means that there is in principle nothing gradual about them; half an entry ticket is no entry ticket. Rights of access may be more or less widely available, but as such they are clearly defined. Entitlements grow or decline in steps rather than in a linear fashion. There is in fact a sense in which they do

11

not 'grow' or 'decline' at all, but are established or removed, given or taken away.

This is precisely what distinguishes entitlements from the other side of the Martinez Paradox, the things to which people are entitled. It is not easy to give these 'things' a name, especially if the entry tickets which we call entitlements include basic rights as well as real incomes. Amartya Sen the economist wisely confines himself to commodities or 'commodity bundles'. He would probably not find it difficult to extend the notion to a wider concept of welfare supply, as long as this is susceptible to economic measurement. But entitlements can open doors to non-economic 'commodities' as well. The right to vote, for example, is an entitlement, and it makes a great deal of difference whether this is granted in a one-party state in which one has to say yes to a predetermined slate of official candidates, or in a multi-party democracy. Other examples are more complicated. There is an entitlement to education. Does it mean that alternative schools or courses must be offered to give the entitlement substance? In any case, 'commodities' or even 'welfare' are clearly unsatisfactory concepts to describe the whole range of material and immaterial choices which may be opened up by entitlements. I shall use the term 'provisions' to encompass these choices.

The word 'choice' as commonly used can describe both the act of choosing ('I make a choice') and the objects from which to choose ('what is the choice?'). Provisions are choices in the latter sense only. They are in other words the supply of alternatives in given areas of activity. These alternatives are themselves highly structured: by what the imagination of markets contrives, by what people want, by what economists call taste and by organized preferences of many kinds. From time to time, I shall discuss the structure of particular provisions in greater detail. Throughout, provisions will be defined as 'things' which can grow and decline incrementally. In principle, the concept is quantitative rather than qualitative, economic rather than legal or political. Provisions can vary in at least two respects, one being quantity or amount, the other variety or diversity. The two are related in intricate ways which again will be discussed as the need arises. The fact (for example) that the number of newspaper copies sold goes up from say ten million to twelve million means little if they are all official party papers toeing the same line, or tabloids of the same vacuousness; an increase from ten to twelve independent newspapers sharing the same total circulation may involve more growth.

The idea of distinguishing between entitlements and provisions is not exactly new. No claim for originality is made here, merely one for usefulness. Not so long before Amartya Sen wrote his study of famines, Fred Hirsch published a book called *Social Limits to Growth.*[7] Its central thesis is based on the distinction between a 'material economy' or 'material goods', and a 'positional economy' or 'positional goods'. The former are the subject of economic growth in the traditional sense, while the latter are intrinsically scarce. No amount of equality in regard to material goods can therefore do away with positional inequality. Hirsch himself refers to Roy Harrod's terms 'democratic wealth' and 'oligarchic wealth'. In these as in other cases, the key distinction is one between economic and social or political factors.

As one ponders the distinction, other familiar concepts fall into place. Privilege and deprivation are concepts from the world of entitlements, and so is Tocqueville's notion of democracy as a condition of fundamental equality of status. Citizenship is a set of entitlements. The language of supply-side economics on the other hand belongs in the world of provisions; innovation, incentive, competition are a part of this vocabulary, as is the notion of choices in education and health care. Some concepts straddle the two worlds; they will be of special interest for this analysis. Both wealth and poverty can be relative advantages or disadvantages in terms of provisions and draw more absolute, entitlement boundaries of privilege and deprivation. The Industrial Revolution was in the first instance a revolution of provisions. It led to great increases in the wealth of nations. The French Revolution on the other hand was a revolution of entitlements. It established a new stage in the progress of the rights of man and the citizen. In the eighteenth century, and in the interests of the bourgeoisie, the two may have come close. Since then, they have fallen apart. The Martinez Parad x tells the story by the contrast between provisions without entitlements and entitlements without provisions.

Life Chances

The obvious answer to Minister Martinez was of course a question: Why can't you have both access for all and plenty of goods? Why indeed? The minister thought that the provision of goods was but a matter of time, and of the lifting of the US embargo and boycott. He may have been overly optimistic even in theory. Of course it would make a difference if the United States and other OECD countries decided to help Nicaragua rather than hold it down. But the underlying issue remains. Let us state it again in terms which refer to Nicaragua but have wider application as well.

Somoza's Nicaragua was for some time a country of considerable economic growth. At any rate this is the story told by macroeconomic data. But only a minority benefited from this growth. There were thresholds of participation not just in the political process but also in the economy; these formed rigid barriers to access. Growth did not filter through, because the entitlement boundaries within Nicaraguan society were simply not permeable. The same is true in many developing countries. The old belief that if one transfers money to a Third World country it may in the first instance make the rich even richer, but will in due course trickle down and create a middle class, was simply wrong. There is no limit to the richness of the rich, nor to their cynicism with regard to the poor. Even well-meaning World Bank projects tend to benefit the haves, partly by their limited use and partly by corruption, and leave the have-nots in the lurch. Unless traditional entitlement structures are broken and elements of a civil society created, macroeconomic growth means little for the many, however satisfactory the International Monetary Fund may find the statistics.

But when these structures are broken, all is not over. For one thing, very few countries indeed have managed to find a fairly straight route to both civil society and market economy. Perhaps there are only two, Britain and the United States, and even their histories raise questions. How universal was Britain's civil society when the country's economy flourished? How market-like was the Imperial economy? And how civil was American society during the years of slavery and even after? Most recent attacks on the authoritarian defence of entitlement barriers have ended in the emergence of new forms of privilege, such as a *nomenklatura* of self-appointed and self-perpetuating functionaries. Many fear that this is happening in Nicaragua today. In any case, it is a mistake to believe that once political pressures are eased, economic expansion will follow as a matter of course.

(This may be the problem with General Secretary Gorbachev's hopes of economic restructuring as a result of cultural openness.) Economic progress requires a whole panoply of pushes and pulls which concern that most mysterious factor, human motivation. Even the carrots of supply-siders and the sticks of guardians of discipline will not necessarily do the trick. People must want more, and at the same time be prepared to forego immediate pleasures for greater delights in the future. These are two big obstacles, and politics alone does little to overcome them. One thinks of the Protestant ethic and the spirit of capitalism, of breaking people's accommodation to the cycle of poverty, of inventiveness and entrepreneurship.

Two quite different schools of thought have in fact grown up around the distinction introduced here. There is the provisions party, which believes that the greatest need is for economic growth, for an increase in goods and services, their quality and diversity. They like to think of the task of mankind as a positive-sum game. Progress can be painless. One has to make an effort, of course, but if one does there is a prize. The main issues are in any case economic in the sense of the need to push the frontiers of scarcity out so that all can have more. The entitlement party does not agree. It insists that there are harder choices, and that sometimes zero-sum games have to be played in which one side pays for the gains of the other. Progress is not a common effort to move the frontier of scarcity, but a battle of groups for chances of participation. It is measured in terms of the number of people who have access to markets as well as to the active public and social life generally. The main issues are thus political in the sense that they call for deliberate action to establish rights and redistribute goods.

The two parties can be found all over, and often within one and the same political grouping. Between the eighteenth-century revolutions and about 1848, many liberals belonged to the entitlement party. They did not worry unduly when the Burkes and Tocquevilles reminded them of the cost of their revolutions. 'We have abandoned whatever good things the old order could provide but have not profited from what our present state can offer.' Nicaragua all over again? America at any rate, as the French aristocrat Tocqueville saw it in the 1830s. But soon the fighters for more entitlements turned their attention to provisions. Liberals considered that enough was enough, or rather they split.

15

Some did not even see a need for adding political participation to equality before the law, let alone, half a century later, the services of a welfare state. Others continued to fight for these entitlements, though perhaps with declining enthusiasm. Another entitlement party entered the scene, in the form of socialism. In different forms and shapes the battle continues to the present day, not least as one between 'New Dealers' and 'Neoliberals', or Keynesians and Friedmanites.

There will be many opportunities in the course of this analysis to return to the two parties, but it is time that we took the story a step further. Distinctions are fine, but their main use is in putting them together again and learning something in the process. Let us assume that we could describe levels of entitlements and provisions by a number on a scale from 1 to 10. Let us decide furthermore, with a degree of informed arbitrariness, that in Somoza's Nicaragua the level of entitlements could be described as 2 out of 10, and that of provisions as 6 out of 10. Arguably, the position is reversed in Ortega's Nicaragua, that is, entitlements 6 and provisions 2. If one multiplies the two (which also requires a number of assumptions), the level of human welfare would seem to be much the same in both; two times six equals six times two. Has nothing been gained – or lost – at all?

This would be a very silly case to argue. Yet the experiment in social arithmetic has a point. It is that in order to advance human welfare one needs both, entitlements and provisions. People need access to markets and politics and culture, but these universes also have to offer numerous and manifold choices. No society can be regarded as truly civilized which does not offer both.

I referred to human welfare as requiring both entitlements and provisions. There is need for a concept to describe the combination of the two. The concept of welfare as it is used by welfare economists may be said to do just that by adding some social indicators to the measures of national accounting. However, words have their histories, and welfare will forever have connotations which are not intended here. (Curiously, they are entitlement connotations, even in the technical discussion of the welfare state.) I propose to use another term for the purpose. It is 'life chances'. Life chances are a product of entitlements and provisions. In principle it should be possible to measure them. In practice, countries can at least be described in terms of the level of life chances which they offer, as can groups, categories, classes within them.

Here I have to ask the indulgence of readers for adding a note which is addressed to those who may have read some of my earlier books. Several years ago, I published a collection of papers under the title *Life Chances*. This rather attractive notion appears here and there in the literature, including a few times in the work of Max Weber. At the time, I defined the concept by two elements which are qualitatively different, though historically related in complicated ways, 'options' and 'ligatures'. Options are the choices which people have open to them; ligatures are the co-ordinates which give these choices meaning. Clearly, ligatures are the more complicated notion. I had in mind those deep cultural ties which help people find their bearings in the world. In the past, and for many even today, they have to do with family, locality, religion; but there are other linkages of deep culture which can take their place. My concern at the time was a world of numerous choices but little meaning, an existentialist world in a sense, in which every act is an *acte gratuit*, a mere gamble into nothing. I act therefore I am. This is a worrying and difficult subject which clearly has a great deal to do with the modern world. What some call the return of the sacred demonstrates the need for meaning in disoriented societies. It also suggests risks. Where God appears to have died, false gods are not very far away. They have misled many, and some have followed them all the way to Jonestown. Perhaps the mass murder-suicide of the 916 American followers of Reverend Jones in Guyana is symbolic of a world without ligatures.[8] Thus, I have nothing to retract from the point that choices have to have meaning in order to be more than gratuitous constructs of the scientific mind. Ligatures are a part of life chances in the full sense of the notion. For purposes of social analysis, however, I have since concentrated on the other side of the concept as I originally introduced it, on options. The present discussion is an attempt to refine the notion of options and make it somewhat more operational.

In one sense, life chances are options both in their entitlements and in their provisions aspect. This is what is meant by chances as against results or accomplishments or the real actions of people. Entitlements by giving access offer opportunities. Even a university degree or a guaranteed minimum income is in this connection not a purpose in itself but a precondition for pursuing other goals, whether individual or social. The same is true for provisions. Goods and services and a variety of other desirable things must be available; but no society should try to prevent the ascetic from renouncing them, or the hermit from withdrawing in disgust. There is an undertone of liberty in the concept of life chances. A society which tries to enforce life styles, which controls the actual lives of people, is not a free society, whether such control is exercised by Big Brother and his secret police, or merely by a moral tyrant of social democratic persuasion. There are differences between the two, but a free society is one which offers chances and does not impose ways of using them. The task of liberty then is to work, and if need be to fight, for an increase in life chances. At times, this requires above all attention to entitlements, at other times provisions come to the fore, but at all times there is more to be done. There are never enough life chances for enough people. The liberal who ceases to seek new opportunities ceases to be a liberal.

These are, perhaps, fine words, or at any rate fine prescriptions. But as we proceed to putting the concepts introduced in this chapter to use, let there be no doubt about one point. The distinctions between politics and economics, chances of participation and standards of living, entry tickets and the choices which await the entrants – in short, between entitlements and provisions – are useful. But despite appearances to the contrary, there is no trade-off relationship between the two. The contrast between an entitlements party and a provisions party was not intended to suggest that one can only be had without the other, and that the Martinez Paradox poses an inescapable dilemma. Although the emphasis may change with the times, and there are conditions in which one must opt for one or the other, the whole point about the modern social conflict is that it can advance both. It can increase life chances. The task of liberty at the end of the twentieth century is once again to find levers for advancing entitlements and provisions at the same time. This is what the reformers of the inter-war period, William Beveridge and John Maynard Keynes, have done in their time. Other names come to mind as one looks back over the nineteenth century, all the way to Wilhelm von Humboldt. What I have called the twin revolution of the bourgeoisie in the eighteenth century belongs in the same liberal textbook of modern history. It also gives occasion for tying up a few conceptual ends which had to remain loose so far in the interest of advancing the central argument.

Modernities

'The bourgeoisie has played a most revolutionary role in history. This book has been inspired by contemplation of this irresistible revolution advancing over every obstacle and even now going forward amid the ruins it has itself created. When royal power supported by aristocracies governed the nations of Europe, society, despite all its wretchedness, enjoyed several types of happiness which are difficult to appreciate or conceive today. The bourgeoisie, wherever it has got the upper hand, has put an end to all feudal, patriarchal, idyllic relations. It has pitilessly torn asunder the motley feudal ties that bound man to his natural superiors. It has drowned the most heavenly ecstasies of religious fervour, of chivalrous enthusiasm. But in abandoning our ancestors' social state and throwing their institutions, ideas and mores pell-mell behind us, what have we put in their place? All fixed, fast-frozen relations, with their train of ancient and venerable prejudices and opinions, are swept away, all new-formed ones become antiquated before they can ossify. All that is solid melts into air, all that is holy is profaned. Men of religion fight against freedom, and lovers of liberty attack religions; noble and generous spirits praise slavery, while low, servile minds preach independence; honest and enlightened citizens are the enemies of all progress, while men without patriotism or morals make themselves the apostles of civilization and enlightenment.'

Who is this strange author who combines familiar turns of phrase with less familiar ones into a curious mixture of praise and indictment? I confess to having done a dreadful thing and commingled two of the great nineteenth-century authors into one textual artefact, even leaving out some inconvenient bits. They are of course the authors of the *Communist Manifesto* and *Democracy in America*, Marx and Tocqueville. (It takes a separate note to reconstruct the original texts from this artefact.[9])

No one would confuse the two in the normal course of reading. The French aristocrat and sometime republican minister of state was a reluctant modern, impressed by America but fearful of its infectiousness; the German academic and sometime revolutionary organizer was a cynical modern, unimpressed by anything real but hopeful of radical transformations. Yet the two were sufficiently close in their assessment of the gist of modernity to make the attempt to merge their texts not entirely implausible.

For one thing, both Marx and Tocqueville recognized that the twin revolution of the bourgeoisie meant a farewell to a more idyllic past and its heavenly ecstasies. Man's departure from his self-imposed infancy is also a departure from the warmth of stable human relations across frontiers of status. 'All that is solid melts into air.' 'All fixed, fast-frozen relations are swept away.' Ancient ligatures are broken. Tocqueville the aristocrat felt the loss more acutely, but even Marx betrays a slight frisson of nostalgia when he describes the premodern world which is now forever gone.

What has stepped into the breach when chivalry, loyalty, mutuality collapsed under the weight of new interests? Deep down, Marx and Tocqueville agree on the answer but one is tempted to say that they differ to agree. They certainly reach their answers in different ways. Marx predicts a revolution of entitlements but his interest is almost entirely fixed on capitalism, the great modern force of provisions. Tocqueville on the other hand looks back to a life of rich choices lost with the *ancien régime* but wonders above all whether democracy, or equal entitlements for all, will ever be able to allow such a wealth of provisions.

These then are the elements of the classical theories of social dynamics: modernity (by many other names), the great forces of capitalism and democracy, and as a guiding light for the future, versions of civil society. Let us dwell on them for a moment to clarify recurrent concepts and to emphasize the critical methodological bias of this essay, which is that concepts must not be confused with realities. There is no capitalist and no democratic society; even modern society is a notion which is but imperfectly realized at the best of times; and civil society will forever remain a task.

In the Preface, I have traced the word 'modern' to the author of the motto of this essay, George Hakewill (who refused to 'vilifie modernitie', it will be remembered, in 1635), and beyond. In fact, the founding father of the gallery of modern heroes which I am going to assemble as the argument progresses is Erasmus of Rotterdam. Erasmus was (probably) born in 1466 and he died in 1536. He wanted reform, though not the Protestant Reformation, which was really a revolution. He managed to leave his religious order and, much later, to resist the cardinal's purple, but he remained an author and adviser of great influence who drew upon himself the hopes of progressives as well as the fear of the establishment (though he led a fairly established life and sometimes treated his more radical admirers with cruel disdain). He straddled a great era of change with all the ambivalences of that position. While unlocking the door to the modern world, he also held it tight to make sure that it would not be broken down by the many.

Erasmus was nothing if not mobile. He crisscrossed Europe at a time at which such voyages could be most uncomfortable, especially those to his friend Thomas More across the English Channel. Even his mobility tells a symptomatic story. If there is any one feature which definitions of modernity have in common, it is movement. This includes people's movement across geographical spaces as well as up and down the social scale. Modern people are able to leave their inherited place. Sir Henry Maine thought that he had discovered his own law of history when he wrote in 1861 in his *Ancient Law*: 'We may say that the movement of the progressive societies has hitherto been a movement from Status to Contract.' Social 'laws' tend to have more exceptions than their discoverers like; certainly not all societies have gone in this direction, nor has any one society completed the path. There is South Africa; there are race issues in many parts of the world; there is the unfinished history of gender; and there are of course many distinctly premodern societies. But a tendency to make social positions negotiable rather than preassigned is unmistakable. There are still 'rich men in their castle' and 'poor men at their gate', but few believe today that 'God made them high or lowly / and order'd their estate'.

All this has often been described; it is indeed the original theme of social science. In this essay, the aspect of modernity which will occupy us most is that it has changed the quality of entitlement barriers. In modern societies the presumption is that entitlements are not of the caste or estate variety. Instead, one is dealing with barriers which do not need to be broken to be shifted. Once the revolutions of modernity have taken place, entitlements too become in principle negotiable. The negotiations are often hard, they break down, they lead to clashes at the ballot box as well as on rostrums and in the streets. But the modern social conflict has lost some of the absolute qualities of historical divisions. (Where it still seems absolute, it is typically about the movement from status to contract.) Conflict too has become more fluid. It is the domesticated force for change.

It would be tempting to argue that democracy and capitalism are necessary consequences of modernity, but history does not allow such kindness. Without contract (in Maine's sense) neither democracy nor capitalism would be possible, but there are several other patterns of modern society. Sometimes it appears that it was not the latecomers to the modern world who chose – or had to choose – a *Sonderweg*, their peculiar way forward, but that the early moderns found a unique path to modernity. The charm of the 'Protestant Ethic and the Spirit of Capitalism' is precisely in its application to those who embraced the Calvinist ethic, notably in Britain, and despite all allusions to France, 'Democracy in America' is after all about America. Thus, democracy and capitalism are particular ways of advancing the causes of entitlements and (material) provisions in the modern world and need to be seen in a context which includes tyranny and socialism as well as many hybrids, to which we shall have occasion to return.

The ambiguities of democracy have often been pointed out. Tocqueville was not talking about constitutional checks and balances, let alone parliamentary government, and modern theorists of political democracy are not concerned with the basic social condition of equality which Tocqueville had in mind. I do not believe that there is a satisfactory way of resolving such ambiguities. Wherever conceptual precision is needed, I shall therefore avoid the word 'democracy'. The institutional political issues associated with it will be discussed in Chapter 3 and a mixed constitution will be advocated. Democracy in Tocqueville's sense, on the other hand, is the subject of Chapter 2 on citizenship.

With respect to capitalism, there is no such easy way out of problems of definition. The concept is actually not particularly ambiguous. It describes an economic system which is characterized by three main elements: *private actors* co-ordinate their economic activity through *the market* in order to achieve accumulation and *growth*. There are other ways of putting this linkage, such as Peter Berger's handy phrase, 'production for a market by enterprising individuals or combines with the purpose of making a profit'.[10] Somehow or other, private property, markets and growth always figure. Capitalism need not be industrial; the first two centuries of modern capitalism were primarily commercial, and the recent capitalist upsurge has been more financial than industrial; but certainly industrial capitalism has dominated the time since the Industrial Revolution on which this analysis is focused. Moreover, capitalism is always about more for more, and among the models of economic growth it is the most successful.

I have said and will say again that there is no capitalist society, and that no real condition deserves the description 'capitalist' (with whatever qualification). This means first of all that no historical society has displayed the traits of economic growth by private initiative in markets sufficiently to warrant such a description. Versions of capitalism may have been the driving force of economic and social development in some countries, but actual modes of development were almost invariably mixtures of forces. Those who praise Germany's economic success before 1913, or Japan's after 1945, may use the word 'capitalism', but public actors played a major part in both, and whether the prevailing systems of co-ordinating economic activity in these countries are properly described as markets is open to doubt. Socialism also aims at creating growth, by public rather than private actors, plans rather than markets, and discipline rather than incentives. In economic terms, this is not a very effective method, but it clearly has compensating advantages, or else it would not have survived for so long. Also, there are as many variants of really existing socialism as there are of really existing capitalism.

The statement that there is no capitalist society has another meaning. For capitalist methods to work, certain social preconditions must be given. One is contract rather than status as the basis of labour relations. Opportunities of market participation

23

are not a matter of course, nor is the 'spirit' which enables people to put growth first and consumption second. However, one must beware of the assumption that market economies presuppose market societies. Some of the most successful capitalist economies have flourished under authoritarian and highly inegalitarian social conditions. As the Nicaraguan example shows, there is not even a case for assuming what Adam Smith called the 'natural progress of opulence'.[11] Smith, as usual, is not naïve in this matter. His statement on the spread of prosperity includes an important proviso; it occurs 'in a well-governed society'. Even for the founding father of capitalism, something else has to be given for provisions to become entitlements.

That something else is civil society. The concept will accompany us throughout this essay. It will be discussed in some detail in the next chapter, and it will recur until in the final chapter the case for a world civil society is made. A civil society is a society of citizens in the full sense of the word. It is a product of civilization rather than nature. When David Hume made this point about the word 'civil',[12] he could already look back on a tradition which was probably begun by John Locke's *Treatises on Civil Government*; at the same time he inspired Adam Ferguson's *History of Civil Society*. Civil societies are invariably modern; they are not necessarily capitalist, though they offer opportunities for initiative and growth if they are to deserve the name; they are democratic at least in the sense of providing basic rights for all. Thus the connections between the life chances of modern societies and civil society are numerous. Above all, there can be no liberty without the conditions of civil society. Tocqueville mustered all his courage to describe the possibility of a modern civil society, without making it sound terribly attractive, whereas Marx deferred its advent to noman'stime and thereby made it unreal. Both have rendered us a disservice. Immanuel Kant knew better what the union of justice and liberty demands and he called it civil society.

2 · Citizenship and Social Class

Origins of Inequality

Life chances are never distributed equally. We do not know of a
society in which all men, women and children have the same
entitlements and enjoy the same provisions. We do not even
know of one in which all men have the same status. Probably
there cannot be such a condition. 'Similars do not constitute a
state,' said Aristotle. If all were alike, or even nearly alike, there
might be human sand dunes or other molecular formations
brought about by the elements, but there would be no structure,
no meaning, no progress. Society is necessary because different
people have to create common institutions to survive and
advance their lot. Their differences matter at least in so far as
their various interests encroach on each other, if not because
some are able to impose their will on others whether by force or
the evil eye.

To reflect upon these matters has become popular again in the
late twentieth century. All of a sudden, the social contract has
been unearthed by philosophers, economists and political
theorists. For the most part, the reason for this interest differs
today from what it was two, three and four centuries ago.[1] Then,
authors from Hobbes to Locke and on to Hume and Rousseau
were arguing that some elements of a deliberate social order are
necessary. In the midst of civil upheavals, they tried to establish
the rule of law and civil government. Today, the sense is
widespread that government and the law are everywhere. The
dominant 'contractarian' question is how little government
would suffice to guarantee law and order. Even those who do not

25

exactly advocate a minimal state insist that reasons must be given for social institutions such as property or democracy. The rediscovery of the social contract arises from the search for fundamental structures in a jungle of superstructures of many kinds.

This is as it should be as long as one point is well understood. The social contract is not an unchanging skeleton of the body politic. It is not there once and for all, but itself subject to change. Even the American constitution – the nearest to a deliberate social contract in modern history, and of course in part a result of the eighteenth-century debate on the subject – had to be adapted by amendments, court rulings and practice to stay alive. The social contract is not the basis of society but the subject of history. It is written and rewritten by each generation. Its lasting elements are at best a grammar of society; everything else is variable, capable of improvement but liable also to take a turn for the worse. The question is not whether we should return to the everlasting articles of the social contract, but how we can write such articles anew to advance liberty under changed conditions.

Still, a little grammar helps one understand the language. We need not pursue the question of natural inequalities of humans here, save to say that people's motives and interests differ, and that all societies have found ways of organizing these differences in ways which involve both co-ordination and subordination. The division of labour co-ordinates different tasks to common effect; social stratification subordinates some to others by applying a scale of values on which some rank lower than others. Both, but notably subordination, require a group and an agency which set the tone. Some speak of hegemony, others simply of power. In the grammar which is used here, the old distinction between a 'contract of association' and a 'contract of domination' is at best of analytical usefulness. In practice it is difficult to think of human association without an element of domination. Where there is society there is power.

Certain authors like to use a less orthodox grammar and separate the two contracts. They dream of an association freed of all elements of domination.[2] Theirs is the language which appeals in revolutionary moments of elation. It has little use at other times, except to prepare people for unusual days which cannot last. Like all absolute perspectives it detracts from the tasks before real people in real conditions. These have to do with the domestication, not the abolition, of power. Of course, power is never benevolent. Society is not nice, but it is necessary. The question is therefore how power and the inequalities generated by it can be turned to advantage in terms of liberty.

Modern societies have gone some way towards this objective. Aristotle's statement about similars who do not constitute a state was not as bland as its isolated citation sounds. The early chapters of his *Politics* abound with statements which we would regard as entirely unacceptable. For Aristotle, slaves are not a part of the state, because they are 'by nature' slaves. Women differ some-what from slaves, but again they are 'by nature' inferior to men. Children, the sons of free men at any rate, grow up to be citizens, but are not citizens yet. There is obviously an issue of inclusion here which has accompanied the history of mankind through the centuries, and of which many would say that it is still unresolved. It is clear, however, that modern societies have a more generous concept of who belongs and who does not than Aristotle did.

How did this come about? Even the benevolent reader of this chapter and the two subsequent ones will not fail to notice a melancholy weakness of social analysis. There is a theory of how change comes about, and there is history. The theory is not bad, in that it directs our attention to certain actors and motives, and even helps us anticipate the eventual outcome. But the ways of human progress are not so simple. Things happen for reasons not foreseen in the theory and at times at which they should not have happened at all. This chapter is rather more theoretical, and therefore simple and clear; the next ones will explore some of the vagaries of the actual politics of citizenship and freedom.

The unequal distribution of life chances is a result of structures of power. Some are in a position to lay down the law by which the standing of others is measured. For many centuries, it looked as if very few were able to do this; the rule of kings remained virtually unchallenged by the people. Even then, there were good rulers and bad ones (and great rulers somewhere in between). Gradual-ly, more people came to be involved in making the law, though it was still administered by a minority. The difference is not only one of times, but also one of places. A degree of democracy was characteristic above all of certain islands of association in the oceans of domination. They were often co-extensive with cities, from the Greek *polis* to the medieval *burgh*. The rise of modernity can be described also as the gradual spread of such experiences. As the power of a few was brought under the control of more and ultimately of the many, inequalities lost their fateful, ascribed character and social positions became at least in principle attainable as well as sheddable. The route from status to contract was also one from status to class.

It is as well that society is not nice. If it was, men and women would, as Immanuel Kant put it, 'live an Arcadian, pastoral existence of perfect concord, self-sufficiency and mutual love. But all human talents would remain hidden forever in a dormant state, and men, as good-natured as the sheep they tended, would scarcely render their existence more valuable than that of their animals.' Man's 'unsociable sociability' is the sting which produces the antagonisms from which progress flows, including more life chances within an improved social contract. Power generates not just inequality but by the same token conflict. It creates interests in change as well as interests in the status quo. But such interests find different expressions in a world of hierarchy than they do in a world of contract. It would be instructive to speculate in another context about the premodern social conflict. Was it merely a battle of elites? How important was the formula of bread and circuses for maintaining power? When did elements of class begin to enter the scene? In the eighteenth century they certainly did. With the revolutions of modernity the quality of conflict has changed. As a result, large numbers of people are involved, and visible conflicts become the motive force of change. Class conflict enters the scene.

One little noticed internal contradiction in Marx's theory of class mars the stringency of the theory but testifies to the honesty of the author. In the *Communist Manifesto*, Marx and Engels talk briefly about different epochs. As the bourgeoisie had to turn feudal relations of production upside down, they say, in order to help new forces of production break through, so the proletariat will have to put an end to bourgeois relations of production. I have argued earlier that neither Marx nor his followers ever identified the forces of production which had the proletariat as their herald and bearer. But there is another point. The bourgeoisie can hardly be described as the oppressed class of feudal society and compared to the proletariat in bourgeois society. The

28

Third Estate may have lacked political rights, but the recognized estates had long been economically dependent on its services when the revolutionary grumblings began. In fact, the proletariat has a unique place in Marx's schema of history, and the authors of the *Communist Manifesto* knew it: 'All previous historical movements were movements of minorities, or in the interest of minorities. The proletariat is the self-conscious, independent movement of the immense majority.' Leaving hyperbole and the hang-up with epochs on one side, it is not unfair to translate this into the statement that class, in the sense of open political conflicts based on social position and involving large numbers of people, is a modern phenomenon.

The origin of the class conflict then is to be found in structures of power which no longer have the absolute quality of entrenched hierarchy. The subject of the class conflict is life chances. More precisely, it is the unequal distribution of life chances. Those at the disadvantaged end demand from those in positions of advantage more entitlements and provisions. The struggle, first latent and barely visible, then open and fully organized, leads to a wider spread of both. But it has above all one effect which describes the history of modern societies from the eighteenth century to the present: it transforms differences in entitlements into differences in provisions. From qualitative inequalities we move progressively to quantitative inequalities. Status barriers give way to degrees of status. This is the story which has to be told in greater detail before the next stage in the history of modern conflict can be described.

Enter Citizenship

One of the more important developments which accompanied the rise of modernity was the creation of the nation-state. The process was in most cases the deliberate work of monarchs and their first ministers, but it was in the evident interest of a social group which could not rely on traditional territorial powers. The nation-state was also a necessary vehicle for the establishment of the modern contract in the place of feudal bonds. It provided the framework for law and the institutions to uphold it. Not uncharacteristically, the first modern societies were also the first nation-states, and those who came later had as much trouble with problems of nationality as with those of citizenship.

No contemporary of the second Thirty Years' War, or even of the wars between the new nations of the post-war period, would call the nation-state an unmixed blessing. Many would not call it a blessing at all. But they are wrong. Historically at least, the nation-state was as much a necessary condition of progress as it unfortunately turned out to be a source of regression and inhumanity. The alliance of nationalism and liberalism was a force for emancipation during the revolutionary decades from 1789 to 1848. To this day, no other guarantee of the rule of law has come to the fore than the nation-state, its constitution of checks and balances, due process and judicial review.[3] Not the least advantage of the nation-state was that it generalized the ancient idea of citizenship.

The citizen is the city-dweller, and in the first instance the (male, free) inhabitant of Athens in the fifth century BC. When the first dead were brought home from the Peloponnesian War, Pericles spelt out to the survivors the values for which their loved ones had fallen and described the constitution of the city.

> 'Its administration favours the many instead of the few; this is why it is called a democracy. If we look to the laws, they afford equal justice to all in their private differences; if to social standing, advancement in public life falls to reputation for capacity, class considerations not being allowed to interfere with merit; nor again does poverty bar the way, if a man is able to serve the state, he is not hindered by the obscurity of his condition.'

The translation of Thucydides' report on the speech is perhaps a little too modern,[4] but many of the characteristics of citizenship can be found in the famous funeral oration: equality of participation, equality before the law, equal opportunity and a common floor of social status. It was to take a long time, and harsh battles, before any modern nation was brought close to this ideal; but then one remembers that Athens was exceptional and fought a very different Sparta, that within Athens the majority even of grown-ups were 'by nature' excluded from citizenship, and that the great experiment did not last. Its significance was that it established the possibility of a great idea, for there is no better way of doing that than by making things real in one place. Citizenship was not a utopian idea; it was the development of an ancient experience.

The experience was never entirely lost. Contrary to some, I would not praise the Romans for 'the wit to distinguish between civil rights – rights of equality before the law – and political rights – rights of membership in the sovereign body'.[5] Once this distinction is made, civil rights tend to evaporate into distant skies of morality whereas rights of membership quickly turn into the duties of subjects. But there is a Roman history of citizenship; there are the Italian cities, the Hanseatic cities and others during the Middle Ages. The difference is that for many centuries the principle was dormant. It served to defend the few rather than to envelop all. The momentum of the principle of citizenship begins with the creation of political units within which civil rights and civic participation become necessary elements of the constitution. We are back to the nation-state.

Citizenship describes the rights and obligations associated with membership in a social unit, and notably with nationality. It is therefore common to all members, though the question of who can be a member and who cannot is a part of the turbulent history of citizenship. Its turbulence is still much in evidence. It has to do with the issue of lateral or national (as against vertical or social) exclusion and inclusion.[6] It affects people's identity because it defines where they belong. More often than not, it involves drawing boundaries which are visible on maps or by the colour of people's skin or in some other way. These are processes which quickly raise the temperature of human relations. Lateral exclusion has probably given rise to more violence than social exclusion. Disputes about definition are also among the more intractable human conflicts.

There is no shortage of examples. Multiracial societies are the exception rather than the rule even in the modern world. Civilization has not led to a noticeable decline in people's desire to be among their own. Few societies have managed to integrate as many ethnic groups as those of North America; but even there, the hyphen – Italian-American, Polish-American etc. – has become as important as American citizenship, and the blacks mind that they alone do not seem to have one. After the Hapsburg Empire, the United Kingdom is an outstanding example of a country which includes several nations. This is acceptable in Wales, just bearable in Scotland and the source of civil strife in Ireland. The concept of national self-determination which emerged from the great carve-up of empires after the First World War has confirmed the strain towards homogeneity which seems characteristic of human societies. It has also weakened the force of citizenship by detracting attention from its rights in favour of mere membership. I am a Latvian, Tyrolean, Basque, etc., and liberty must wait until that is recognized . . .

Perhaps it was wrong to imply that modern societies should find it easier to live with difference than earlier ones. Are the Quebecs and Irelands, the Lebanons and Belgiums not issues of fiercer conflicts today than 100, let alone 200 years ago? Versions of these issues are moreover evident everywhere. Has a Jewish convert from a reformed community a claim to Israeli citizenship? Can an Egyptian immigrant be trusted to run a Swedish business? Should asylum seekers be given even the most elementary rights of membership? Do they not belong in camps, like the boat people in Hong Kong, or the Cambodian refugees in Thailand? Some countries are more border-conscious than others; perhaps they have special identity problems. But everywhere it appears that as traditional bonds become weaker, boundaries of membership become more important.[7] The subject is complicated. Mobility plays a part in it, as the characteristic social role of the century increasingly seems to be that of the migrant for the more fortunate, and of the refugee for the unlucky. As one considers the result, it is hard to conclude that mankind has made great strides of civilization. A civilized society is one in which common citizenship rights combine easily with differences in race, religion or culture. It is also one which does not use its civic status as a weapon for exclusion, but regards itself as a mere step on the road to a world civil society. We shall not lose sight of the dream as we take stock of the real world.

Citizenship then is a set of rights and obligations for those who are included in the list of members. The phrase 'rights and obligations' comes easily, but has its pitfalls. Clearly, I am not simply talking about a value, an ideal. Citizenship is a real social role. It provides entitlements. Entitlements are of course rights, such as the right to conclude a free contract, or the right to vote, or the right to an old age pension. But what is meant by obligations?

One obvious obligation of citizenship is to comply with the

law. (I am leaving the question of civil disobedience on one side, though it does not alter the basic proposition.) But it has long been argued that this is not enough. One recent author has made the point forcefully that what is wrong with the welfare state is the neglect of obligations in favour of entitlements.[8] Obligations should include not just compliance, but also 'civility', 'activity and competence'. The 'common obligations of citizenship' encompass 'both political and social duties', and among the social obligations the most important is work. Indeed, apart from 'law-abidingness', 'learning enough to be employable', 'fluency and literacy in English', 'contributing . . . to the support of one's family' and 'work in available jobs for heads of families . . . and for other adult families that are needy' are all part of the 'operational definition of citizenship in its social dimension'.

I believe this view is fundamentally mistaken and destroys an important concept if not, by its application, the rights of people. The objections could be argued in terms of the history of work, to which I turn in a later chapter, but they can be made in general terms too. Citizenship is a social contract, generally valid for all members; work is a private contract. In societies in which the private contract of labour does not exist there is no citizenship either. This is true for feudal relations of dependence and for some versions of really existing socialism. It is no accident. For when the general rights of citizenship are made dependent on people entering into private relations of employment, these lose their private and fundamentally voluntary character. In an indirect but compelling manner, labour becomes forced labour. It is imperative that the obligations of citizenship are themselves general and public as it were.

This is not to say that they are necessarily confined to compliance with the law. Paying taxes has become an obligation associated with membership, although (income) taxes are levied only on those who can afford them. (The argument put forward here is by implication an argument for civic rather than work taxes.) It may well make sense to ask all citizens to give some time of their lives to the community. Conscription is the obvious example, though some form of community service could be one method of dealing with issues which the market does not resolve by itself. Such service, whether military or civilian, is of course also 'forced labour'. But it is strictly circumscribed and in all respects a part of the public domain in which citizens exist.

Thus both the rights and the obligations of citizenship can vary over time. However, they are under all conditions not only public but in principle universal. Moreover it is an important issue of liberty to what extent they may include calls on what people actually do rather than on what they have the right to do. Probably, such demands should be minimized rather than maximized. Compulsory voting is a dubious interpretation of citizenship rights. In principle the rights of citizenship are not conditional, but categorical. What citizenship offers does not depend on the readiness of people to pay a price in the private domain. Citizenship cannot be marketed.

These caveats are important when it comes to understanding the related concept of civil society. The term has a long and distinguished history. From Aristotle to the eighteenth century, it was used interchangeably with the political community, the body politic, the commonwealth, or even the state.[9] Then people – liberal people – began to distinguish between society and the state. One of the productive forces of the bourgeoisie was society as against the state, or more precisely a new society against an old regime. It was but a small step from this confrontation to an understanding of civil society which associated the notion with market exchanges and capitalist economic relations generally. The ambiguity of the German term, *bürgerliche Gesellschaft*, helped such misunderstandings; to some, the *citoyen* and the *bourgeois* appeared as two sides of the same coin. In fact, they are not. The two coins may have been minted at about the same time, but they are two coins, and it is conceivable that one will lose its currency long before the other.

There is no reason, in other words, why civil society should cease to be desirable, or real, once the bourgeoisie has left the social and political stage. This means in turn that the eighteenth-century distinctions may have served their purpose, but need not be maintained. The separation of civil society from the state is, like that of the contract of association from the contract of domination, analytically useful but misleading in practice. Civil society is not a private game of intelligent discourse apart from the institutions of government, let alone against them. It is rather the inclusive concept for social units in which citizenship is the guiding principle. All members possess certain equal entitlements which have the quality of social norms. They are enforced by sanctions and protected by institutions. This is effective only if there are structures of power to back them up. The search for a civil society, and ultimately a world civil society, is one for equal rights in a constitutional framework which domesticates power so that all can enjoy citizenship as a foundation of their life chances.

T. H. Marshall's Case

As we turn from the outer or lateral boundaries of citizenship to the inner or social ones, we encounter another issue of membership. It is Aristotle's issue, or rather the one which he left unresolved when he suspended slaves and women and children from his polity. One of the themes of the modern social conflict has been the extension of citizenship to more members of society. One way of describing this process is to tell the story of suffrage. First, property qualifications or tax classes were abolished for men and the right to vote extended to all adult males. The process took more than a century even in countries which started it early. Then the fight for women's suffrage began in countries which had limited voting to men. While the suffragettes may seem a quaint memory today, they represent a stage in a difficult battle which in most countries was not won before 1919, and in some, like Switzerland, considerably later. Eventually, adulthood was redefined, and the voting age lowered to twenty-one and further to eighteen years.

This is only a part of a difficult story. Many civil rights issues in the developed world have been issues of inclusion. The right to vote meant little to segregated blacks in the American South, and perhaps to American blacks generally. Action was needed to bring them in, by literacy programmes and by forcing employers to give blacks a chance. The process has remained incomplete to the present day, and some see a reversal of trends. Women's rights too are not confined to suffrage. They touch on deeper cultural obstacles to equal participation and require both a change in attitudes and one in prevailing norms. The road from the assertion of equal rights to the acceptance of comparable worth is long. Then there is the vexing issue of the place of children in the scheme of citizenship. The simultaneous attempt

35

to give them more rights and to grant them exemptions has not worked very well. Contemporary societies are loath to deal with the incompatible facts that most crimes of violence are committed by people who are not held fully responsible as citizens for reasons of age or incompetence.

If I turn to class at this stage, this is not to detract from the importance of these issues of citizenship, much less to claim that minority and women's rights are essentially questions of class. The reason is rather a sense that the crucial momentum of change in the last two centuries has been the extension of citizenship to new dimensions of social position. Advocates of minority rights or women's rights will object, and they may have a case, but I would argue that their fight makes sense only if citizenship has become a full and rich status. The class conflict for the extension of the entitlements of citizenship is the precondition for extending the range of those eligible for them.

The English sociologist T. H. Marshall has told this story in a series of lectures given in 1950 which provide one of the gems of social analysis. I have borrowed the title of his lectures for this chapter, *Citizenship and Social Class*.[10] The lectures were given in Cambridge in honour of T. H. Marshall's (unrelated) namesake, the economist Alfred Marshall, which fact led the lecturer to begin with a question raised by the author of *The Future of the Working Classes* in 1873: 'The question is not whether all men will ultimately be equal – that they will certainly not – but whether progress will not go on steadily, if slowly, till, by occupation at least, every man is a gentleman.' The question sounds a little dated, not only to women who would have an equal claim to be ladies (or gentlewomen). Since we are here concerned with entitlements one must wonder also whether they actually progress 'steadily, if slowly', or in bursts and stages. But T. H. Marshall merely uses the quotation for his own formulation of the problem which is close to ours in concept and language. He distinguishes between what he calls 'quantitative or economic inequality' and 'qualitative inequality'. The former may not disappear, but the latter can, and if it does the former will lose its sting. The way to bring about this result is to include more people as members of society with more rights. This has in fact happened. 'The basic human equality of membership . . . has been enriched with new substance and invested with a formidable array of rights . . . It has been clearly identified with the status of citizenship.'

This then is Marshall's thesis. Modern social change has transformed patterns of inequality and the conflicts resulting from them. What used to be qualitative political differences between men have become quantitative economic ones. This has happened in two stages, by the revolution of modernity itself, and by the transformations of the modern world (to use our words rather than Marshall's).

Marshall begins by discussing feudal hierarchy with its legally defined privileges and exclusions. This is the world of status which when invaded by modern contract fell apart. In the old world, entitlements formed an apparently immutable pattern of inequality. 'The impact of citizenship on such a system was bound to be profoundly disturbing, and even destructive.' It meant the end of legally defined entitlement barriers, no less. But no more either. It did not mean the end of inequality. Marshall says somewhat apologetically, 'it is true that class still functions' once the principle of citizenship has been established. There is no need to apologize. In some ways, class only begins to function on the basis of common citizenship for all. It is the driving force of the modern social conflict.

It may help to avoid confusion if I add at this point that the modern class conflict too has to do with entitlements. Many remnants of an earlier age are left over, including titled families and local landlords who enjoy privileges long after these have lost their legal sanction. New entitlement barriers emerge which may not have the binding force of the law but are nonetheless solid obstacles to full citizenship rights for all. They include real incomes as well as social discrimination, barriers to mobility as well as to participation. The modern social conflict is no longer about removing differences which (in Marshall's words) 'have the essential binding character of the law'. The principle of citizenship has destroyed such differences. (At least, it has done so 'in principle'.) The only legally binding status left is in fact that of citizenship. The modern social conflict is about attacking inequalities which restrict full civic participation by social, economic or political means, and establishing the entitlements which make up a rich and full status of citizenship.

T. H. Marshall distinguished three stages of this process, which he called civil rights, political rights and social rights, and being lucky enough to be English he could make the otherwise suspiciously tidy claim that it is possible 'to assign the formative period in the life of each to a different century – civil rights to the eighteenth, political to the nineteenth and social to the twentieth'. Perhaps there was more overlap between the three even in Britain, but the distinction remains useful.

Civil rights are the key to the modern world. They include the basic elements of the rule of law, equality before the law and due process. The end of hierarchy means the beginning of civil rights. No one is above the law, all are subject to it. The law constrains power and those who hold it while giving those in a temporary or permanent minority position a haven of integrity. The discussion about whether the rule of law can be defined in purely formal terms or requires certain substantive elements will never end. Due process in the United States is a formal concept which has nevertheless served to protect human rights; many other countries have found it preferable to take up the ancient notion of natural rights and embody these in the preamble to their constitutions. 'We hold these truths to be self-evident . . . .' Certainly, a purely formal notion of the rule of law can be abused. Hitler started his regime with an Enabling Law to abolish the rule of law. Despite such twentieth-century ambiguities, the notion that all members of society are citizens, all citizens are subject to laws, and all are equal before the law was the first definition of citizenship.

It was also a necessary condition of Western versions of capitalism. Free wage labour presupposed the modern contract. Markets work only to the extent to which people have access to them as equal participants. This is not to say that everyone has to have access; for many decades capitalism meant increasing provisions for a minority. It is not to say that civil rights are a sufficient condition for growth either. Neither the Protestant ethic nor entrepreneurial initiative or technical inventiveness follows from civil rights. But if the eighteenth-century bourgeoisie had any one subject which tackled both entitlements and provisions, it was civil rights. Civil rights were and are one of the strategic changes of the modern world. They are therefore the first necessity for all countries embarking late on the course of modern development.

The most obvious weakness of civil rights is that the laws in which they are embodied may themselves be biased. They are intended to be rules of the game, but some rules of the game benefit one side more than the other. The labour contract is an obvious example. What does 'free and equal' mean if one party needs labour to survive whereas the other can pick and choose, hire and fire? Unless all citizens have an opportunity to feed their interests into the law, the rule of law leaves serious inequalities of entitlement. This is why political rights were a necessary supplement to civil rights. They include not only suffrage, but also freedom of association, freedom of speech, and the whole panoply of rights discussed by John Stuart Mill in his treatise *On Liberty*. The political public corresponds to the economic market; its structures are similarly complicated and similarly imperfect; but in the first instance it has to be open to all. Political rights are the entry tickets to the public.

Liberal reformers fought for both civil and political rights. Not all were prepared to 'attach political rights directly and independently to citizenship as such'; some thought that civil rights were sufficient and politics was the task of the chosen few. But, on the whole, reformers recognized that the rule of law and universal suffrage were conditions of liberty. However, most did not want to go any further. The largest free country – and civil society – never fully accepted that the story of citizenship does not end here. In the United States, a notion of opportunity prevailed which interpreted equal starting chances restrictively and subsequent choices extensively. Civil rights, political rights and the open frontier summed up the American concept of liberty. To some extent they still do. The poor deserve help if they help themselves; otherwise their condition is their affair. In Europe, the twentieth century is marked by a different development. Whether the logic of citizenship and the class struggle or the tradition of an all-embracing state inspired the process, members of society were deemed to need more than civil and political rights. Social rights were added so that the status of citizenship came to include, as Marshall put it, 'a universal right to a real income which is not proportionate to the market value of the claimant'. It is an entitlement.

The underlying argument is clear enough. Civil rights are not only curtailed by the exorbitant power of some, but also by the economic weakness of many of those who have them. It makes a difference whether one can afford to defend one's interest, or one's honour, in a court of law or not. Political rights mean little if people lack the education to make use of them. They can also have a social and economic cost which prohibits their use. Unless everybody can live a life free of elementary fears, constitutional rights can be empty promises and worse, a cynical pretence of liberties which in fact stabilize privilege. The conclusions to be drawn from the argument are not so clear. Whereas civil and political rights can be established as such and embodied in laws or even constitutions, it is less easy to see how social rights can be entrenched. Some have tried, but neither a minimum wage nor the right to work nor other social 'rights' have proved very durable.

In this connection it is telling that the case for social advances has often been made in terms of provisions. When Keynes pleaded for a more conscious management of demand, he did not argue for higher real wages as such, but for purchasing power as an engine of growth. The debate about educational expansion in Europe in the 1960s began not as one about education as a civil right, but as one about educational opportunity and economic growth. In widely publicized OECD papers, it was argued that there was a correlation between gdp growth and the proportion of graduates. It is worth mentioning also that the notion of social rights, or of transfer payments as an element of citizenship, blurred the line between equality of opportunity and equality of results. T. H. Marshall anticipated Fred Hirsch's questions when he wondered whether social citizenship rights had not gone beyond the original intention of 'raising the floor-level in the basement of the social edifice' and 'begun to remodel the whole building' so that they 'might even end by converting the skyscraper into a bungalow'.

Why not? one might ask. The quick answer is that inequality is a medium of liberty if it is inequality of provisions rather than entitlements. It fills the supermarket, which is highly desirable especially once everybody has access to it. But our initial concern here is with what the extension of citizenship rights has done to class. We assume for the moment that the process itself is a result of class conflict. The have-nots of the rudimentary civil society have organized to push their demands for political and eventually social rights; the haves have reluctantly given way. As a result, the progress of citizenship from the civil through the political to the social sphere is also a process of 'class-abatement'. Indeed, at the end of the day, what is there left for classes to struggle about? T. H. Marshall is cautious in his conclusions. Still, he leaves no doubt that citizenship has brought many changes affecting class. 'They have undoubtedly been profound, and it may be that the inequalities permitted, and even moulded, by citizenship do no longer constitute class distinctions in the sense in which that term is used for past societies.' They are economic inequalities which are subject to market conditions, not social inequalities which require political action. The classless society at last?

A Perfect World?

T. H. Marshall gave his lectures in 1950. Like many sociologists, he anticipated social trends as much as he observed them. During the 1950s, several authors would claim that modern societies had reached the end of the class war, and perhaps of class. We shall encounter some of them again in Aron's world (see Chapter 5). The striking thesis hinges in part on definitions. But if one associates class with modern entitlements, it might indeed have seemed for a while that the battle was almost over. In the early centuries of the modern age, modernity itself was at stake. Legally entrenched differences in entitlements – privileges – had to be broken and the principle of citizenship established. Then the struggle for giving this principle civil, political and social substance began. From the point of view of the 1950s, it was quite successful.

The gist of this struggle was to eliminate inequalities of entitlement. This was done by bringing about two related changes. One of these had to do with raising the floor on which everyone stands. The other concerned the ceiling for those in an exceptional position of wealth or prestige. The point in both cases was to decouple civic status from economic position. Put differently, constitutional rules had to be introduced to prevent the translation of wealth into the power to deny the citizenship rights of others. Other measures were designed to empower all citizens to participate in the economic, social and political process. The combination may be described as the domestication of power. Numerous particular developments of the last two centuries find their place in this story. Apart from those already mentioned they include tax and antitrust laws, the separation of Church and state, parliamentary committees of inquiry and administrative law as well as the traditional foundations of democratic constitutions.

The basic idea throughout is that inequalities of provisions are acceptable if and when they cannot be translated into inequalities of entitlements. There is a degree of functioning wealth which gives those who have it illegitimate power, and there is a degree of poverty which deprives those who suffer it of civic participation, but between the two, distinctions of rank and of income do not give rise to the same kind of conflict. Little has been said about provisions in this chapter. Yet more than one question could and should be asked. For example, why did T. H. Marshall not relate the progress of citizenship to the advances of economic perform-ance? Would one have been possible without the other? Is not the key factor the rising level of general prosperity? Does not class detract from the individual opportunities for increasing life chances? Is not the American example the model for the rest? (In the words of Werner Sombart's book of 1906: *Why Is There No Socialism in the United States?*) And if one looks at things the other way round, are not citizenship rights an optical illusion in view of continuing inequalities? Should one not focus on the fact that inequalities of income distribution, of educational oppor-tunity, of the incidence of social mobility appear to have changed little in the last decades?

This is quite a mouthful of partly contradictory questions. Yet they can probably be reduced to two. One is analytical. How do increases in provisions affect entitlements, and vice versa? The other is normative. Why should the unequal distribution of provisions be acceptable as long as it cannot be translated into unequal entitlements? The normative question goes to the heart of liberal theory. So far, I have merely asserted that qualitative inequalities are incompatible with free societies, whereas quanti-tative inequalities may even be a stimulus to growing life chances. The analytical question goes to the heart of the story told in this book.

Adam Smith believed that there would be a 'natural progress of opulence'.[11] He thought that the market entailed the force for its own extension, so that in the end inequalities are swept away 'and a general plenty diffuses itself through all the different ranks of the society'. One notes the paradox: there is a 'general plenty' but there are also 'different ranks of society'. Prima facie, this could be the opposite of the picture drawn here with the help of T. H. Marshall; it could mean equal provisions in a structure of unequal entitlements. On reflection, however, this makes little sense. After all, what are entitlements for, if not for provisions? Perhaps what we really see here is an early version of a curious weakness of much economic analysis. Almost by definition, it concentrates on the provisions side of change. Economics is the science of provisions. Great claims are made for increases in provisions, in incomes, standard of living and welfare. Who would deny that the long economic miracle since the Industrial Revolution has changed the social scene? But underlying social structures are almost anxiously held constant, as if the whole approach of economics would collapse if they changed.

Moreover, this is true independent of the political persuasion of economists. Friedrich von Hayek praises the pathbreakers, but assumes that others will lag behind. For him this is bearable because 'even the poorest today owe their relative well-being to the results of past inequality'. At the other end of the spectrum, Robert Heilbroner is concerned about those who are capable of 'denying to others access to the goods which constitute wealth', but regards the fact as a kind of law of nature, because wealth for him 'is a social category inseparable from power'. The de-coupling effect of citizenship does not occur. In between Hayek and Heilbroner, Fred Hirsch bemoaned the failure of an extension of 'material goods' when it comes to the lasting scarcities of 'positional goods'. Again, the assumption is that inequalities of entitlement are inevitable.[12]

In fact, they are not. One must not confuse the shortcomings of economic analysis with those of reality. Capitalism – the growth of provisions – does not solve all problems, nor does it create them. Adam Smith was wrong in expecting too much from the 'natural progress of opulence', and Karl Marx was wrong in expecting the contradictions of capitalism to lead to the dramatic dissolution of the Gordian knot of provisions and entitlements. As a rule, the two revolutions of modernity do not merge into one event, nor is there one theory to explain them both. The theory of class conflict and that of the incompatibility of new forces and old relations of production are after all two theories. Markets fail to achieve entitlement changes, and governments fail to achieve increases in provisions, but it would be wrong to hold them responsible for what they cannot do. True, the separation is not total. Civil rights provide access to markets and thereby help their extension; rising incomes are a necessary condition of an entitlement to a decent standard of living. Time and again, we shall seek the points at which the twain meet, because they are the levers of strategic change. But 'the twain' they remain. Different processes advance provisions and entitlements. For example, active minorities – pathbreakers, entrepreneurs, innovators – play a much more important role in the progress of opulence than that of classes. The story of citizenship does not invalidate economic analysis (unless it makes exorbitant claims for encompassing everything); it must be added to it. The same is true the other way round. The creation of a common floor of entitlements and the domestication of power do not make the separate study of economic growth superfluous; they merely supplement it. Political economy is perhaps too facile a concept for what we need; politics and economics are as close and as far apart as entitlements and provisions. Social analysis however falls short if it simply holds either constant; it is in some ways always about their interrelations.

Whatever citizenship does to social class, it does not eliminate either inequality or conflict. It changes their quality. Several authors have compared the result to a marching column. People have their place at very different points in the column; but since the whole column is moving, the last will eventually reach the point at which the first were before them. Some state this with delight, others with irony, again others with frustrated anger.[13] When the last reach the point which the first passed some time ago, will it still be the same? The marching column is too orderly a simile. In fact, it is an economist's metaphor since it holds the relative position of everyone constant. It would be more apposite to think of one of those shambolic urban marathons which paralyse large cities once a year. The chaos is not total; some start in front and try to win the race; some have just joined to have fun; many want to prove that they can do it. There are surprises and disappointments. The important point is to be a part of the race.

Is not such a state of affairs the best of all possible worlds? The question was bound to arise in the reader's mind as I went along taking more and more citizens into the modern marathon. It is fundamental to this essay. While the answer that will be given must disappoint those who expect a straight yea, yea or nay, nay, it is nevertheless clear. Moreover, the line of argument which responds to the expectations or suspicions of perfection can now be sketched. It will be extended, embellished, illuminated, but its direction is clear.

In one sense, the world of citizens is a perfect world. It is hard and costly to achieve. The process involves many pains and aches, of which some are literally unbearable. Even the scourge of totalitarianism has something to do with the halting progress of modernity. There is also the price in ligatures which Marx and Tocqueville described so vividly. But the establishment of civil, political and social citizenship rights for all marks true progress. If it is coupled with significant growth in the quantity and diversity of provisions it creates a highly desirable state of civilization, and of liberty. Even the best of all possible worlds is however not perfect.

In the first instance, the process is far from complete. Three major issues remain on the agenda of citizenship and entitlement struggles. The first arises from the fact that much remains to be done to assure all members of even the OECD societies of their citizenship rights. The old class struggle is by no means fully played out. Boundaries of membership give rise to violent struggles. The rights of women and of minorities remain under-recognized. Such conflicts may involve playing out old themes rather than adding new ones, but they concern millions of human beings and need to be fought and won.

The second issue may on the contrary be a sign of things to come. The modern society of citizens has created new social problems. While it may have seemed to some as if everyone was on board, or a part of the race, it suddenly emerged that not only had some been left behind, but new groups were pushed to the margin and beyond. Persistent poverty and long-term unemployment are new issues of citizenship, and the old instruments of the social state do not seem able to cope. It is not easy (yet?) to tell what form the conflicts arising from a new exclusion will take. They are not likely to be traditional class conflicts because those at the margin are scattered, disorganized and weak. But they represent a living doubt in the contract of society which cannot fail to affect the rest. Perhaps law and order is the subject which tells the story.

In the meantime, those who are included are discovering new kinds of entitlement issues. They enjoy full citizenship rights but are also affected by threats to their natural environment, by the deterioration of their habitat, perhaps by the absence of certain services as a result of the cartel of special interests. Such deprivations do not constitute classes, because they affect everyone. The few who can escape them by moving to the South Seas are hardly relevant, and may even be in for surprises there. But everyone is affected only with a part of his or her social existence. A disparity of social position has been replaced by 'disparities of realms of life'.[14] The resulting conflicts mobilize everyone to some extent, though there are always activists for a cause. The resulting social movements or, more modestly, civic initiatives add an element to modern conflicts for which class-based institutions are ill prepared.

The third issue is the biggest of all. Perhaps socialism in one country is possible, even if it is not viable; but a civil society in one country is strictly not possible. Let there be no misunderstanding. Of course, one can and must start at home building a civilized society of citizens. But as long as this is confined to the boundaries of nations it is also coupled with attitudes, policies and rules of exclusion which violate the very principles of civil society. The historic task of creating civil society will be complete only once there are citizenship rights for all human beings. We need a world civil society.

This is the second or third time that I have mentioned the notion which some will regard as hopelessly utopian. Whatever it is, utopia it is not. As Pericles' Athens turned citizenship from a dream to a reality on which to build modern societies, so the civil societies of Europe and North America and some other places on the globe prefigure what is evidently possible everywhere. The process will take time and strategic action, but it is worth embarking on. We have to embark on it if we do not want to see the achievements of citizenship jeopardized. It is unfortunate that even our instruments of analysis are geared to the national boundaries of progress. When one says 'society', this is usually a euphemism for the territorial boundaries of nations. Social analysis is to all intents and purposes national analysis. (It is only honest for Germans to call economics *Nationalökonomie.*) As we try to tackle wider interrelations, we flounder. The study of international relations (note the expression!) has yet to become a serious subject, and there are only rudiments of genuine international law. Some instructive studies of war have been written, though fewer of peace, and numerous stilted vacuities about strategy in the nuclear, or any other age. The application of economic approaches to the global scene has suffered from an overdose of ideologies of the establishment of the International Monetary Fund or the equally established left of dependency and decoupling theories. These are overstatements of course, but I believe they overstate a valid case. It would be wonderful and important to know more about the conditions and processes of extending civil society. This would include an understanding of conflicts which involve geographically dispersed groups, of entitlement struggles and the growth of provisions worldwide. Knowledge does not necessarily lead to action, but it might help. In any case, there is a vast field for theory as well as practice in an issue which figured prominently even in Immanuel Kant's project for a 'general history with cosmopolitan intent' 200 years ago; it is to create a general civil society under the rule of law.

It is clear then that citizenship has changed the quality of the modern social conflict. Remnants of class in the old sense continue to be with us and may even provide the underlying pattern of social and political antagonisms for some time to come. But increasingly they are overlaid with other, less familiar contests. It is certainly possible to use the term 'class' for them also. After all, inequality and power continue to be forceful factors making for divergent interests and strife. Often, a farewell to class is coupled with an overly idyllic picture of things to come. But if one retains the concept of class after citizenship, one has to qualify it and spell out the difference. I shall handle this question without undue claims of certainty. For purposes of analysis, it is sufficient to note that the days of entitlement conflicts are not over. Though most differences of income and status may have become gradual, and some of the old barriers are still there, new ones have been erected. In the world at large, such barriers of privilege remain the key issue. Citizens have not arrived, they have merely gained a new vantage point in the struggle for more life chances.

3 · Politics in Industrial Society

Moments and Motives of Change

Social structures of class and the resulting conflicts about citizenship enter the lives of ordinary people, and the history books, by way of politics. Arguably, this is more true for the history books than for people's lives. People have a strong sense of superiority or of injustice even before they express it in public. They act in accordance with their interests whether there are parties to organize them or not. Social forces are more than a figment of the sociological imagination. But they become visible, tangible and above all practical only when they are expressed in political divisions and decisions. At that moment, they also encounter other, complicating forces and influences. Class is not the only basis of political interest. Events occur which distract the attention of most from issues of citizenship. Above all, the logic of the political process adds unforeseen dimensions to the struggles of class. In this chapter, I want to explore the process by which the subjects and social configurations of conflict are translated into political action.

This perspective adds new facets to the modern history of citizenship. Plotting its progress from the early nineteenth century to the 1970s, one makes a number of discoveries.[1] The first is that the progress of changing entitlements is jerky. It is not incremental or gradual but occurs in steps. Every major change in entitlements is associated with a memorable event. This is especially so with respect to hard entitlements which become entrenched in law. The extension of suffrage in Britain is an example: in 1832, the Reform Act reduced and standardized income and property qualifications; in 1867–8 and again in 1884–5 further reductions in qualifications were enacted; in 1918, universal and almost equal suffrage was introduced for men over twenty-one and women over thirty; in 1928, it was extended to women over twenty-one; in 1948, the 'university seats' and certain other anomalies were abolished; in 1968, the voting age was lowered to eighteen years. Similar stories could be told about the introduction and extension of general and post-primary education, or about the core elements of the welfare state. In some countries, a minimum wage is stipulated by law. Where this is not the case, and unless wages and salaries are totally indexed, negotiated settlements which are legally binding determine people's incomes. Softer entitlements are not so clearly associated with specific events. The main steps on the road to citizenship are, however, identifiable. Often, they are celebrated dates of constitutional, political or social change.

The second discovery one makes in tracing the progress of citizenship is that by and large it truly is progress. There are long periods in which little happens, but when something happens, it is usually an improvement. Events which undo earlier achievements are rare and dramatic. Nazi Germany not only meant the abrogation of civil rights and political entitlements, but also involved the reduction of certain social citizenship rights, but then it resulted from a major, and possibly unique constitutional crisis. In general, citizenship is sticky. (Keynes described real wages as sticky. He meant that they tend to resist pressure to push them downwards. Today we know that this is more true in Europe than in the United States, which means that in Europe the entitlement character of real wages is more pronounced.) Once citizenship has advanced to a certain point, the probability is that it will stay there, and if it does not, a rupture of political continuity has occurred.

In both these respects, the story of entitlements differs from that of provisions, especially of goods and services. Economic development can be plotted as a smooth curve and is subject to conjunctural fluctuations.[2] In recent decades, the invention of economic policy has complicated the picture, as has the political cycle of economic fortunes associated with elections. Even so, it remains a fact that there is no simple parallelism between economic growth and the extension of entitlements. Major changes of entitlement structures occurred during the inter-war period when economic development was at best indifferent and fluctuated around the level first reached in 1913. Significant advances of citizenship took place when the economic outlook was quite uncertain, in 1918–19 for example, or again between 1944 and 1950. The provisions party likes to argue that unless there is growth there cannot be change. Curiously, both Marxists and advocates of capitalism insist on the primacy of economics over politics. In fact, the relations between growth and change are more complicated where they exist at all.

What has motivated the advances of citizenship if it was not the desire to make a growing cake of provisions available to more people? Some critical years have already been mentioned, 1918–19 and the years after the Second World War. Why should wars give rise to improvements in the lot of the many? Keith Middlemas has explored this question in considerable detail in his book *Politics in Industrial Society* from which the title of this chapter is borrowed.[3] There are at least two reasons why wartime politics produce reforms. One is ideological in the sense that it has to do with attitudes. The twentieth-century wars were not fought by small segments, but involved the near-total participation of the population in the war effort. Among ruling groups, this led to the conviction that those who had given so much without being politically or socially enfranchised had to be rewarded. They had to be given citizenship rights, as Winston Churchill put it at the end of the First World War. The view was not confined to one side in the war. 'It is a political impossibility', Max Weber wrote in 1917 as he outlined his ideas for post-war German democracy, 'to relegate returning soldiers to second place in their electoral rights by comparison to those strata which were able to maintain or even improve their social position, their wealth and their market opportunities while others gave their blood in the trenches to protect them.'[4]

The other relationship between wartime experiences and social reform is more practical, and is Middlemas's central theme. In Britain at least, the 'wartime social pact' presupposed the organization and co-ordination of the main parties to decision-making. Governments actually had an interest in stronger trade unions – contrary to Bismarck's strategy, British Conservative leaders recognized the advantages of organization over diffuse threats of violence – and also promoted the formation of employers' associations. As an alliance was forged between the three main actors, the 'corporate bias' emerged which has dominated almost fifty years of (British) political life. The bias could be sustained only if all had at least some of their interests recognized. This meant in the first instance recognition of the interests of the hitherto disadvantaged and their organizations. Middlemas argues that even the post-1945 Labour government did little in the field of redistribution and welfare policies that had not been discussed and largely agreed by the three partners of the corporate effort during the war.

Two particular points have to be added. Britain was fortunate in having leaders during the crucial period of both wars who were not only strong but also aware of the need for social change, Lloyd George and Churchill. Moreover, there were blueprints for change which by accident or by design met precisely that window of opportunity which divergent and normally antagonistic social groups shared at particular times. The names of Beveridge and Keynes will reappear in this book as exemplars of strategic change. For both, wartime coalitions and opportunities provided the stimulus for developing proposals which raised the life chances of many.

Not all entitlement changes, of course, were introduced by wartime coalitions or governments which felt some special national responsibility for the deprived and the disenfranchised. If one looks at the dates at which key elements of the welfare state were first enacted, one finds extraordinary divergence, and no obvious relationship to cataclysmic national events. Take health insurance: Germany 1883, United Kingdom 1911, France 1930. Or pension insurance: Germany 1889, France 1910, United Kingdom 1925. The German example is particularly striking. During Bismarck's rule, political entitlements remained at best stable and very limited; there was legislation to ban socialist organizations. At the same time, the working classes were given certain social entitlements. One was used to balance the other, and both in the interests of a conservative, indeed para-feudal ruling class.

The example takes us closer to the core of the issue raised by the confrontation of class theory and historical reality. Class conflicts and social changes were clearly not unrelated during the period under review here. Bismarck would have denied that he recognized in any way the conditions predicted in the *Communist Manifesto*; he found it hard enough to come to terms with their translation into the idealistic language of Lassalle's *Workers' Programme*. At the same time, he knew that he had to do something to pacify the increasingly unruly children of the new industrial age. He responded to social pressure. This was even more clearly the case at some of the other relevant dates: France 1910, Britain 1911, Britain 1925, France 1930. Thus the pressure of conflict was there, as was the action of change; but the bridge between the two is made of unexpected material, and at times it is difficult to find at all.

What happens in such situations is easier to describe than to explain or even to interpret. Social conflicts are undoubtedly real. There are clashes of interest between disenfranchised groups and those who defend the existing franchise. Pamphlets are published, meetings are called, suffragettes march in the streets, and ageing former liberals argue solemnly that those who have no property must not vote, or that women are physiologically inferior, or that protesters must be confronted with the full force of the law. In the end, however, something gives. The reason is not that the whole country is on fire, or even that the disenfranchised have gained a mysterious majority in the legislature. Their majority remains invisible in the corridors of power, and yet those who for long resisted change their minds. They do it grudgingly, partly because they hope to relieve a pressure which has become a nuisance, partly because they believe that they can turn the protest energy to their own advantage.

Thus there are several ingredients to political change. One is the force built up in more or less organized social movements which may, but need not, include political parties. Another is a situation which is ripe for change, and in which there is a kind of budding consensus. One would probably not find it by opinion research, but once action for change is taken, a majority feel that this is what they had wanted all along. This is why those who take the action are so important. They appear to be swimming against the tide, but in fact they have merely sensed the turning tide earlier than others. At first sight, they seem to offend their own supporters. One thinks of Winston Churchill saying after the war that 'socialism' (he meant the welfare state) must be allowed to run its course; or of Konrad Adenauer promoting co-determination in German industry; or of Charles de Gaulle turning *Algérie française* into an independent state. After the event, we know that they have unified rather than divided their countries.

For movements dedicated to systematic change this is a depressing scenario. But then, such movements are often in for depressing experiences anyway. The 'iron law of oligarchy' comes to mind by which Robert Michels suggested that those who seek power inevitably have to pay a price in democracy. One can lose one's effectiveness in two ways, by being too far removed from the seat of decisions, and by being too absorbed. In a sense, socialists have experienced both in their history. Keir Hardie, August Bebel, Jean Jaurès were leaders of social movements who changed perceptions but were not involved in taking decisions. Ramsay MacDonald, Hermann Müller, to a lesser extent Léon Blum, held high office, but will not go down in the history books as the great reformers. One must wonder whether enlightened conservatives and determined liberals are not in the end more effective agents of change.

This touches on a sore subject, which is the relationship between class theory and elite theory. Absolute claims have been made for both, but they shed little light on real processes of change. Absolute opposition to either is also not very helpful. Classes probably provide some of the energy and direction of social change. They cannot be ignored, and the substance of the interests which they defend can give one a sense of where things are moving. However, someone has to translate these interests into actions and move things along. There are many studies of the limitations of elites. They are self-recruiting; their members have similar biographies; most of them have degrees from the same select group of colleges or universities and in the same subjects; they know each other and speak a common language in more ways than one. But somehow these studies do not seem to get to the heart of the political process. Members of socially homogeneous elites are quite capable, under certain circumstances, of taking unorthodox radical decisions. Indeed, it is often the newcomers who are reluctant to stick their necks out and who therefore conform more than necessary. The more confident people are of belonging, the less need do they have to be purely defensive, and the more open they can be to the interests and impulses of social forces. Such reflections can lead to outrageous

53

conclusions. Homogeneous elites may be more effective agents of change than pluralistic ones. In any case, sensitivity to the order of the day is an important element in the picture sketched here, and it does not come automatically with having the support of a noisy movement.

Politics in industrial society is about mediating these various elements in an effective way. Parliaments have their function in this context. They assemble organized social forces, select leaders and provide them with opportunities, force them to listen. If they are sensitive and lively, they may even make leaders aware of the moment of action. However, the interplay of social forces, parliaments and elites remains liable to be disturbed in a variety of ways. Without losing sight of the main theme, I want to pursue this subject a little further, availing myself of the help of the most insightful author on the subject, Max Weber.

Max Weber and the Problem of Modern Politics

Max Weber has a place in the small pantheon which I am incidentally setting up in this book. Like Beveridge and Keynes (and like Wilhelm von Humboldt more than a century earlier) he was a straddler, precariously combining in his life scholarship and politics, theory and practice. Weber suffered more than the others from the conflicting demands of these worlds. His ascetic, puritanical streak made him try the impossible and keep the two apart, value-free science and passionate politics. The heroic attempt was bound to fail, but this is not to say that it was wrong. Weber was also a strategic reformer. He tells us that he began as a conservative and later became a liberal; immediately after the First World War, he even calls himself a 'radical', and advocates 'an entirely radical social democratization'. His name is associated with the fight against unrestricted submarine warfare, but then above all with the debate about Germany's post-war constitution. In 1917, he wrote a series of articles for the *Frankfurter Zeitung* on 'Politics and Government in the New Order of Germany'. They were intended for Germany after the war, and along with the famous lecture on 'Politics as a Vocation' (1919), they are a useful basis for setting out the problem of modern politics.[5]

Max Weber was a German. He had travelled, and of course read widely, but the experience of Imperial Germany determined the way in which he defined the problem of modern politics. There was the towering figure of Bismarck. Weber felt a characteristically liberal ambivalence towards him. Bismarck had achieved much for Germany, but in the process he had destroyed as much at home as he had built abroad. In particular, he had left no room, either institutionally or in terms of political culture, for modern leaders operating in a modern framework. Weber deplored the mediocrity of German leadership after Bismarck, and regarded it as a result of the Founder's peculiar mixture of weakness and strength. It was also a result of the social and political phenomenon of bureuacracy which, more than all others, informed Weber's thinking about modern politics.

Weber was obsessed with the role of bureaucracy. Whatever subject he tackled, he soon got on to its perniciousness. Mention feudal lords and absolute kings, and he will turn to their administrative machinery and its innate tendency for separation and autonomous power. Mention Bismarck, and he will launch into a detailed attack on the *Beamtenherrschaft* which followed him, bureau*cracy* in the emphatic sense, and the general 'will to impotence' which accompanied it. Mention 'rationalization' including the logic of capitalist development, and he will turn to the institutional nature of modern organization with its rules, its office personnel and the rest. Mention power and legitimacy, and he will describe the pattern of 'rational' or 'legal' legitimation by an administrative staff with certain characteristics of office, qualification and career. There is clearly an element of Prussian experience in the obsession, but there is also a vision which has lost none of its compelling awesomeness by seven decades of history. It is the vision of bureaucracy as a 'cage of bondage' for future generations. If bureaucracy is left to its own considerable resources, it will involve a perfect administration which is also total in the sense in which the word was to be used in 'totalitarianism', or in Goffman's 'total institution'. People are mere cogs in the wheels of a 'living machine', dependent and impotent.

Weber was curiously weak on the world before bureaucracy, and perhaps this is one of the points at which his German-ness tells. He had no real sense of the market, or of the political

55

marketplace for that matter, including the rough-and-tumble of American politics. But his singlemindedness added to the dramatic quality of his questions: 'How is it possible at all, in view of the overpowering tendency of bureaucratization, to save any part of any "individualistic" room for manoeuvre?' Weber is not asking for a literary or philosophical reply; his interest is in politics and political institutions. He therefore translates the general question into two more specific ones; I shall call them the questions of democracy and of leadership.

Weber raises the question of democracy from an important, though limited angle. In view of the rising indispensability and consequent power of the civil service he wonders how there can be 'any guarantee that there are powers which hold in check and effectively control the monstrous preponderance of this stratum which continues to grow in importance'. 'How will democracy even in this limited sense be possible at all?'

Democracy means many things to many people, and if the word is taken literally, it means something which probably cannot be. One may even wonder whether there should be a condition in which the people can be said to rule. The general will has for good reason created first confusion and then concern as Rousseau, Kant and Hegel gave it three quite distinct interpretations. If it is thought to be a substitute for institutions, permanently recreated by unconstrained discourse, it makes the sceptic think of anomy, the tyranny of the majority, and also straight autocracy. Where there is no domesticated power, crude power is likely to step in; where there are no institutions, arrogant claims will hold sway. If one wants to avoid the emotions and metaphysics of such debates, one had better consider democracy in a more limited sense. It has to do with feeding into the political process the interests and views of the many, and with legitimacy.

Max Weber reminds us that the simple model of social forces, including social classes, providing energy and direction, and elites reconciling their interests with the needs of the moment, is too simple. The nature of elites is not the only possible obstacle to the functioning of the model; though Weber has an apposite comment on the inability of 'nervous regimental commanders' to 'represent the interests of those in their charge to their superiors'. The bureaucratic threat is even more serious. For example, it can paralyse the mediators between the people (*demos*) and power (*kratia*), parliament. Parliament can become a mere talking shop in which representatives give vent to their grudges and wishes, but nothing happens as a result. This of course is how Bismarck saw the German *Reichstag*; but the European Parliament of the 1970s and 1980s is an even more pertinent example. Parliament can also become an ingredient of a part-corporatist and part-bureaucratic ball of wax in which all initiatives melt away into business as usual. Such bureaucratization of parliaments is a serious issue everywhere. It tends to turn those outside, 'the people', away from their political institutions and give rise to a new set of social movements which are soon faced with the same set of problems.

Two processes constitute the democratic minimum, as it were. One is the input of popular views and interests into the political system, the other is the control of those in power and their administration. If either democratic input or democratic control are blocked, a constitutional crisis ensues. The democratic minimum is not the application of some nice idea or sweet dream. It is the most sensible way of making sure that change can take place without revolution. In this sense, democracy is simply more efficient than other forms of government. Familiar complaints that democracy is slow and wasteful – 'if it wasn't for parliament and the press we could do what needs to be done quickly and effectively' – are at best uninformed; at worst they encourage people to support political regimes which are intrinsically unstable precisely because all is quiet within them. If on the other hand the noise rises above a certain level in countries which have adopted the democratic minimum, this is the price not of democracy but of it having gone wrong.

'Parliaments', Max Weber said, 'are in the first instance representations of those over whom bureaucracies rule.' Democratic fundamentalists will not like such language, yet it makes sense to the realist both in terms of input and of control. However, there are other constitutional arrangements. Referenda and plebiscites can be abused by conservatives as well as demagogues; but they cannot be dismissed. Control of power involves administrative review and judicial action as well as straight parliamentary procedures. The media are important in fact and perhaps should become more important in constitutional theory. An untidy structure of social movements and special interest groups, lively debates in universities and demonstrations by angry crowds in the streets is part and parcel of civil society. Democracy is almost by definition untidy, and whoever will not let it be is likely to get something worse.

Democracy, however, was not Max Weber's main concern. He worried more, and had more to say, about the second institutional question arising from his overriding concern, which has to do with 'what bureaucracy as such cannot achieve'. It takes Max Weber to his favourite subject of leadership. Subsequent history has not made it easier to use the word which Max Weber uses freely; but whether one likes it or not, the question has to be answered. It is the question of innovation, initiative, the readiness and ability to do things. As Schumpeter was to answer this question for economic development by extolling the virtues of the 'entrepreneur', so Weber answered it for public affairs by praising the social figure of the 'politician', the person who pursues 'politics as a vocation'.

It is worth mentioning that I am not concerned here with Max Weber's (in many ways obscure) concept of charisma, and of the legitimation of power by extraordinary claims to inspiration and standing. It is a part of Weber's routine analysis to point out that bureaucracy can predominate, but not lead. Indeed, bureaucracy is by definition headless. To be sure, many of those who are formally in charge of modern bureaucracies are themselves bureaucratic characters. But this is the problem; it creates rudderless, mediocre polities which are administered but not run. Bureaucrats are supposed to execute loyally and competently the decisions taken by others. There may be situations in which officials have to point out to their leaders that they regard instructions as wrong; but in the end they must either do what they are told, or go. Governments as well as other associations get their sense of direction from those at the top, the 'leading men', 'leading spirits', or just 'leaders'.

Weber never tires of adding further colours to his canvas of what leaders should be like, what talents they need, what conditions they should accept or reject, and under which circumstances they are most likely to emerge and to succeed. He is clearly fascinated himself by the 'sense' which he imputes to leaders, 'of holding a nerve fibre of historically important events in one's hands', and thus he proceeds with some gusto to the discussion of the three qualities of politicians: 'passion', 'sense of responsibility', and 'sense of proportion'. Like many young politicians of the time, my father bought the first edition of *Politics as a Vocation* in 1920, and underlined these passages with a red pencil. 'Passion' is not the 'sterile excitement' of intellectuals, but deep dedication to 'a thing', 'a cause', an 'it' in any case, *eine Sache*. The 'sense of responsibility' means that the politician knows that he is in charge; it is also an allusion to the 'ethics of responsibility' which the politician applies rather than succumbing to the demands of an 'ethics of conviction'. Pure morality has no place in politics where the actual consequences of actions matter; it is not enough for the politician to have the right beliefs, he or she must have an awareness of constraints, possibilities and ramifications. This requires judgement and a sense of proportion. 'Politics is made with the head, not with other parts of the body or soul,' Weber says, but given his own passions, he cannot sustain it for long: 'Truly, while politics is made with the head, it is certainly not made *only* with the head.'

Weber does not spell out in any detail the nature of the problem with which leaders are faced in a bureaucratic world, though he would probably agree if one used a metaphor from space travel. The leader who finds himself 'in charge' of a bureaucratic empire has to avoid two risks. One is that he enters his sphere of action at too steep an angle and burns up in the process; he becomes a bureaucrat himself. The other risk is that the angle is too flat, and he is thrown back into orbit; he remains a distant little light in the skies. The angle has to be right for the leader to be effective and maintain his or her integrity. Weber wondered whether there are constitutional arrangements which would make such a result more likely. This is why he supported those who introduced the direct election of the President and his emergency powers into the Weimar constitution of Germany. Some have, foolishly, held him partly responsible for the way in which President Hindenburg used these powers before and during 1933. Perhaps the absence of a real presidential system – or alternatively, a fully fledged parliamentary democracy, Westminster-style – was the greater shortcoming.

All answers to the problem of modern politics are controversial. A generation of democratic fundamentalists will be particularly worried about the independent role given to the political class not only by Max Weber but in this analysis also. They would like to think of those in relatively elevated positions as no more than a wholesome steam rising from geysers which reach deeply into the people's earth. Public debate has lost much subtlety since the nineteenth and early twentieth centuries. This is understandable in view of the experiences of recent decades. There is nothing subtle about tyranny, war and genocide, nor about the essentials of peace and liberty. However, the problem of modern politics as Max Weber defined it does not go away. It is, quite simply, how to combine democracy and innovation in the face of the increasing threat of bureaucracy.

The constitution of liberty has to respond to this problem. It has to find a way through the siren songs of the Scylla of democratization and the Charybdis of autocracy, but at the same time beware of the vast sandbanks of bureaucracy in the shipping lanes of progress. Such metaphors are often a little too neat. This one makes it sound as if constitutional liberals must not deviate by even one degree from the safe course forward. In fact there is more than one course. Once again, the imagination of reality exceeds that of theory, and it is instructive to indulge in it as we take the analysis forward.

On Mixed Constitutions

The American constitution must have pleased Max Weber. The presidency is pure leadership, Congress is pure democracy, and the role of bureaucracy is minimized by a ('spoils') practice which enables an incoming administration to fill all key positions with staff of its own choosing. The latter, to be sure, was not Max Weber's ideal of bureaucratic organization; he preferred the Prussian ethos of state officialdom, and perhaps the British concept of civil service. But the United States system seems to provide a neat institutional answer to the problem of modern politics.

And so it does. Despite the fact that not all presidents were or are great leaders, and that Congress has got deeply entangled in its own bureaucracy, and sometimes in esoteric games of status and money rather than democratic representation, the American constitution has worked extraordinarily well for more than two centuries. Moreover, the social basis of American politics should please theorists of modernization. Mobility is the birthmark of America; most Americans come from families in which someone at some not too distant stage took the courageous decision to brave traditions and often pressures at home, and then the oceans and Ellis Island as well. (The one notable exception, the descendants of black slaves, are different for this reason alone.) Americans have remained mobile. Such mobility was coupled from the outset with democracy *à la* Tocqueville, that is to say a fundamental condition of equality in which traditional ties of dependence were conspicuously absent.

To complete the picture with a somewhat more surprising observation, even theorists of class have reason to be pleased with the American example. 'The emphasis on "classlessness" in American political ideology has led many European and American political commentators to conclude that party divisions in America are less related to class cleavages than they are in other Western countries. Polling studies however belie this conclusion.' S. M. Lipset has traced such studies back to 1936; but long before that time, political conflict in America followed the model.[6] 'Even before the development of the two-party system in its present form, the political issues dividing the society tended to have a class character.' Lipset reminds us that even Tocqueville was not unaware of this fact. On closer inspection, Tocqueville said, party political controversies in America are not as 'incomprehensible or puerile' as they appear. 'The deeper we penetrate into the inmost thought of these parties, the more we perceive that the object of the one is to limit and that of the other to extend the authority of the people.'

Is the United States then a case study in pure democracy? Many authors have thought so and offered explanations in terms of wealth, or provisions in our terminology. Lipset created one of the dominant theories of the 1960s and 1970s when he stated (in 1959) 'that democracy is related to the state of economic development. The more well-to-do a nation, the greater the chances that it will sustain democracy.' When a critic pointed out that the United States in 1820, France in 1870, and Sweden in 1890 were hardly highly developed countries, but were democracies, Lipset used a strange crutch to save his theory and argued that these democracies had emerged before 'a worldwide communications system' made comparisons with others possible. But then, there is the British example, especially in the inter-war period. There is India. One might be forgiven for arguing almost the opposite case: democracy allows countries to play economic zero-sum games in freedom.

In any case, the American example tells a different story. It is that of a combination of civil rights and the open frontier. Both these concepts are meant here in a definite and uniquely American sense. Civil rights are close to what Tocqueville had in mind when he called the basic condition of equality, 'democracy'. They are rights of inclusion, citizenship rights, but strictly confined to the civil and a part of the political sphere. American history demonstrates how virulent citizenship even in this limited sense can be. If one side wants to limit and the other extend the authority of the people, then the class struggle may well become violent, as it often did in American history. The early constitutional battles, the Civil War, and the civil rights movement of the 1960s are three outstanding events in a long history of the struggle for citizenship. The Constitution and the Bill of Rights, the Civil Rights Act of 1866 and the Fourteenth Amendment, and the Civil Rights and Voting Rights Acts of 1964–5, as well as the Supreme Court rulings on affirmative action and related subjects in the 1960s and 1970s, are landmarks in an unending struggle for more entitlements for all.

But throughout one must note that Americans were reluctant to extend these entitlements into the social sphere. To be sure, the United States too has developed rudiments of a welfare state. Both President Roosevelt's New Deal and President Johnson's Great Society had to do with social rights. There is Social Security for the old, Medicare and Medicaid for many, Aid for Dependent Children and much else to prove the search for more comprehensive entitlements. But if one probes American attitudes to social policy, one soon makes a striking discovery. Americans do not like the notion of entitlements, which is widely used to describe and to discredit people's claims to help from the community. They prefer to think of social policy as assistance which is (unfortunately) needed in order to enable some people to be fully self-sufficient. The assumption is that self-sufficiency can be achieved without many social citizenship rights. This in turn means that people are not really entitled to social services, but are involved in a contract, and one which moreover resembles a private rather than the social contract. They are helped on the understanding that they are prepared to make their own contribution, and that essentially means, to help themselves.

Thus civil rights in America are strictly about the entry ticket to economic, social and political life, not about what happens afterwards. Everything that occurs inside, as it were, is left to a great struggle of all against all, the rat race as some call it, that attitude which has made social Darwinism so important not only in American thought. This is where the other side of the picture comes in, the open frontier. A restrictive interpretation of citizenship works because – and as long as – there are opportunities for individual advancement. American social mobility was never quite as extensive as the American dream suggests, though the dream had its own effect on people's attitudes and perceptions. American geographic mobility is not a myth; people do get if not on their bikes then into their cars and move from Detroit to Houston to San Diego.

However, they cannot move further west without falling into the ocean. They can move back, of course; there are spectacular examples of the reconstruction of apparently dying towns and regions in the east and the north. Above all, the open frontier has one other name which brings it closer to the rest of the world; it is 'economic growth'. As long as there is a chance to produce more provisions, there is also – given the entry ticket of civil rights and the absence of formal entitlement barriers – a chance for the individual to earn more, and to satisfy more of life's desires. There is a peculiarly American balance of elementary citizenship and seemingly unlimited provisions. This balance, and not mobility as such, let alone wealth or a particular stage of economic development, was the secret of American democracy.

In many ways, it still is. But the hurricanes of the 1970s have not left the United States unaffected; as this analysis proceeds to more recent times, the weaknesses of America's strength will emerge. First, let us cross the Atlantic, where one encounters a very different condition. In some respects, the country from which early Americans borrowed their experiences, if not always their theories, Britain, is a marked contrast to the United States. Its hallmark is political conflict without economic success. Whereas in America, politics for a long time did not really matter very much in people's striving for more life chances, Britain has tended to relegate economic advancement to second place. It is therefore a prime example of a country in which politics matters, though one cannot always be certain whether it matters as a great drama, a stage for acting out social divisions and national aspirations, or as an actual method for the allocation of life chances.

It is hard to describe the British constitution. In the twentieth century in particular, authors are torn between emphasis on the reality of the 'corporate bias' and the appearance of 'adversary politics'. However, in a comparative perspective, one cannot fail to be struck by the importance of innovation, change and leadership. From time to time, the British positively enjoy radical political leadership and they have built a system which enables such leaders to get into power and act out their idiosyncrasies. The method of election is a part of this system; it makes large majorities in parliament possible with little more than 40 per cent of the vote.[7] The power of the executive is not separated from that of the legislature; the prime minister has an almost automatic majority in parliament, and above all the important residual right to have it dissolved. An adversary style of debate is symbolized by the arrangement of benches in the House of Commons where government and opposition face each other. All this leads to curious distortions in what I have called the democratic input. The electorate can express its views only through the given channels of essentially two parties which are in most respects opposed to each other. It also limits the other side of the democratic minimum, control, although over time elections have led to alternations of power. But the innovative impetus in the system remains strong. What is more, bureaucracy in Britain – the Civil Service – has long been a model of a serving rather than a dominant administration. It has even prepared alternative legislative projects before elections, so that whichever party gets in can begin to implement its programme without delay.

The first observation to make in the context of this analysis is that the British constitution has proved remarkably resilient in times in which the economic fortunes of the country were at best relatively bad and at worst truly miserable. Even when people in Britain 'never had it so good', those in other parts of the world, including the nearby world of European competitors, had it much better. In the 1890s, Britain led the league of national income per capita by quite a margin, but eighty years later, the German figure had increased thirty-four times, the French seventeen times, the corresponding British figure only eight times; Britain had fallen from undisputed leader to the relegation zone of the premier division of the world economic league. Yet even during the inter-war period, there was never a real threat to the institutions of representative democracy. Post-war unemployment, the general strike, the depression, blackshirts and communists, the National Government and the split of the Labour Party certainly put British democracy under strain, but none of the many immigrants from Germany and other countries under totalitarian rule or occupation had any fear for the durability of Britain's unwritten constitution. After the war, Britain all but missed out on the economic miracle, but democracy reached a new height of success, with important reforms as well as periods of respite, and a near-perfect two-party game at Westminster.

Many theorists of democracy would not allow such a contrast between political stability and (relative) economic decline. This suggests one of two conclusions. Either theories of democracy are, to their detriment, insensitive to cultural difference, or Britain's secret was that it was not a democracy at all. In any case, it would seem that the Westminster system of adversary politics is almost perfectly suited for playing zero-sum games. Somehow the notion – implicit in the 'economic theory of democracy' from Schumpeter to Arrow and beyond – of political parties outbidding each other during campaigns, running into trouble when they can no longer deliver, but stimulating the economy in the process, does not seem to describe British politics between the late nineteenth century and the 1970s. Significant changes were of course brought about in this time. We have seen how the two wars have produced a surge of entitlement changes. T. H. Marshall's book about the extension of citizenship rights was after all an analysis of the British experience. Is there a wider lesson here? British politics has long been the politics of entitlements, not of provisions. It was geared to rights and privileges, not to economic growth. Such issues are often zero-sum games, where the gains of some have to be paid for by the losses of others, whereas the politics of growth runs into deep water when it no longer has a positive sum.

The peculiar features of British politics are not just the result of procedural arrangements but have deeper roots. They reflect an essentially static socioeconomic condition. This has often been described as a system of class; but if class points to the dynamics of social conflict, then the British condition was clearly something different. In Britain, people had settled into their 'classes' as if they were pre-industrial estates. They complained about their position, but they were also proud of their 'class', including not least the working class with its strong culture. In fact, the history of class in Britain could well be written as one of the defence of, and demand for entitlements for which economic position was never regarded as adequate compensation. Even in the 1960s, David Lockwood and John Goldthorpe described the 'affluent worker' as better off but still 'class conscious'. At the same time, there was much talk about an 'establishment' which had kept its privileged position despite modest economic success.[8]

This static, almost estate-like structure was probably the result of a peculiar turn of social and economic events in the second half of the Victorian era. Perhaps one can call it, with Martin Wiener, 'the decline of the industrial spirit'.[9] In any case, the country which had given rise to the modern revolution of industry somehow got tired of it after two or three generations. There was an enormous spurt of innovation; there were great social upheavals; but then people settled into a mould which had more in common with that of the eighteenth than with that of the twentieth century. The sons of entrepreneurs became the new gentry, country life and all; and the sons of the miserable inmates of workhouses became the terraced-house working class. Both had their clubs, their pastimes and their pride, and neither was clamouring for unlimited opportunities of economic improvement. It took more than the sons of entrepreneurs to make for a strong Conservative Party; there were middle-class groups, some aspiring, some happy to stay where they were. In general, however, the two-party system as a game, a theatrical display of social divisions, with entitlement changes as its major subject, expressed this condition perfectly.

The past tense in which the British story has been told requires a brief explanation. The British political game and its social foundation were never quite as stable as I have depicted them here. However, in recent decades, both have turned out to be highly precarious. Several things happened within a short time. Certainly, people came to compare their lot with that of others of whom the 'worldwide communications system' made them aware. Minority groups of immigrants added a new element to city life, and to the position and consciousness of the working class. The 'politics of economic decline' in the end raised questions of governability. Young middle-class groups (not all 'upwardly mobile urban professionals') demanded that traditional moulds be broken. Two Tory prime ministers set out to do so; the first, Edward Heath, was soon discouraged by English tradition and made his much-discussed U-turn, whereas the second, Margaret Thatcher, had no qualms about sacrificing Britain's social and political civilization on the altar of economic success. Attention was and is turned away from entitlements and towards the view that growing provisions will solve all problems, with consequent divisions of an unfamiliar explosiveness.

But this takes us beyond the great divide of the 1970s before the points in between have been made. For significant periods of modern history, the constitutional mixtures of Britain and America were as different from each other as they were both successful. The combination of civil rights and economic growth in one case, and of innovative politics and a poor growth record in the other, turned out to be stable and acceptable. One gave little scope to the political process, the other much; one was emphatically modern in that it presupposed and favoured individual mobility; the other was in many ways half-modern; but both recognized the principle of citizenship and the need for change. The mixtures were viable. The German mixture was not. It was on the contrary such that its faultings gave rise to a series of sociopolitical earthquakes which shook first Europe and then the world. The post-war Federal Republic of Germany is the first German state which appears to have stable and democratic constitutional conditions.

Even present-day West Germany has not been able to rid itself entirely of bureaucracy, the most serious failure to come to terms with the problem of modern politics. For a long time, what I have called the democratic minimum has been missing in Germany. There was neither effective control by elected politicians nor a regular input of views and interests of the many. This meant that they had to look for other outlets which were extra-parliamentary at first, anti-parliamentary soon after, and made the constitution the issue rather than the basis from which to act. At the same time, leadership tended to be ineffectual as an instrument of considered change. One of the prime concerns of many in positions of authority was to be recognized as competent experts, almost as good as government officials. As a result, the machinery of government had a tendency to creak to a halt, only to be set in motion again by dramatic change, and by idiosyncratic leadership. In so far as the constitution of liberty is about change without revolution, Germany failed to come to terms with it.

The story behind this failure has so often been told that I hesitate to repeat it, except that other countries to the present day have followed a similar path, so that there is a lesson to be learned. It is a story of economic growth without civic entitlements. Thorstein Veblen analysed it as early as 1915 in his *Imperial Germany and the Industrial Revolution*.[10] This is a book of divination as much as information, but its main point is no less valid for its source.

According to Veblen, Germany combined a 'nearly unbroken medievalism of the institutional scheme', and in any case a 'State of the dynastic order' as well as the corresponding values, with rapid, borrowed industrialization. The 'industrial arts' were as a result 'wholly out of consonance with their institutional scheme, but highly productive, and so affording a large disposable margin for the uses of the dynastic State'. In Germany, a ruling class with largely feudal credentials tried to make industrialization its own affair. This is very different from an industrial class adopting some quasi-feudal values and moulding them in its own image. Germany provides the first major example of industrialization from above, authoritarian industrialization as it were. Its driving force was neither the free contract of labour based on civil rights for all nor the innovative entrepreneur operating in a market, but the feudal lord (the infamous *Herr im Haus*) and the obedience of his subjects.

Many, from the last tsars to contemporary Latin American dictators, have tried to imitate the German model of upholding an old ruling class and its values throughout the process of modern economic growth. In Europe and Latin America, most have failed. Even if they succeeded in getting their economies going, they paid the price of unstable political conditions.

I have referred earlier to Bismarck's gamble with the substitution of welfare for citizenship rights. It did not work. Citizenship proved to be the stronger force; welfare paternalism could not hold down the class struggle forever. But when it appeared in 1918 that after a traumatic war Germany might be ready to join the modern world, two things happened. One was that economic conditions became unstable and unsettling. Some blamed the war, some the reparations; in any case, the recovery from hyperinflation in 1923 was soon overtaken by the great depression. In so far as people linked these events to the experience of democracy, their conclusions were not happy. The other event was the discovery that 1918–19 had been rather less than a revolution. Whatever doubts one may have about Mancur Olson's claim of a near-total continuity of important structures from the 1870s to the 1930s, there was enough continuity to make many wonder about the virtues of democracy.[11]

In an awesome way, it took Hitler's National Socialism to complete the revolution of modernity for Germany. This thesis of mine (in *Society and Democracy in Germany*) has often been criticized, but I would still maintain its essence which is that all remaining premodern barriers of estate and Church allegiance, of authoritarian benevolence without civic participation, of immobility and traditionalism were brutally destroyed by a regime which needed total mobilization to maintain its totalitarian power. The effects of this great dismantling process were not immediately evident; in retrospect one is struck by how short this disastrous episode of history was. But it meant that, in the negative sense of the absence of traditionalist obstacles, German democracy had its first real chance after 1945. The fact that soon after there were two Germanies, and that for reasons not of their choosing they went two very different ways of modern political organization, is a sobering reminder of the limits of social analysis.

If the British example defies textbooks of democracy, the German one defies those of capitalism. But again, the German economic miracles before 1913 and even after 1948 were perhaps not very good examples of capitalist growth. In both cases, though especially before the First World War, the agents of growth were large bureaucratized organizations, the banks, instant big businesses, and government. Entrepreneurs and politicians were conspicuously absent – *pace* Bismarck and Adenauer – and so was the democratic input. For many decades, Germany's rulers were reluctant to grant the people the entitlements which go with a modern civil society. A bureaucratic version of the rule of law was inherited from Prussia, but it was not coupled with civic participation or parliamentary control. As a result, the country vacillated between autocracy and bureaucratic ossification. It could have done with a dose of class struggle to vitalize the constitution of liberty; but this impious wish is hardly relevant after the event. Even today, the risk of Max Weber's cage of bondage is greater in Germany than elsewhere, though the burned earth left behind by Hitler has allowed the construction of one civil and wealthy society on German soil.

The (West) German route to liberty adds a painful variant to the more acceptable ones of Britain and the United States; there were others still. For the last two centuries, France has vacillated between emphatic demands for more democracy and a penchant for authority. This has not favoured a steady process of development, but it has enabled the country to scrape by several incipient revolutions (after 1789 of course) and at the same time avoid the worst abuses of modern power. Switzerland has undergone a mysterious process of change under a surface of tradition and stability. It is hard to identify Swiss leaders who have moved things forward, or even the social forces behind them, but the movement has happened. Perhaps the entire political class of the country worked for progress, while the people provided through referenda the inertia of conservation.

The answer to the problem of modern politics is thus not to be found in a single word. Many use the word 'democracy', but on inspection this describes only a part of the answer. I prefer Friedrich von Hayek's phrase, the constitution of liberty, though not necessarily in his definition.[12] The advantage of this notion is that it describes the objective of the solutions which we are looking for, liberty, and the means by which this objective is sought, a constitution in the wide and not necessarily formalized sense of the term. The constitution of liberty has three indispensable elements. They are the rule of law, democracy and leadership. The rule of law makes people citizens, equal members of civil societies. Democracy enables citizens to make their voice heard. It gives them the right, and at times of crisis the duty, to say what they want and what not. The positive side of democracy, what people want, is better suited for festive speeches about political culture, but the apparently negative side, control, criticism and protest, may well be more important for freedom. Leadership keeps societies moving. It helps prevent them from getting stuck in the cage of bureaucracy; it also cuts through the perpetual discourse of total democracy. By the interplay of democracy and leadership civil societies remain open.

A fourth factor, economic growth, is not strictly an ingredient of the constitution of liberty, though its presence helps. History shows that it is also helped by civil societies with open structures. It is a favourable light in which the constitution of liberty can be cast, though the necessary ingredients of this constitution have shown strength at times of economic gloom, and growth has often not sufficed to bolster the rule of law, or democracy.

As for the practical history of the constitution of liberty it has brought about many variants. The rule of law may be procedural or substantive; civic participation may be direct or representative; initiatives may grow out of political parties or presidential powers. Constitutional arrangements have to respond to the history, culture and other unique conditions of particular societies. They are hard to translate from one country to another. This is not an alibi for sundry violations of the essentials of liberty; on the contrary, it means that the formal presence of certain arrangements says little about their reality. Moreover, the purer constitutions are, the more reason there is for suspicion. It is all too easy to cover up privilege, or stagnation, with a beautiful text. Really existing liberty is usually untidy. One of the few conclusions to be drawn from the inspection of examples of modern politics is therefore the praise of mixed constitutions. Perhaps I should have said 'of some mixed constitutions'.

4 · Temptations of Totalitarianism

The Vanishing Proletariat

July 1914 was a fateful month in the modern history of Europe and perhaps the world. When it began, the advanced nations had experienced several decades of economic growth. Civil rights had not followed suit everywhere but demands for full citizenship were strong and the guardians of privilege began to give way. No one could have any doubt about the reality of the class struggle. Progressive liberal parties had turned their attention to the social question; socialist parties were increasing their electoral strength. There was change in the air. At the same time, the great powers – Britain, France, Germany, Austria-Hungary, Russia – were at peace. Progress seemed if not inevitable then at least probable.

On 28 June, Archduke Franz Ferdinand of Austria had been assassinated in Sarajevo. At first, few appreciated the possible ramifications. There was agreement in the capitals of Europe that Austria was entitled to take revenge on Serbia for the outrageous act. Vienna's ultimatum was noted with a degree of apprehension, though the French President embarked on his journey to Russia as if no major threat was imminent. Some began to talk about a limited war in the Balkans. Talk of war aroused sleeping dogs which became more vicious by the day. Alliances were confirmed and new ones explored. The air became electric. Soon the military were alerted, and as the wires between the capitals heated up, stages of mobilization were passed. Suddenly, everyone spoke of war, with excitement, with horror, and in the end with a curious fatalism. In the final days of July, the capitals of Europe agreed that war had become inevitable. When Kaiser

Wilhelm of Germany tried to stop the process at the last minute, his generals told him that this could no longer be done. *Alea iacta*. This was nonsense, but generals are bureaucrats, and bureaucrats quite like to shrug their shoulders over the course of events while letting them have their way. Kaiser Wilhelm of course was not exactly Max Weber's ideal politician; so war was declared.

Britain's foreign secretary Edward Grey coined the phrase during those summer days: 'The lamps are going out all over Europe; we shall not see them lit again in our lifetime.' He was right in more ways than one. The story has to be told here precisely because it is not simply one of the unfolding modern conflict. Attempts to explain the First World War as the imperialist extension of capitalist greed, or the ascendancy of National Socialism in Germany as a desperate capitalist ruse to safeguard power, miss most of the points. If ever economics became the handmaid of politics, it was during the second Thirty Years' War. This is not to say that social conflicts were absent, or that class conflict, the struggle for citizenship and the desire to improve life chances had become irrelevant. But their relevance appeared in strange deflections. At the end of the day, when Europe lay in ruins and the nuclear age had been inaugurated by the death of hundreds of thousands in Hiroshima and Nagasaki, the conditions were ripe for the orderly democratic class struggle and a unique economic miracle. Until then, obstacles to modernity, to the extension of citizenship, the growth of life chances, and liberty apparently had to be removed in explosive and violent ways.

One of the lights that went out all over Europe was the revolutionary illusion. It did not go out all at once and continued to flicker into the 1930s, but its strength was gone much earlier. Instead of 'the revolutionary illusion', I might have said 'hope'. It is true that the star of hope was dimmed by events in 1914 and the following years. But here the subject is 'hype' rather than hope, the hyperbole of hope which expects a totally different world to emerge soon. Hope is an indispensable motive force for action. It is also necessary to tie hope to real social forces and political groupings if it is not to remain a mere dream. We need an image of the future and a notion of how we might get there. The hyperbole of the revolutionary illusion, on the other hand, combines faith in

73

the inexorable march of progress with a utopian vision. It takes people out of the real world and in effect if not in intention away from freedom.

For many, the key to such hyperbolic hopes was the concept of the proletariat. Marx was far from the only author to have endorsed it, but he above all others had paved the way from reality to utopia. 'The conditions of bourgeois society are too narrow to comprise the wealth created by them.' The bourgeoisie therefore has to destroy productive forces in order to survive, until the crises brought about by such destruction turn against it; for 'not only has the bourgeoisie forged the weapons that bring death to itself; it has also called into existence the men who are to wield those weapons – the modern working class, the proletarians'. In response to an increasingly nervous bourgeoisie, the proletariat (according to Marx) will grow in size, in homogeneity, in misery and in organizational strength. Like the bourgeoisie in feudal society, the proletariat in bourgeois society is 'the class that holds the future in its hands'. But unlike the bourgeoisie, the proletariat will not set up another minority rule. With bourgeois relations of production, it will destroy all previous relations of production and the superstructures that went with them. Thus, the proletarian revolution will 'have swept away the conditions for the existence of class antagonisms and of classes generally, and will thereby have abolished its own supremacy as a class. In place of the old bourgeois society, with its classes and class antagonisms, we shall have an association in which the free development of each is the condition of the free development of all.' And so on, in the *Communist Manifesto*, in the enthusiastic poetry of the time, in the songs of the labour movement, and the call to proletarians of all countries to unite.

Instead, the representatives of the proletariat voted for the war credits in the parliaments of their respective countries. The socialist parties of France and Germany were undoubtedly doing what their voters wanted them to do in August 1914. Instead of creating a different world, the workers went to war for the world that is. And who could be surprised? When did the poor and downtrodden of the earth ever create a world in their image? Is it not a patronizing intellectual fallacy to impute to the most needy utopian fantasies rather than real interests? The poor seek a place in the sun, this sun, today's sun, rather than the lights of some unknown world. Being told that they carry the future in their hands does not feed them or house them. It is therefore quite natural that their dreams are built on what they see in the present. The industrial working class and its political organizations certainly were a force for change, but this change meant the unfolding of a principle which was already present, citizenship.

Some were surprised, to be sure. Many intellectuals had fallen for the revolutionary illusion. Intellectuals played an important part in the second Thirty Years' War which is why they will come up often in the present story. A number of leaders of the labour movement were either intellectuals themselves or taken in by their hyperbole. The fears of the powers that be mirrored such extravagant hopes. But somewhere between 1914 and the 1930s, between the initial acceptance of the war of nations by socialist parties and the ascendancy first of Stalin in Russia, then of Hitler in Germany, the proletariat all but disappeared as a lodestar of hope for a different world.

The vanishing act of the proletariat had several facets which point to social developments which are important enough to be recounted. One of these may well be a simple fact rather than a development. Those who wrote and sang about the new world of the proletariat apparently knew little about the real views of working people. Contrary to abstract belief, they tend to be intolerant rather than tolerant, nationalist rather than internationalist, hostile to libertarians and protective rather than freedom-loving and open. 'Both evidence and theory suggest that the lower strata are relatively more authoritarian, that they will be more attracted to an extremist movement than to a moderate and democratic one, and that, once recruited, they will not be alienated by its lack of democracy, while more educated or sophisticated supporters will tend to drop away.' Who can undertake to contradict Lipset when he points out that the 'gradual realization that extremist and intolerant movements are more likely to be based on the lower classes than on the middle and upper classes' has 'posed a tragic dilemma for those intellectuals of the democratic left who once believed the proletariat necessarily to be a force for liberty, racial equality, and social progress'?[1]

Disappointment with working-class attitudes was accompanied by an even deeper disillusionment with the organizations of the labour movement. When Robert Michels first published his *Sociology of Political Parties* in 1911, his main thesis was no longer entirely new, though it was still shocking. It was simple really, suggesting that socialist parties are not very different from other parties and organizations; but the implications upset many. 'Whoever says organization, states a tendency towards oligarchy.' The masses cannot lead, and once they form parties and trade unions they are led by a minority. Representatives rule over their electors, delegates over those who gave them their mandate. Michels dug deep into human nature and the imperatives of society to back up the simple observation that a party is a party is a party. It is not always clear whether he was upset about society in general or about avoidable weaknesses of its real manifestations. Either way, he concluded that the labour movement had become a part of the normal political process. Social democracy was born. What this meant was put in airy but telling language by Georg Lukács when in 1922 he deplored the process of 'real political organization' which 'forces the proletariat back into its immediate existence where it is merely a component of capitalist society and not at the same time the motor that drives it to its doom and destruction'.[2]

Michels's juxtaposition of oligarchic leaders and a mass of members had another implication. It hinted at a description of the hallowed proletariat as being without structure or culture. It was simply a mass. The 1920s were a time also in which the allegedly atomized masses were discovered as the scourge of modernity. Gustave Le Bon's *Psychology of Masses* was still widely read; José Ortega y Gasset wrote his *Revolt of the Masses*. Theodor Geiger, in his book on *The Mass and Its Action*, tried to defend the many by reintroducing an emphatic notion of the proletariat as the bearer of revolutionary tidings, but his later books show that he barely convinced himself. Many were more inclined to follow Werner Sombart's assessment of the proletariat as a 'qualityless mere-quantity'. The 'omnibus proletarian' is by now 'the same colourless and characterless figure in London and Rome, in Moscow and in Paris, in Berlin and in Vienna'.[3] The road from hyperbole to cynicism is not very long.

Real social developments did not help the remaining believers in the proletariat. Economically, the inter-war period was one of mixed fortunes, but some redistribution took place. As a result, a portion of the working class moved at least outwardly into a middle-class existence. The word *embourgeoisement* gained currency. In any case, Marx's thesis that in due course the proletariat would be one huge homogeneous class was proved wrong. Industrial progress required new skills; the distinction between skilled, semi-skilled and unskilled workers was more than a formality.

Industrial progress, and economic development generally, also led to the massive growth of a 'new middle class' of private and public office workers. It had first been noticed before the First World War, and continued to preoccupy social analysts throughout the 1920s. Clearly, the growing new middle class – as well as the stubborn survival of an 'old middle class' of self-employed craftsmen, small shopkeepers, farmers – made nonsense of the assumption that sooner or later the overwhelming majority of all people would be drawn into a largely undifferentiated proletarian existence. True, the working class was still growing; in many advanced countries it comprised about 50 per cent of the population. But other strata were growing more rapidly, and their social position was by no means clear. When Emil Lederer and Jakob Marschak published their influential study of 'the New Middle Class' in 1926, they were still arguing that it was wrong to call the salaried groups a 'buffer between big capital and the proletariat', and that the new service class had found its place in existing trade unions along with traditional workers. Six years later, Theodor Geiger was the first to show that things were not quite so simple. While in many practical respects white-collar or blackcoated employees were like workers, they not only wore white collars or black coats but also had their own characteristic sociopolitical 'mentality'.[4] This led them to support a party which was equally opposed to the rule of capital and to the proletarian revolution, the Nazi party.

To complicate matters further, really existing socialism began to sow doubts in the minds of true believers. In the 1920s, there were two kinds of socialism. One was social democracy in government. Whoever still believed in the imminence of the millennium could hardly fail to recognize that this was not going to be brought about by Reichskanzler Hermann Müller and Prime Minister Ramsay MacDonald. The Soviet experience raised even more serious issues. Some took a very long time indeed to recognize the true nature of the Soviet regime, but the process of disillusionment began in the 1920s when the first travellers brought back their tales, and many started to wonder about the dictatorship of the proletariat, the length of the 'period of transition', and Stalin. An increasing split in the labour movement of free countries, and notably the vicious attacks by communists on social democrats, did not help.

If one had one's eyes open and one's feet on the ground, the meaning of these developments was not hard to fathom. I have described it as the gradual extension of citizenship rights to those who were initially deprived, by a combination of social pressure and strategic political reform. The working class was anything but an unstructured mass. On the contrary, from being an 'unconnected set of individuals exposed to the elements like desert sands' it had become a 'powerful, confident, well-established part of society'. In the process, it had not only found its own position much improved, but had also 'changed the character of the bourgeois economy in a significant way'. The man who used such language in a retrospective analysis published after 1945 has a claim to a place in the pantheon of strategic reformers which incidentally emerges in this book. It was Karl Renner, a leading 'Austromarxist' in the 1920s, who truly had his eyes open and his feet on the ground.[5] He was to be the first President of Austria after the Second World War.

Others did not find it so easy to abandon the revolutionary illusion. The contortions to which some went (and a handful still go) in order to save a lost theory are extraordinary. They range from the strenuous denial of change through the notion of an 'externalized proletariat' in the developing world to a new ethereal Marxism. The proletariat, according to this line of reasoning, was never intended to mean real working people, but something much more abstract, 'the collective worker', work itself, even the totality of social relations. Such evaporation of reality meant the abdication of intellectuals as a political force. It is therefore of little interest.

However, the void which the vanishing proletariat left in the minds of intellectuals must not be underestimated, nor should it be discounted because only intellectuals felt it. What the critical guardians of interpretations and visions think and say is not just a part of an esoteric world of the mind. It is that too, and with the

growth of the modern intelligentsia, a set of jargons has developed which at times seems designed to restrict audiences
rather than extend them. Language here is a means of identi-
fication and not of communication. Even so, intellectuals are
seismographs of social change, and sometimes they are catalysts
and ferments too. Intellectuals remain instrumental for any
liberal solution of the problem of modern politics, because they
translate the interests of social movements into the language of
decision, they interpret decisions to the public, and through all
that they maintain a critical detachment from leaders, bureaucrats and popular interests alike which is an indispensable
lubricant of openness.

That is, if they maintain such detachment. The history of the
second Thirty Years' War is as much a story of intellectual
betrayal as it is one of the liberal mind. The revolutionary illusion
itself was a form of treason of the intelligentsia. Hyperbole and
utopia pave the way for ideology and tyranny. Some of those who
tried to fill the void left by the vanishing proletariat with other
forces of history were relatively harmless. Today, we have got
used to the fact that every so often an author proclaims the
revolution of yet another group, of managers, scientists, 'yuppies'. Increasingly, intellectuals themselves figure prominently in
the world view of intellectuals. Karl Mannheim started the
fashion in the 1920s with his bestseller on *Ideology and Utopia*
which left only the 'free-floating intelligentsia' as a subject of
hope. Was he too 'free-floating' perhaps? Recently published
evidence suggests that even Mannheim, the Jewish sociologist
from Frankfurt, wavered for a period in the face of Hitler's regime
before he finally emigrated to London. The void in the mental
budget of hyperbole was a dreadful temptation. When Robert
Michels published the second edition of his book in 1925, he had
already embraced the fascist movement of Mussolini. If the
masses cannot rule, then let us be ruled by unadulterated
power . . . Hyperbole remains, though it is transferred from the
proletarian illusion to the reality of total power.

Totalitarianism

In the years between 1914 and 1945, things happened which defy
normal categories of analysis. The attempt to talk about them in a

calm and matter-of-fact way seems to ignore the pain of the victims and of those who cannot forget their fate. Was it fate? For those who suffered, it may have appeared so, especially since so many went their last way in the midst of a great silence at home and abroad. But of course their murder was man-made. The holocaust was man-made, as was the 'harvest of sorrow' in the Ukraine, and the Gulag, to say nothing of the wars themselves, the First World War, the Second World War, and the Spanish Civil War in between, where the two totalitarianisms met, still on a human scale, and where many remaining illusions were shattered.

Explaining totalitarianism is not easy. It falls right outside the progress from traditional to rational power, from authoritarianism to the constitution of liberty. Many have struggled even to describe its features: 'an ideology, a single party typically led by one man, a terroristic police, a communications monopoly, and a centrally directed economy'.[6] Is it really just another 'form of government' or even 'mode of legitimation'? One thinks of Hitler's German National Socialism and Stalin's Soviet Communism. Both were full of contradictions, 'blood and soil' but also 'total mobilization', emphasis on solidarity but also brutal power, romantic antimodernism but also an architecture of frightening 'modernity', sentimental songs of yesterday and tomorrow in cold military formations. There were unmistakable differences too. One attracted the traditional right, the other the traditional left, however much their patterns of power may have merged until in 1939 a diplomatic alliance between Nazi Germany and the Soviet Union became possible.

I shall argue that European totalitarianism was uniquely characteristic of the two decades between the world wars. There are obvious reasons for this. The First World War not only brought Lenin to power in Russia, but also led to the Treaty of Versailles and the incomplete democracy of Weimar. The Second World War grew out of totalitarian power and its expansive claims. While the roots of totalitarian ideologies may go back to the eighteenth century and beyond, it was during the inter-war period that these ideologies became virulent. The less obvious question is why this should have been so. It has led some to metaphysical invocations of the Russian soul and the German character. I have little use for such fantasies, but would instead take a hard look at politics and society in inter-war Europe.

In doing so, one makes a surprising discovery. Among those who have tried to discover the social structure of totalitarian regimes, one idea stands out. It is that totalitarianism is the result of the replacement of older social structures by structureless 'mass' societies. 'Totalitarianism', wrote Leonard Schapiro, 'is a new form of dictatorship which grew up in the conditions of mass democracy after the First World War.' (We have seen how the proletariat of old was said to have merged into the post-1918 mass.) Hannah Arendt took up a theme of Franz Neumann's when she traced totalitarianism not only to the 'structurelessness of a mass society' but to the 'specific conditions of an atomized and individualized mass'. In his very last (unfinished) article, Neumann returned to the idea and described totalitarian techniques *inter alia* by 'the atomization and individualization of the individual, which involves negatively the destruction or at least weakening of social units based on biology (family), tradition, religion, or co-operation in work or leisure; and positively the imposition of huge and undifferentiated mass organizations which leave the individual isolated and more easily manipulable'. Characteristically, several authors on the subject quote with approval Tocqueville's fears of the tyranny of the majority and the risks of a new 'democratic despotism'.[7]

The analysis corresponds to the experience of those involved. 'I became converted because I was ripe for it and lived in a disintegrating society thirsting for faith,' Arthur Koestler says in describing his conversion to communism.[8] The theme is familiar. It has to do with modernity and the loss of ligatures. An antimodern streak, a revolt against modernity is indeed unmistakable in the temptation of totalitarianism. But we must not be misled by easy language. Structureless mass societies? What were these authors talking about? Europe in the 1920s? Surely there is something wrong here.

Tocqueville wrote of course about the United States where feudal structures had never existed and individualist values had been enshrined in the constitution. If there was one mass society in the 1920s, it was American society. However, America adopted Model T Fords and early Hollywood products, and perhaps the attitude of 'keeping up with the Joneses' which David Riesman was to describe much later as 'other-directedness', but it did not become either fascist or communist, nor was it ever at risk.

81

Germany and Russia in the 1920s, on the other hand, were hardly prototypical modern mass societies. Weimar Germany was shot through with active remnants of an earlier age, East Elbian landlords and industrial cartels, estate-conscious civil servants and stable church allegiances. In the Soviet Union, the 1920s and 1930s were a time of the deliberate destruction of surviving pre-modern structures; but no one would describe Russia in 1917 or the Soviet Union in 1927 as a modern mass society of atomized individuals. Totalitarianism was tempting not to atomized modern masses (if such existed or exist anywhere) but to those who got stuck halfway between old and new, who had lost one without having found the other and then fell for the false promise of the best of both. Its ingredients are incomplete modernity, the treason of intellectuals and the lure of leadership.

In his essay on 'National Socialism as a Temptation', Fritz Stern summarizes the programme of the Nazis in terms which give a sense of these ingredients: 'The class struggle would be overcome; the people would be united again; a powerful *Führer* would rule the Third Reich; enemies of the state would be driven from the land; and the Jews, who were responsible for Germany's woes, would be excluded from the national community; there would be no more parties; the *Führer*, as a forceful dictator, would embody the will of the people.'[9] Instead of the modern social conflict the promise of the womb of community, with a narrowly defined identity to allay the fear of freedom, and a modicum of paranoia to settle remaining self-doubts, plus of course the Führer.

The temptation lay in setting an end to the discomforts of an incomplete civil society at a time of uncertain economic growth. Those tempted were above all people – voters – who had lost their place in an old scheme of things without having found one in a new order, in that sense 'displaced strata'. Many Nazi leaders were recruited from socially rootless families. Their supporters came from certain lower-class groups which were 'never integrated in the total society', small businessmen and other self-employed who were equally upset about organized capital and organized labour, white-collar people torn between their aspirations and their position, and those 'conservative and tradition-alist elements' who wanted to preserve a world without modern politics.[10] Neither citizens nor classes account for the rise of

National Socialism, but the disoriented products of a faulted structure of old and new. Their problem was that they were groups without a home rather than atomized masses of individuals.

The treason of liberal values was not confined to intellectuals. Many weaker souls thrived in the long shadow of leaders who allowed them to punish helpless victims with their frailty. The totalitarian era was also an era of cowardice. Cowards paved the way, carried the flag and executed the crimes for the leaders. They are despicable while blind activists and erring idealists are frightening. Intellectuals however betrayed more than partisan values; they betrayed the civil society which made them possible. It was a dreadful sight which must not be forgotten.

In the German case, one thinks above all of the spring and summer of 1933 when few managed to resist the enthusiasm of the time and many fell for a strange retrospective doubt in liberty. In some cases, this was not surprising. Ernst Jünger had advocated 'total mobilization' and advanced the anti-proletarian ideal of 'the worker'; Carl Schmitt had reduced politics to relations between friend and foe; Hans Freyer had explicitly called for a 'revolution from the right'. Martin Heidegger's justly infamous inaugural lecture as Rector of Freiburg University in 1933 praised times in which teachers had to abdicate in favour of soldiers, indeed philosophers in favour of stormtroopers. Even Thomas Mann, though outside the country, went through a short phase of cautious curiosity. None of these were Nazis, but they were fellow-travellers along with hundreds of others.

The temptations of communism are much better documented, if only because those who succumbed have been less hesitant to write and speak about their past. In his introduction to *The God That Failed*, the book of confessions by Koestler and Gide, Wright and Silone, Spender and Fisher, Richard Crossman speaks of 'despair and loneliness' as 'main motives for conversion to communism' and then makes the extraordinary, though probably correct statement:

'But, whatever name you use, the idea of an active comradeship of struggle – involving personal sacrifice and abolishing differences of class and race – has had a compulsive power in every Western democracy. The attraction of the ordinary political party is what it offers to its members: the attraction of Communism was that it offered nothing and demanded everything, including the surrender of spiritual freedom.'[11]

It is important to note the element of masochism, of self-destruction in this temptation which combines extravagant hope with total submission.

One could write the history of the inter-war period as the history of successive 'Kronstadts', to use Louis Fisher's (all too real) metaphor for events which led to the disenchantment of the tempted on the left. The massacre of Kronstadt in 1921 did not put off many of the early believers whose abstract, almost aesthetic creed made them accept that you cannot have an omelette without breaking eggs. (Even after his break with communism, Stephen Spender wrote: 'Perhaps violence, concentration camps, the perversion of the sciences and the arts are justified if these methods result eventually in making the classless society.')[12] The murderous path of de-kulakization and collectivization in the Ukraine and elsewhere has only recently been fully documented. The show trials of the 1930s had their effect on some; but the more important disillusioning events were the deliberate break-up of the anti-fascist alliance by communists which became evident to many during the Spanish Civil War, and then the Hitler–Stalin Treaty of 1939. Some of course stayed on; there are few limits to temptation. They stayed on until Khrushchev's great denunciation of Stalin, or the Hungarian Revolution of 1956, or even the Prague Spring of 1968.

Other factors entered the story of European totalitarianism apart from the dislocations of incomplete modernity, the lure of leadership, and the treason of intellectuals. There are important differences between the Soviet Union and Nazi Germany. But in important respects the two were also similar. The reader will have noticed that when Franz Neumann speaks of 'the atomization and isolation of the individual' in connection with totalitarianism, he uses the words transitively. In other words, this is what totalitarianism does, not why it exists. Totalitarianism as a process – Hannah Arendt would say, 'totalitarianism in power' – atomizes and isolates people, and has to do so in order to maintain its grip. Totalitarianism is not the result of an atomized society, but is creating it; it is therefore, in Trotsky's words, a 'permanent revolution'. Hannah Arendt makes a point of great importance in this context when she says that

> 'the totalitarian ruler is confronted with a dual task which at first appears contradictory to the point of absurdity: he must establish the fictitious world of the movement as a tangible working reality of everyday life, and he must, on the other hand, prevent this new world from developing a new stability; for a stabilization of its laws and institutions would surely liquidate the movement itself and with it the hope for eventual world conquest.'

It is worth pondering this statement with respect not only to Hitler and Stalin, but also to post-totalitarian Soviet Russia and China's 'cultural revolution'. If the observation is correct, it also means that totalitarianism is in fact not a viable form of government; it is not built to last. Instead it deserves Franz Neumann's description of the National Socialist Behemoth which is at first sight so unlikely: 'an unstate, a chaos, a condition of lawlessness, of rebellion and of anarchy'.[13]

The totalitarian condition is the incompatibility of privilege without context and citizenship without anchor; a society which seems unable to go either forward to the civil society or back to more traditional patterns. The totalitarian process resolves the incompatibility by destroying all surviving traditional or authoritarian structures. But it does not put anything durable in their place. It accomplishes the negative part of modernization without creating its positive counterpart. Totalitarianism is pure destruction. This is why the temptation is great to look at it in terms of psychopathology. Totalitarian leaders take their nations to collective suicide, having murdered many others on the way. Less metaphorically put, the permanent revolution is also a permanent state of emergency; in fact, it is that more than a revolution. Such a state cannot be maintained forever. It either leads to some form of routinization, thus to that stability which 'would surely liquidate the movement itself', or it leads to catastrophe which is most likely to mean war.

Totalitarianism is thus an extreme possibility of the organization of disorganization, a regime of anarchy. One may wonder whether it ever existed anywhere. Nazi Germany during the war probably got fairly close to being totalitarian; but the intrinsically totalitarian trends of wartime government had to be added to what the Nazis had done in six brief pre-war years. Stalin too was helped by the war in cementing his rule of terror which in some ways was even more perfect than that of the Nazis because it was less predictable in Moscow who would be the next to hear the knock on the door than it was in Berlin. Mussolini's totalitarianism never got very far beyond the use of the word; and Franco's fascism increasingly turned into that hybrid, a modern autocracy, which has since become so frequent in Latin America and elsewhere. Mao Zedong had a huge country to deal with; yet he went a long way in the totalitarian direction. On a smaller, but no less cruel scale, Pol Pot, Idi Amin and a number of post-war rulers come to mind.

Some resisted the totalitarian temptation. Of those who did, many paid with their lives. Solzhenitsyn's *Gulag Archipelago* leaves one with, among other sentiments, a sense of those whose names are not remembered but whose deeds should be. Solzhenitsyn himself of course stands for the resurrection of an older Russia rather than for the creation of a modern civil society. This was true also for the core of the German resistance. The revolt of 20 July 1944 was about decency and the rule of law, but not about the constitution of liberty. The way forward was pointed by the few who were not a part of totalitarian systems and were never tempted. Perhaps they had to be rugged individualists. Hannah Arendt was one of them. In the next chapter, more will be said about Raymond Aron. Friedrich von Hayek could write his *Road to Serfdom* in 1944 with a clear intellectual conscience. And in his distant exile in New Zealand, Karl Popper produced the great book of wrath against Plato, against Hegel and Marx, against all those who cannot bear freedom, *The Open Society and Its Enemies*.

Popper's message is simple and yet profound. We live in a world of uncertainty; we try and we err. No one knows quite what the right way forward is, and those who claim to know may well be wrong. Such uncertainty is hard to bear. Throughout history, the dream of certainty has accompanied the reality of uncertainty. Great philosophers have fostered this dream. Plato painted the picture of a state run by philosopher-kings, in which those who know have the say. Hegel, and Marx after him, claimed to speak on behalf of history when they pronounced that what is reasonable either is already real or will be that after the proletarian revolution. But these are false prophets. They cannot know what you and I cannot know. The real world is one in which there are always several views, and there is conflict and change. Indeed, conflict and change are our freedom; without them, freedom cannot be.

'Arresting political change is not the remedy; it cannot bring happiness. We can never return to the alleged innocence and beauty of the closed society. Our dream of heaven cannot be realized on earth. Once we begin to rely upon our reason, and to use our powers of criticism, once we feel the call of personal responsibility, and with it, the responsibility of helping to advance knowledge, we cannot return to a state of implicit submission to tribal magic. For those who have eaten from the tree of knowledge, paradise is lost. The more we try to return to the heroic age of tribalism, the more surely do we arrive at the Inquisition, at the Secret Police, and at a romanticised gangsterism. Beginning with the suppression of reason and truth, we must end with the most brutal and violent destruction of all that is human. There is no return to a harmonious state of nature. If we turn back, then we must go the whole way – we must return to the beasts.
It is an issue which we must face squarely, hard though it may be for us to do so. If we dream of a return to our childhood, if we are tempted to rely on others and so be happy, if we shrink from the task of carrying our cross, the cross of humaneness, of reason, of responsibility, if we lose courage and flinch from the strain, then we must try to fortify ourselves with a clear understanding of the simple decision before us. We can return to the beasts. But if we wish to remain human, then there is only one way, the way into the open society.'[14]

Times which strip all skin and fat and meat away from the bare bones of the social contract are also times in which fundamental questions are raised. Sometimes they are answered.

Dictatorships and Simple Standards

Hitler is dead, and so is Stalin. The question is whether it can happen again. Can totalitarianism visit the same country twice? If the analysis suggested here is correct, it cannot. Once a totalitarian regime has run its destructive course, the conditions for its emergence have gone forever.[15] Of course, the analysis may not be correct. It certainly has several implications which need to be spelt out. One is that the Soviet Union today is not totalitarian, nor has it been since Stalin's death. How then do we describe the regime? Another implication may sound like the historicist assumption that history is a one-way street; once modernity, always modernity. Can the assumption be sustained? Before I go on to the world after the second Thirty Years' War, the profusion and in part confusion of terms has to be put in order: authoritarianism, totalitarianism, democracy, bureaucracy, autocracy. These are the political forms within which the modern social conflict unfolds. One does not have to have a theory about them, but one has to be clear about their meaning.

In November 1979, Jeane Kirkpatrick published an article which not only helped her gain the position of United States Ambassador to the United Nations, but also provided the incoming administration of President Reagan with a rationale for its departure from the foreign-policy assumptions of the President's predecessor, Carter.[16] The article, entitled 'Dictatorships and Double Standards', was in fact a preemptive strike in a war of deputies. It was an attack on views expressed and policies promoted by Carter's National Security Adviser, Zbigniew Brzezinski. Jeane Kirkpatrick recounts Brzezinski's view of the underlying political trends of the world (in his book *Between Two Ages*) in a way which suits her own purpose. Brzezinski believed (she argues) that modernization was an irreversible process. It was therefore bound to destroy premodern, authoritarian regimes before long. The immediate result of such destruction was often not pleasant; it might even be communism; but America had to be on the side of history rather than try in vain to resist its course. In any case, only modern societies can eventually become democratic, and most of them will do that given half a chance.

The model is familiar indeed. The route to modernity is also one from authoritarianism to democracy, though it sometimes leads through the purgatory of totalitarianism. Jeane Kirkpatrick does not share the view. Whatever modernization may do or not do, she sees the world divided in different ways. There are a few, very few, democracies. 'Decades, if not centuries, are normally required' for people to acquire the habits and institutions of a democratic order. Perhaps Britain and the United States are the only examples. Otherwise, there are mainly autocracies. Of these, two kinds must be distinguished; traditional or benevolent ones, and revolutionary or malevolent ones. Jeane Kirkpatrick has no illusions about either, though she emphasizes the distinction. 'Generally speaking, traditional autocrats tolerate social inequities, brutality, and poverty while revolutionary autocracies create them.' But she regards the miseries of traditional life as more bearable for ordinary people, because they are familiar, whereas revolutionary autocracies destroy everything known and customary in the process.[17]

Jeane Kirkpatrick's objective is foreign policy. Having set out her clever, if somewhat cynical views, the conclusions are clear. Roosevelt is supposed to have said about Somoza, or perhaps Trujillo: 'He is a son of a bitch, but at least he is our son of a bitch.' Kirkpatrick puts the same view in more academic language. 'Groups which define themselves as enemies should be treated as enemies,' and vice versa. Much of the heated debate about her article centred on these conclusions.[18] This is understandable since they can be read as an ideology of United States support for the autocracies of corrupt families or generals in Latin America and elsewhere. They are an invitation to let short-term geopolitics override all moral considerations. Even apart from morality, Kirkpatrick's conclusions can lead to practical difficulties when, as happened in the Philippines, 'people power' sweeps the autocratic friend of Washington away.

The underlying analysis of political systems remains important even if one disagrees with its foreign-policy conclusions. However, the model which I have implied and at times made explicit is different. It reserves the term 'authoritarian' (following Jeane Kirkpatrick's teacher Franz Neumann) for regimes in which a relatively small traditional stratum exercises power because it has always been that way. As long as people do not clamour for participation, they are looked after by the elite, though there are good times and bad times and above all kindly as well as nasty rulers. Such authoritarianism is hard to maintain in the modern world. In the Kirkpatrick debate, it has fairly been argued that there can be no justification for claiming 'irreversible' trends.[19]

The disintegration of an authoritarian regime under the on-
slaught of demands for entitlements and needs of economic
growth can take a long time and remain quite incomplete.
Germany was one example; perhaps Japan provides another.

Germany and Japan remind one of a type of political organization which we have encountered in many parts of the world.
From time to time, I have called it modern autocracy. This, more
than authoritarianism, is what we find in Latin America and Asia
today. It is the rule of self-appointed rather than traditional elites
which try to invoke ancient values and at the same time to
channel new-found wealth into a limited number of pockets. A
deliberate policy of growing (economic) provisions is coupled
with equally deliberate restrictions of civic entitlements. There
are many indications that this kind of regime cannot last very
long. One generation or even two is of course enough for those
who suffer; but the risk of either the totalitarian aberration or a
democratic opening-up is never very far. In that sense, Brzezinski
may have been a better adviser than Kirkpatrick by discouraging
the superficial confidence of the thoughtless in the stability of
modern autocracies.

It could be argued that the term 'modern autocracy' should
really be reserved for socialist regimes. In any case, once societies
have crossed the Tocquevillean threshold of modernity, once the
bug of equality has been planted in them, they are faced with
three political risks. These are the absolute versions of the three
elements of the problem of modern politics which are leadership,
administration and participation. The absolute version of leadership is *autocracy*. Pure autocracy probably only exists in
Machiavellian fantasies, but a tendency for the inevitable oligar-
chies of power to harden and try to turn all social action to their
benefit, to the defence of their position, is endemic. In some
constitutional and cultural circumstances this tendency is given
more leeway than in others. If administration is given unlimited
scope, the result is *bureaucracy*. Absurd as it may sound to say
that a service class becomes the ruling class, there are signs of
such developments all over the modern world. Max Weber's
nightmare remains apposite. Participation in its extreme form
would lead to the most unstable of the three risks, *democracy*.
This may seem a disturbing use of a popular word, and I do not
propose to turn it into an antidemocratic theory, but the rule of the

people in the strict sense is either the tyranny of the majority or the immobility of the permanent participation of all in everything. The risk is slight, for democracy in this sense cannot be.

The real risks of the world arise like real opportunities from mixed constitutions. Really existing socialism is not totalitarian, but it is a leaden mixture of autocracy and bureaucracy. A political class, the *nomenklatura*, has grown out of and formed an alliance with a vast bureaucracy which is in charge everywhere. Both feed themselves in the first instance and the rest of the people only to the extent to which they must. For the majority, really existing socialism is a pretty pure form of what it pretends to have overcome, exploitation, except that the regime is sufficiently incompetent in economic matters to make sure that there is not a great deal to exploit. The question is why such a system could gain such wide currency in the modern world and prove relatively stable. One can but speculate about answers. As traditional authoritarian (or colonial) regimes collapse, there are not many alternatives, and *nomenklatura* rule may appear more attractive than that by corrupt autocratic families. The impersonal hand of bureaucracy reduces obvious vulnerabilities. In the end, a forbidding concentration of power can be combined with slow improvements in provisions. There may also be inklings of democracy which open the system a crack without threatening to dislodge it.

Countries of the free world face their own risks. If one extrapolates real developments a fairly long way, they can probably be described as the entropy arising from a combination of bureaucracy and democracy. If the reality of the rational administration of lives is coupled with the illusion of democratic participation, then nothing moves any more. In his gloomier moments, Max Weber had his own theory of irreversibility and called the bureaucratic cage of bondage 'unbreakable'. Certainly, it cannot be broken unless the will and the protest of the people is translated into innovation and strategic change. Democracy alone is never enough to shift or control bureaucracy. The sclerosis notably of European countries may have been overstated by some, but it is hard to deny that the decline and fall of nations has something to do with their inability to keep going, to explore new ways, to increase life chances both by raising common entitlements and by expanding diverse and varied provisions.

91

This is what the constitution of liberty is intended to do. There is no formula for it, though we know the ingredients. In the face of the great threat of bureaucracy, a lively interplay of leadership, control and popular input is more important than ever. (It is not certain that we have found appropriate institutions anywhere.) The rule of law remains an indispensable condition of liberty. Both citizenship and the supply of opportunities for choice, economic and otherwise, are tasks which are never accomplished. Intellectuals must maintain their independence in order to play their critical part. The list makes one somewhat more sympathetic to Jeane Kirkpatrick's exclusive concept of free societies. Only a handful of countries have been able to create enduring constitutions of liberty. But despair of the task is as irresponsible as the claim of irreversible trends; it is arrogant where the latter is historicist. It may well be that 'democratic institutions are especially difficult to establish and maintain', and even that it is wrong to try and 'force complex and unfamiliar political practices on societies lacking the requisite political culture, tradition and social structures', but it is hard to see why a successful country should not be 'the world's midwife to democracy'. The constitution of liberty is not a privilege but an obligation.

At the end of the second Thirty Years' War the world was weary and aching everywhere. It was a testimony to human resilience that the survivors did not just roll up their sleeves and begin to clear away the rubble to build new houses and new lives, but also thought about the kind of world in which they wanted to live in order to avoid the recurrence of the wars. The post-war international system did not last; it was cracked early by the incipient Cold War and largely broken when the United States abandoned it in the 1970s and 1980s. However, the idea of this system should not be forgotten. The United Nations as an organization to promote both peace and human rights; the International Monetary Fund and the General Agreement on Tariffs and Trade to guard the rules of the game of growing economies; the World Bank system as an instrument for promoting development – these were not bad markers on the road to a world civil society. The world needs more, not less internationalism, and perhaps a 'Society for the Prevention of Another July 1914' to promote it.

5 · Aron's World

Industrial Society

When the second Thirty Years' War began to give way to the *trentes glorieuses*, the survivors felt as if they had passed through a nightmarish North Atlantic gale in mid-winter and were now sailing into the Caribbean sun. It was hazy at first – after all, no one knew how long the new climate would last – but soon the sun shone brightly on glittering seas. The change in people's lives was dramatic. For many years, turbulent times had forced their rhythm on most; now they were masters of their own destiny under increasingly predictable conditions. For decades, survival had been the order of the day; now it was consumption, and upward social mobility.

A personal memory makes the point. In the late autumn of 1918 my father held forth from an orange crate outside the town hall of Hamburg on the virtues of democratic socialism. He was seventeen years old and thus a little apprehensive when soon afterwards his party sent him to organize a trade union in the coal mines of Upper Silesia. Still, he seems to have discharged this task sufficiently well to earn himself a job with the party newspaper, access to courses in workers' education, and years later the candidacy first for the Hamburg Diet, then for the German *Reichstag*. Having voted against Hitler's Enabling Law, he, along with other Social Democratic members of parliament, was detained by the new State Police. After his release, he decided to move with his family to the more anonymous Berlin. However, normal life did not last long. After years of harassment my father was finally arrested in the wake of the attempted coup of 20 July 1944, tried before the infamous *Volksgerichtshof*, and sentenced to seven years' prison. He survived, was liberated by Russian soldiers and put in charge of the energy supply first of Berlin, then of the Soviet zone of occupation. He also became deputy chairman of the East German Social Democratic Party. This was in May 1945. Nine months later, having refused to agree to the forced merger of Social Democrats and Communists into what came to be the Socialist Unity Party, he was hurriedly flown out of Berlin by the British to Hamburg where he started yet another life. But time had taken its toll. He saw only the beginnings of the altogether different world into which his children grew, for he died in 1954.

Raymond Aron was four years younger than my father. He came from a different country, a different class, and also from a different 'race' (to use the misleading language of the time), though it was only the circumstances of the 1930s which made him realize that he was not just a Frenchman but also a Jew. He shared the *École Normale* with Jean-Paul Sartre, Paul Nizan and others. Aron managed to steer clear of the temptations of totalitarianism throughout his life. In 1924, he joined the Socialist Party for a brief period at the age of nineteen. It was to remain his only party-political affiliation. In the following six years he passed through the stages of academic preparation as well as military service. Aron believed in the reconciliation between France and Germany, and so he went as a *Lektor*, teaching French culture, first to Cologne in 1930, a year later to Berlin. At that time, Aron discovered his other vocation as a journalist, and began to write pieces for example about the 'anti-proletarian revolution' of National Socialism. On 10 May 1933, he watched, along with Thomas Mann's son Golo Mann, the burning of books by the Nazis on the Unter den Linden. 'The flames were the symbol of barbarism in power.' In August of that year, Aron returned to Paris. He wrote the influential little book on *Max Weber and German Sociology* which showed him to be the first of many who wanted to follow in the footsteps of Weber's explosive mixture of theory and practice. Soon after the beginning of the war, Aron fled to Britain. For a while, he became editor of *La France Libre*. But he never got on with General de Gaulle, who came to be the commanding figure of French politics. Perhaps this is why Aron's own political career remained confined to a few months in the personal office of the Minister of Information in de Gaulle's 1945–6 government, André Malraux, before he resumed his life between scholarship and journalism.

Aron lived to see and to describe for contemporaries both thirty-year periods of the century. He followed his much-admired teacher Halévy and called the era of tyrannies by its name, emphasizing the bond of totalitarianism which informed the 'meeting of two revolutions' in the Hitler–Stalin Pact. But this was only one theme of his fertile intellectual life. His biographer distinguishes, somewhat awkwardly perhaps, between Aron 'the philosopher in history' (1905–55) and Aron 'the sociologist in society' (1955–83).[1] Certainly, Aron's first forty years or so were shaped by history like the lives of many contemporaries; and he thought deeply about the events around him. It was only after the Second World War that he could focus on society as a process capable of rational understanding and even as a rational process. Characteristically, from that time onwards his life became very largely the story of his books and his lectures rather than of events outside his control (and the one exception, 1968, found him unprepared). In his famous Sorbonne Trilogy of lectures in 1955–6, he gave the term 'industrial society' a new and emphatic meaning. The *Eighteen Lectures on Industrial Society* document the mood of the time well. They tell the story of expanding provisions by economic growth which marked the years from the late 1940s to the mid-1970s.

Growth was of course no new experience. The story of modernity is the story of expanding provisions throughout. Erasmus wrote in the early sixteenth century: 'Nowadays the rage for possession has got to such a pitch that there is nothing in the realm of nature, whether sacred or profane, out of which profit cannot be squeezed.' The age of discoveries was also an age of the expansion of trade. Not just quantities of gold and silver, but commercial expectations led to an early expansion of banking. Leonardo da Vinci mapped the way for centuries of invention and innovation. New kinds of companies were founded, with joint stock for many and limited liability for all. The productivity of agriculture increased.

However, all this was not only precarious, but also a mere prelude to what was to come in the eighteenth century. The Industrial Revolution marks the beginning of what one might call democratic growth. This of course is my subject in this book, the conflicts and confluences of entitlements and provisions. The modern story is usually told in terms of provisions only. Walt Rostow may have aggregated more uncertain data than is good for exactness in his composite indices of world industrial production and world trade since 1700; but the picture which emerges from his exercise is so unambiguous that there can be no doubt about the conclusion. Trade multiplied 500 times after 1720, and so far as production is concerned, Rostow himself speaks of an 'improbable figure': 'Taken at face value, the quantity of manufacturing production in the world increased about 1,730 times' over the 150 years from 1820 to 1971. Although Rostow plays down this figure by pointing out that it involves an annual growth rate of 'only' 2.84 per cent, it remains remarkable.[2]

And yet even these figures are low if held against what happened after the Second World War, during 'the most remarkable two decades of economic growth in modern history'. In today's OECD world, there is no index of welfare which does not show a significant rise in the decades following 1945. In many developed countries, gross domestic product increased by a factor of three or four between 1950 and the mid-1970s. Real incomes grew by an even larger figure. Indeed, this is the time when growth seemed to answer all questions. Growth not only became a universal creed, but an engrained habit of individuals and institutions. Whenever something went wrong or was in need to be done, the first answer was to get more.

The assumption was that more meant more for all, at least in principle. Simon Kuznets first suggested the U-shaped relationship between economic growth and inequality: whereas inequalities of wealth first rise during the process of modern economic growth, there is then a levelling effect. Peter Berger has recently looked at this theory again in the light of comparative data, and essentially found it confirmed: 'As technological modernization and economic growth perdure over time, inequalities in income and wealth first increase sharply, then decline sharply, and then remain at a relatively stable plateau.'[3] Berger claims that the two main causes of this process are technological and demographic rather than social or political, though up to a point political intervention can reinforce the levelling process in the second of the three phases of growth and inequality.

These are, to be sure, economists' theses which have to do with measured income inequalities rather than thresholds of entitlement. The same story could be told in different terms, in which case the U-shaped development would look more like a Z. One precondition of modern economic growth is the presence of elementary civil rights. The momentum of citizenship must be there for capitalism to flourish, if only because the modern contract of labour requires the assumption of equality before the law. The groundstroke of the Z indicates the basic level of economic participation common to all and marks a profound distinction from hierarchical systems of privilege.

However, early civil rights can be, and were in history, coupled with massive inequalities. For one thing, the rights themselves were incomplete; for long, civic equality remained a fiction. For another thing, those who were drawn into the new process of industrial growth either made good and did very well indeed, or found themselves in a no-man's-land between a past which no longer is and a future which is not yet, as it is strikingly visible today in the favellas and tin huts just outside the teeming cities of the developing world. In today's OECD countries, two things happened. The first was that the virus of citizenship became as it were virulent. That extension of citizenship rights has been described in earlier chapters. The other process was the growth of provisions. Thus there was more to distribute in an increasingly open society. This is the process symbolized by the upward-sloping stroke in the Z.

Peter Berger's explanation of this process of levelling in terms of technology and demography means above all that labour becomes more skilled and more scarce as industrial societies progress. These are probably contributing factors, though they underestimate the role of what Berger calls 'political interventions'. To repeat a point made earlier, it is not my contention that there has to be a trade-off between entitlements and provisions. On the contrary, the triumphs of liberty are strategic changes which combine the two. But history has not been very liberal, especially in the twentieth century. The wars, the depression and even totalitarianism have led to considerable entitlement changes. They have been instruments of levelling. There was a hidden agenda of the second Thirty Years' War, and its name is equality. For this reason, the conditions for democratic growth – for an expansion of provisions which benefits a large number of people and in principle all – were never as favourable as after 1945. These conditions did not by themselves suffice to give rise to the economic miracle, but they helped make it a miracle for the majority.

What happened since has often been described, though major differences of interpretation persist. There is widespread agreement on the fact that for some considerable time income inequalities as measured, say, by the relation between the top and bottom quintiles of the population have not changed significantly. (Some figures seem to indicate a 'surge in inequality' in recent years, but even they do not show more than a modest increase in the share of income going to the top 10 per cent.[4]) What does such apparent stability mean? Some think that it shows the persistence of profound social cleavages which require political resolution; others regard it as a sign of the acceptability of remaining inequalities of income, or even argue that such distinctions are desirable as a stimulus to individual and general advancement. To some extent, the concepts of this essay provide a criterion for settling the difference. If inequalities involve entitlement barriers, and the consequent disenfranchisement of large groups, they are likely to give rise to dramatic conflicts. The key question is whether thresholds are mere statistical devices, like quintiles, or real obstacles to mobility. The primary school teacher (for example) who can neither become a head of school nor move out of the salary scale of teachers is constrained by more serious barriers than the small businessman who happens to earn little but may make a lot if he is successful. Inequalities of degree within a common universe certainly present social problems too, but these can be dealt with by the instruments of normal politics. They are, in T. H. Marshall's words, 'quantitative' and therefore do not give rise to 'qualitative' class conflicts. The boundary between the two is not always easy to draw. Perhaps it involves a judgement on the part of those concerned. The American dream defines opportunities as real which may in fact be closed by entitlement thresholds, whereas elsewhere an obsession with class may prevent people from recognizing their chances. Marshall argued that there has been a shift from qualitative to quantitative differences. The question of whether this shift was real, and lasting, will accompany us throughout the second half of this book.

T. H. Marshall wrote, like Raymond Aron, about the 1950s, and the industrial society which emerged at the time. For Aron, this was 'simply defined as a society in which large-scale industry, such as is found in the Renault or Citroën enterprises, is the characteristic form of production'.[5] Much else follows from this definition, including the separation of enterprise and family, an advanced division of labour, the accumulation of capital, rational economic calculation, and of course, growth. Growth is 'the central problem of · modern economics', because modern economies are 'essentially progressive'. Aron adds that 'in most cases, economic growth is accompanied by better distribution'. This is a characteristically cautious statement. If it points to historical coincidences, it makes a certain amount of sense; if it hints at causalities, it is wrong. Growth does not by itself bring about 'better', that is fairer or more just distribution.

One notable and striking feature of Aron's analysis of industrial society is the extent to which he takes growth for granted. He is not obsessed with it: 'I do not believe that growth is an absolute good.' But he regards growth as given in modern societies and likes to use Max Weber's term 'rationality', to make the point. This was not always the case, of course. Even a century ago – or perhaps a century and a half by now – the automatism of rationality was not enough. Aron talks about the 'optimism' of yesterday and today. In the nineteenth century, 'optimism was essentially liberal; people thought that wealth would grow as a result of science, free initiative and competition'. The 'pessimism' of that age was socialist. 'Optimism today, that of Fourastié for example, is neither liberal nor socialist; it is essentially technical. The key to modern economic history is technical progress. . . .'[6]

The significance of this idea runs deep, as we shall see. It is by no means confined to Aron, or to Colin Clark and Jean Fourastié. Daniel Bell's 'post-industrial society' is a result of scientific-technical changes as well, and to the present day there are those who believe that scientific discoveries and their technical application are the common cause of economic growth and social justice. I have not paid much attention to this set of factors in the present essay. The reason is not neglect. It is rather a scepticism born of a simple (perhaps overly simple) observation. Technical change is not a self-propelling process. Inventions have to be

99

applied to make a difference. Like bureaucrats, technocrats may in fact run the world in the absence of democratic input or a sense of direction provided by leaders, but they can only extrapolate and not change course. If one is concerned with changes of course, one must seek the social forces and the actors responsible for using science and technology, or bureaucratic organization, by defining the purposes to which they are put. Rationality alone is never enough to map the passages of liberty.

Aron knew this of course. He had read not only his Weber, but his Schumpeter too. 'In order that an economy should continue to progress, conditions must be such that the economic subjects take the necessary decisions for growth.' There is need for entrepreneurs as well as technical progress, for politicians as well as implementation by administrators. In fact, Aron's main concern was the future of industrial society. He speculated about the risk of a stationary state, about the self-destruction of capitalism, the 'socialization' (as he called the combination of corporatism and the welfare state) of European economies, the retardation of growth. The questions raised by his students as well as his more committed contemporaries who increasingly minded the dispassionate liberal critic forced him to deal with such issues. But they did not deflect him from his conclusions, or from his approach. Industrial societies have a 'tendency to become middle class and to reduce the inequality of incomes. As the standard of living rises there will probably be a tendency for extreme forms of despotism to relax and for demands of social welfare to become more vigorous.' Of course, this may not go on forever. Also, economic growth is not everything. But then, there is always uncertainty. 'Whether for good or evil, we cannot foretell the future.'

Convergence, Socialism and Diversity

The idyllic picture of an industrial society proceeding peacefully to more wealth and welfare for all is misleading for several reasons. One of these is the international context. Aron eventually added to the trilogy of lectures a fourth series on developing countries. The more immediate context was, however, provided by the Cold War. Within two years of the end of the Second World War, the clash of systems championed by the United States of America on one side and by the Soviet Union on the other had reached worldwide dimensions. Aron was not only aware of this clash, but never left the slightest doubt about his own moral commitment to the West and its values. Moreover, he was to become one of the leading theorists of war and peace, and of international affairs more generally, so that he was anything but naive in this matter.

Yet the *Eighteen Lectures* introduce a curious analytical ingredient into this debate, of which one might say that it vitiates the whole approach taken by the lecturer. The entire book is in fact not just about the OECD world, but about the developed world in general in which Aron includes the Soviet Union. 'The key to modern economic history is technical progress,' Aron said in a quotation which I have left incomplete because it continues, 'and this can take place either in a capitalist or in a socialist regime; they are two different examples of the same kind of transformation.' Taking Clark's and Fourastié's notion of the transition from primary to secondary and on to tertiary economic activity as his point of departure, and referring with sceptical sympathy to Walt Rostow's concept of 'stages of economic growth', Aron not surprisingly finds similarities in the socio-economic development of industrial societies in East and West. The confusion of what he calls 'socialization' with socialism, borrowed in part from Schumpeter's *Capitalism, Socialism and Democracy*, contributes to the notion that European societies at least might proceed along a route which is not so dissimilar from that of the socialist countries of the East. One will remember the other quotation about 'a tendency for extreme forms of despotism to relax'. This was also left incomplete, for the very next sentence adds: 'Soviet Russia is even now experiencing the first difficulties of dawning prosperity.'[7]

This was said in 1955, not in 1987. Even today there are serious doubts about the ability of General Secretary Gorbachev to restructure Soviet society and awaken a dormant economy. How much more doubt was in place thirty years earlier when Khrushchev promised to catch up with the United States before long! Certainly, all industrial societies, indeed all modern societies, have certain features in common. Demography and technology are probably among them, although as one becomes more specific variations emerge even on these themes. For the closer

101

one looks, the more one is struck by difference everywhere. Aron chose the 'Renault or Citroën enterprises' to illustrate industrial society, because one was public and the other private, and yet they looked so obviously alike? But their subsequent history cast doubt even on this assumption, for one became stagnant and threatened while the other flourished under a variety of owners. If this can happen in one country, the differences between Russia and America, or Poland and France, or East and West Germany are clearly more serious. A conceptual framework which does not bring out such differences is evidently lacking. There was a manner of thinking about industrial societies in the 1950s and 1960s which needs second thoughts if not radical revision.

Perhaps one should not subsume the Soviet Union under general categories of analysis at all. If one does, however, it is a case of the pains of late development under particularly difficult circumstances. A country with a Westernized but narrow and authoritarian upper class and widespread organized social unrest had lost the war; revolutionary leaders came in from exile abroad and at home; the anatomy of revolution took its course. It brought to power a group which said that it intended to create a world of both participation and prosperity. But soon the latter turned out to be more difficult and the former more unsettling than the revolutionary idealists had anticipated. The politics of preservation of power took precedence over all other objectives. At certain times, this politics looked as if it was going to fail, and perhaps without Stalin it would have failed. But history in the subjunctive mode is never very satisfactory. Stalin came, and with him totalitarianism and the bureaucratic *nomenklatura* which was left to carry on when he died.

We are talking about socialism, of course. 'Socialism' has become a many-faceted word which makes it necessary to distinguish. In the first place there is the socialist dream and the socialist reality. It may not say a lot for the dream that so much of the reality created in its name was a perversion of ideals, but when my father became an active socialist in Germany at the end of the First World War, or Raymond Aron a fleeting member of the French Socialist Party in 1924, they were inspired by hopes of justice in freedom. Within socialist reality, another distinction has to be made. There is social democracy and really existing socialism. On social democracy more will be said presently; it is the extension of the process of citizenship by reform rather than revolution, and under conditions of economic and political diversity. Really existing socialism is an altogether different regime though it requires a third distinction. Some countries have been forced to adopt the regime by an imperialist Soviet Union, and in most of them Soviet tanks were needed at some stage to hold down popular protest. These countries too have today settled down to a kind of bureaucratic autocracy, but they are as far from the socialist dream as it is possible to be. A few countries have developed an indigenous form of really existing socialism, among them the Soviet Union, China, Cuba.

Their pattern of economy and society is not an alternative to that of so-called capitalist countries. It is rather a phenomenon of late and uneven development. Even if one does not agree with Jeane Kirkpatrick's elitist concept of world politics which confines the grail of democracy to the lucky few who could afford to continue the search for centuries, it is true that the number of countries which have managed to advance both citizenship and economic well-being, both entitlements and provisions to a level of life chances which stands the severe tests applied to Nicaragua at the beginning of this analysis, is very small indeed. In most societies which embarked on the path of modern economic development late, the desired outcome of economic growth met with political obstacles. Once the initial problem of a country is defined as political, its economy is very likely to be in trouble. It is ineffectually dragged along by a political class primarily interested in maintaining its power, and a population of subjects of organization and mobilization, but not of participating citizens.

This is the dilemma of really existing socialism in its indigenous form. Of course its autocrats and even its bureaucrats would like their economies to flourish. But they will also deal with first things first, and these are invariably political. They have to do with organization and control, succession and recruitment, obedience and indoctrination, norms and regulations, and also with all those perquisites of bureaucracy which Max Weber was so adept at listing. Setting up such powers means a vicious battle against dilettantes, idealists, critics and rivals. By the same token, relaxing controls in order to encourage initiative involves high risks. In theory it may be possible to conceive of economic participation without political involvement, but in practice the

103

dissociation does not work. From Manila to Seoul and from Singapore to Hong Kong the attempt has failed. In Deng Tsiao-ping's China the encouragement of economic initiative has set political forces in motion which make the rulers wonder. In Gorbachev's Russia on the other hand, the relaxation of political controls has so far not succeeded in bringing about an economic miracle. Entrepreneurs need pushes and pulls, stimuli and incentives which are incompatible with the interests of a bureau-cratized political class.

Socialism is not the other industrial society, but a political method of promoting development. It is a developing-country phenomenon. This is particularly likely to occur where the initial stages of modernization and industrialization have taken place under authoritarian rule. Clearly, provisions can be increased for a minority without economic or political participation by most. But at a certain point this process reaches several limits, often simultaneously. Those who have carried on the process of extending provisions need wider markets; those who have been excluded from the benefits of economic growth want to have their share; and those who have already benefited are no longer satisfied with a modicum of prosperity, but want political rights as well. This is where trouble starts. Suddenly everybody demands a 'political' solution. Those who need expanding markets, the new middle classes and 'the people' enter into a temporary alliance. (The condition is not entirely dissimilar from that of the civic and bourgeois revolutions of the eighteenth century, except that much has happened since and the impatience of latecomers is great.) The resulting upheavals are rarely reformist and peaceful. They are about entitlements, which gives them a special energy. If they set in motion a revolutionary process, the disappointments of revolution are not far.

Thus really existing socialism was never more than a second-best path into the modern world, if that. Today we know that it is also a failure. If it maintains political control, it cannot deliver the economic goods, and if it is serious about economic progress, its political base is threatened. If there is any convergence of systems, it will be on variants of liberty. This may not happen; there is no historical law that all must be prosperous and free. Perhaps people want to be both, but this does not mean that they will get it. It is all too common for people to live in political and economic systems which are second best. Stability does not require moral legitimacy; the absence of active protest is usually enough. Really existing socialism can be stable as long as it combines the heavy hand of bureaucracy with minimal economic progress or even the absence of decline. This is not a happy state of affairs. One must wish those well who want to change it from within and be grateful for small advances.

The idea of a mid-way convergence of systems is thus neither plausible nor desirable. There is no meaningful sense in which one concept, such as industrial society, can be applied to the United States as well as the Soviet Union, nor would the attempt to commingle experiences promise any gain in life chances. For the OECD countries, the developing-country experience of really existing socialism is an irrelevance anyway, and whatever the Soviet Union and China do will be different from the experience of the United States, or Europe, or Japan.

I hope this insistence on difference is not misunderstood. It is neither the abdication of analysis nor the advocacy of relativism, let alone a device for emphasizing hostile and unmanageable conflicts. To start with the latter, it has been a curious intellectual mistake to believe that in order to have peaceful and mutually beneficial relations between East and West, the social and economic systems have to converge. The whole point of international relations, and even of a world civil society, is to manage difference. This includes strong beliefs in one's own values. There can be no relenting in the Western insistence on human rights everywhere, but this insistence justifies neither intervention nor paranoia. Strong convictions do not have to lead to sending marines or tolerating the arms race. Between the ineffectual moralization of foreign policy and cynical *realpolitik* there is a confident line of conduct which superpowers seem to find hard to sustain but which is the only hope of survival in the nuclear world.

Such indications answer the question of relativism by implication. Values need reasons, but reasoned values can and must be defended. The notions of citizenship, life chances and liberty which inform this analysis are more than analytical tools. However, it is a matter of utmost urgency – and itself a value to be defended – that values are not confounded with a particular set of social institutions such as parliament or private property, or with real societies. No society on earth has ever lived up to its values nor is there likely to be one in future. This is why I am so hesitant to speak of free or even capitalist – or socialist – societies, though every now and again such phrases provide a convenient shorthand. The hypostasis of values is the beginning of war. There is good and evil, but there is no kingdom of good or of evil in this world (although the borderline case of murderous totalitarianism has brought some as close to the reality of evil as human societies are likely to come).

This leaves the question of analysis. Is there not a contradiction between the insistence on difference and the avowed intention of this book to present an analysis of the passages of liberty through the last two centuries of history? Certainly, there is a tension. It is that between T. H. Marshall's stages of citizenship and the realities of 'politics in industrial society'. ('Industrial society' indeed!) One can hope to detect strands of meaning in the apparent chaos of events and experiences without denying the uniqueness of each event or experience. For example, I have made much in the last two chapters of two critical thirty-year periods in this century. Yet this attempt to structure historical time betrays a distinctly European, even Central European bias. America's twentieth century looked rather different. For one thing, it was nowhere near as political as the European experience; America could afford a century of concentration on economic provisions instead. For another, the phases were only partly congruent with those of Europe. The First World War began later for the United States and remained brief. What dislocation it brought was soon submerged in the years of 'Coolidge prosperity'. The real shock to Americans came in October 1929 when unemployment was rampant and many people's savings – the American individualist equivalent to the European welfare state – were wiped out overnight. It took the country ten years to return to the level of gross national product and personal income of 1929. Once that was achieved however, growth continued throughout the Second World War and the post-war period. As a result, there was no economic miracle in the 1950s and 1960s, though the net effect of expansion on the level of provisions kept the United States at the top of the OECD league. Despite this quite different experience of two generations, I would hope that Americans can read the present analysis with profit.

The Democratic Class Struggle

The modern social conflict is about citizenship rights for all in a
world of rich and varied choices. It is founded on social divisions,
carried on in the political arena and played out in a multiplicity of
ways depending on specific cultural conditions and historical
situations. We have spent some time on the latter, including the
hidden agenda of redistribution during the second Thirty Years'
War and the different experiences of countries. It is now time to
take up the thread of sociopolitical analysis for the OECD
countries. Their description as such has at last become apposite.
In 1948, the Organization for European Economic Co-operation
(OEEC) was set up in order to help implement the Marshall Plan
and promote European recovery. When the job was done and
Europe had joined the club of the rich, OEEC was re-founded as
OECD, the Organization for Economic Co-operation and
Development. Set up in 1961, the OECD was intended 'to achieve
the highest sustainable growth and employment and a rising
standard of living in member countries', that is in the United
States and Canada, in European countries, in Japan, and in
Australia and New Zealand. I am not sure that the following
analysis applies to all of them equally; certainly Japan is a special
case; but in most the class struggle for citizenship rights was a
reality.

By the 1960s however it was a very un-Marxian reality too. S. M.
Lipset borrowed a term coined by D. Anderson and P. Davidson
in 1943 when he spoke (in 1959) of the 'democratic class struggle':
'In every modern democracy conflict between different groups is
expressed through political parties which basically represent a
"democratic translation of the class struggle" . . . On a world
scale, the principal generalization which can be made is that
parties are primarily based on either the lower classes or the
middle and upper classes.'[8] The idea is simple and striking. There
are social cleavages which give rise to political conflicts. But far
from becoming increasingly violent and disruptive, these conflicts were domesticated by institutions in which they found an
orderly constitutional expression. Political parties, elections and
parliaments provided for conflict without revolution.

Some wondered whether the term 'class struggle' was still
appropriate for this condition. Raymond Aron for example (in the
second lecture series of the Sorbonne Trilogy) denied the

existence of an 'inexpiable struggle' in capitalist society and spoke instead of a healthy 'rivalry' between the better-off and the less well-off, though he too emphasized that democracy means 'to accept conflicts, not in order to appease them but to prevent them from becoming bellicose'. It makes sense to distinguish between the great struggles for entitlements, or citizenship rights, and the incremental claims for redistribution at the margin among those who already enjoy the rights of citizens. Since the traces of deeper cleavages remain present, there is some point however in preserving the concept of class even for the democratic rivalry.

The process which led to this new state of affairs preoccupied many authors in the 1950s. Theodor Geiger, when he wrote about the 'class society in the melting-pot', traced it back to the progress of industrial democracy. Capital and labour, at first irreconcilably opposed to each other, over time formed an organized relationship. Bargaining about wages and conditions, including procedures of arbitration and conciliation, became embedded in a whole system of agreed or legislated rules. The tension between capital and labour came to be recognized as a legitimate principle of the labour market. Geiger calls this process the 'institutionalization of the class antagonism'.[9]

For the post-war generation, the political consequences of such institutionalization have led to a familiar condition. One has got used to the interplay of two political groupings, in the limiting case two parties, each of which has a chance to gain a popular majority in elections. One is more reformist, the other more conservative, one more an entitlements party, the other more a provisions party, though neither goes out of its way to deny the claims of the other or undo what it did. The British example is most clear-cut. The Labour Party won the 1945 election and introduced sweeping reforms; in 1951 the Conservatives got in again and stayed in power until 1964, with one of their four prime ministers telling the people that 'you've never had it so good'; in the end, Labour got back with Harold Wilson's programme of a 'technological revolution'; in 1970 the Tories won with Edward Heath's economic and European programme; in 1974 Labour came back, until Margaret Thatcher defeated Harold Wilson's successor James Callaghan in 1979. Lipset has pointed out that the model is applicable to the United States too, where there were changes in the party affiliation of presidents in 1952, 1960, 1968, 1976 and 1980. In France, the situation was more confused, partly by de Gaulle whose political role is not easily described in party terms, partly by coalition (and, more recently, 'co-habitation') governments, but there were changes too. The German *Macht-wechsel* of 1969 had a somewhat more dramatic quality; then as in Adenauer's first governments in 1949 and 1953, and again in 1982, it was a small third party which 'made' majorities by shifting allegiance; but this too illustrates a variant of the democratic class struggle.

The experience has led to some characteristic extrapolations. In the United States in particular, Joseph Schumpeter's application of economic thinking to politics gained adherents. By way of Kenneth Arrow's theories of social choice, an economic theory of democracy was developed which assumed the near-total opportunism of political parties.[10] Political leaders and their organizations are merely entrepreneurs and enterprises operating in a particular market in which success is counted in votes rather than dollars. Parties cobble together platforms which promise majorities; if elected, they try to put them into effect; they are bound to alienate some in the process and thereby give the opposition a chance. Opinion research takes the place of ideology. Politics is reduced to the competition for votes. In principle, the game can go on forever, because in the absence of a need for overriding group solidarities – of class – there are only issues, and their combinations are a matter of practical convenience rather than social necessity.

The authors of this theory would not deny that it was always an overstatement so far as the description of real politics is concerned. Even in the United States where politics has long been dominated by economic, or provisions, issues, there is a hard core of New Deal Democrats and one of libertarian Republicans. In Europe, socioeconomic status is still a good predictor of voting behaviour. Moreover, the economic theory of democracy fails to come to grips with important side effects of the domestication of the old class conflict, and it overstates the stability of the new condition.

One of the side effects is foreshadowed even in Theodor Geiger's analysis. Having described the institutionalization of the class antagonism he goes on to what at the time (1949) must have appeared a surprising point. Those who have institutionalized their hostile relationship, he argues, have not only thereby taken the sting out of it, but have also formed a cartel to defend their common interests. They may differ somewhat in their views of how the cake of provisions should be distributed, but they are agreed that the cake must be theirs to distribute. As a result, those who are not a part of the cartel are the real victims. 'Misery grows in proportion with the distance of income-earners from the production of goods.' That statement at least is dated. Also, Geiger has to go through considerable contortions to identify those whom he calls 'mere consumers'. It would have helped him to know the notion of 'disparities of realms of life' developed much later by those who wanted to save at least some of the debris of class. They argued (it will be remembered) that important new conflicts do not involve entire social categories so much as aspects of the lives of all. If air and water are polluted, the issue does not constitute a class, but it does give rise to strong sentiments on the part of many, and these sentiments can be translated into political struggles.

On the other hand, Geiger's analysis points to a development which has accompanied the institutionalization or democratization of the class struggle everywhere, that is, corporatism. The basis of the democratic class struggle is organization, and the method is consensus. People do not act as individuals – in this respect too the economic theory of democracy fell short – but as members of parties, trade unions, associations of many kinds. The struggle is carried on by these associations; but it is in fact not a struggle. It is rather an elaborate cartel of organizations. They develop ever new procedures for feeding their particular interests into the political process. In doing so, they discover their common interest in keeping control of the cake. This is the cake of provisions of course, but behind it there lies the control of power by arrangement. In the end, political parties, economic associations, a wide range of interest groups (including those who claim to represent 'mere consumers') as well as institutions which have discovered that without joining in they are bound to lose out, form a huge ball of wax. Citizens no longer know who gets what when and how, though for those who need to know there are well-paid consultants, and for those who want to find out, political scientists.

The risk of the corporatist perversion of the democratic class struggle is that it creates rigidity in the place of movement. Corporatism enters into an easy union with bureaucracy, and both tend to rob the constitution of liberty of its essence, the ability to bring about change without revolution. Every now and again a new actor may enter the cartel of organized interests. Environmentalists for example were hard to keep out in some countries. But fundamentally corporatism takes life out of the democratic process. Arrangement replaces debate, consensus is substituted for conflict.

Such comments probably take us too far in another direction. The fact is that the condition described here is very attractive for the majority of people in the OECD world. They certainly have never had it so good. Traditional class conflicts have receded, though their memory and in some parts their reality lingers on. Diverse interests can be expressed by organized groups which have their place in the scheme of things and see to it that few are neglected entirely. Things move slowly, but then there is no great demand for quicker change. A wide consensus on rules of the game and on substance prevails. The characteristic feature of this consensus is caught well by the economic theory of democracy. For a while it could look as if the days of entitlement politics were over. To be sure, there were, and are still, lively demands for the extension of civil rights to hitherto neglected groups, but the marginality of some of these groups illustrates well that one is no longer talking about great struggles, let alone a revolutionary potential. Involved efforts of overstatement and hyperbole have to be made to turn statistical inequalities into political issues. Aron's world is a provisions world in which conflicts are about a little more or a little less rather than about all or nothing. For the overwhelming majority it literally does not matter much who governs.

Even as I write this I can sense the shock felt by radical-minded readers. They may feel in any case that I have used the word 'class' in a rather cavalier manner, after having insisted earlier on its precise definition. Classes are categories in a common relationship to the exercise of power. They are typically either in or out, and thus in conflict. Such conflict becomes politically relevant if it is about entitlements. The history of citizenship is also the history of class conflict. This was true for the bourgeois struggle for civil rights; it was true more recently for the battle for social citizenship rights. No one who has eyes to see and ears to hear would claim that these rights are truly general in any country of the OECD world. More importantly still, there are new entitlement issues. But it would show a strange sense of proportion not to admit that at some point in the 1960s or 1970s, a great historical force for change had lost its momentum because the principle which it strove to establish had become widely accepted.

Citizenship is the key to this process. Once the overwhelming majority of people in OECD societies had become citizens in the full sense of the word, social inequalities and political differences assumed a new complexion. People no longer needed to join forces with others in the same position to fight for basic rights. They could advance their life chances by individual effort on the one hand, and by representation through fragmented but incorporated interest groups on the other. Not only did the old class affiliations recede, but a new allegiance emerged which includes two-thirds, if not four-fifths or even more, of the members of society. There are many differences between them including inequalities of wealth and income, but there is also a fundamental equality of access. The new class is the citizens' class, if the paradox is permissible, or at any rate the majority class. A chapter of social and political history which began with a profound and potentially revolutionary class struggle led after many travails to the calmer conflicts of institutionalized or democratic antagonisms of class, and eventually resulted in the creation of a majority class of those who belong and can therefore hope to realize many of their aspirations without fundamental change.

1968

In the recent political history of many OECD countries, one date stands out, 1968. The date is partly real and partly symbolic, and its connotations differ in different places. In the United States President Johnson went out of office in a conflagration of glory, turmoil and despair. He had in fact presided over the social programmes of the Great Society which have stood the test of time, but he had also led the country more deeply into the Vietnam War which was to push the United States into one of its deepest constitutional crises. In Europe too, governability, or, as continental Europeans prefer to put it more dramatically, legitimacy became an issue in 1968, though for many it was associated with the capacity of political systems to bring about reform. In France and Germany and some of the smaller European countries, the issue had one name, 'democratization'. This meant in part the completion of the promise of citizenship for all, but the other part was the insistence that rights of participation have to be used to be real. 'We must venture more democracy' (*'Wir müssen mehr Demokratie wagen'*) said Willy Brandt in his first government statement to Parliament as German Chancellor in 1969, and he clearly meant that democracy was not just a state of affairs but a manner of life, an activity and a virtue.

Both in the United States and in Europe, 1968 had much to do with the universities. Student unrest preceded political unrest, and it spread from Berkeley to the London School of Economics and the Sorbonne and the Free University of Berlin. In some places, university reform appeared to be the main issue, at any rate for those who misread the signs of the times. Raymond Aron was among them. He never recovered from what he saw in those troubled May days in Paris. The reason is evident in one sad statement: 'The old Sorbonne deserved to die, but not to be put to death as it was in May 1968.'[11] There are times when one really cannot have one's cake and eat it. The momentum for change was such that reasoned reform was bound to set off processes which the reformers could no longer control. The revolution of 1968 may have been *introuvable*, elusive and hard to identify, but it had many of the trappings of one of those avalanches which cannot be stopped once they have started.

Aron felt above all offended by 1968. He probably did not mean it when he said that the Sorbonne actually deserved to die; he wanted it to flourish in improved form. For him, the death of the old university was an irretrievable personal loss. This was true for many Europeans, and especially for those who had had to struggle to gain a place in it. I can feel with them, although in Germany there are quite a few people who believe that I share responsibility for the murder of the old university. Historically they are wrong. When I pleaded for 'education as a civil right' and took part in programmes of opening higher education for hitherto disadvantaged groups, I was strictly concerned with access and opportunity. Democracy, not democratization, was the objective.

In terms of practical politics, however, the distinction could not be maintained, at least not in Continental Europe. The wave of change soon drowned those reformers who thought that the line between equal opportunities and equal results could be held, or that there could be democracy without democratization.

Aron's experience of the events which were to haunt him for the last fifteen years of his life was a curious mixture of involvement and detachment.[12] When student unrest spread to the streets in the first week of May 1968 he remained uncharacteristically silent. He even refused to appear on television. 'In view of the state of mind people were in, I was not at all sure what to say.' On 14 May he went on a lecture tour to the United States. (De Gaulle left on the same day for a state visit to Romania.) But soon he could not stand being so far away and returned. (De Gaulle also cut his visit short and began his own charade of semi-visibility, including the hurried flight to Baden-Baden to assure himself of the loyalty of General Massu and his troops.) Back in Paris Aron began to feel what he later described as indignation, 'a degree of indignation greater than any I have ever experienced', which says a lot for a man who had watched books burn in Berlin in 1933. He tried to laugh off the 'psychodrama' which unfolded before his eyes as a 'spectacle of revolution' rather than a confused expression of real change; but his laughter sounded hollow. The more one challenged the great man in later years, the stronger grew his resentment. Perhaps in those turbulent days in May 1968 Aron's world had come to an end.

This is more easily said than explained. To the present day, 1968 divides people in many countries of the OECD world. What did it really mean? Was it the revolt of the spoilt children of a new prosperous class produced by the economic miracle? Was it the rise of the citizen against governments which had not realized that the time of subjects was over? Was it the first assertion of value changes which were soon to envelop Western societies? Was it simply a stage in the reform of modern society with institutions which were overdue for change at the centre? Much of this is anybody's guess, though perhaps the passage of time helps give credence to a fairly detached analysis.

The post-war period was one of more options for more people. This could not have succeeded without a firm base in citizenship rights for all which was partly a heritage of earlier battles, partly a result of the post-war social bargain and partly created along with the growth of provisions. But, increasingly, quantitative and economic processes took over. OECD societies became societies of ever more. This left some things to be desired. In the 1960s, more and more people asked for reform. 'After recovery, restructuring' was one of the slogans of the time. Demands for social changes grew, although it was not altogether clear which social forces were behind them. From the outset, the reform movement of the 1960s was not only given a voice by intellectuals, but carried on by intellectuals and concerned with issues which by comparison to earlier social and political upheavals had a somewhat intellectual quality.

This was most evident in so far as the new demands concentrated on universities (as they did in many European countries) and least in so far as the rights of neglected minorities were at issue (as they were in the United States). The last great extension of civil rights may well have been the most substantial change brought about with the force of the social movements of the 1960s. Other changes were more subtle, though describing them as intellectual is not meant to detract from their importance. In European universities, all-powerful professors were dislodged and replaced by a greater sense of the co-operation of equals which found its institutional expression in the German *Gruppenuniversität* in which teachers, students and staff were for a while intended to have an equal say. The churches, and notably Protestant ones, followed suit and became places of debate rather than of preaching. The Catholic *aggiornamento*, powerfully moved ahead by the Vatican Council, responded to similar pressures, all the way to the symbolic removal of the altar from its exalted position into the centre of modern churches, and of course to the hopes and confusions of ecumenism. Everywhere, the assumptions of criminal law and justice underwent a serious re-examination, and in many countries older notions of punishment were replaced by hopes in resocialization. Behind them was the idea that individuals are products of social forces and cannot be held responsible for their deeds. Personalized authority lost its hold, even in such unlikely institutions as armies ('citizens in uniform') or industrial enterprises ('co-determination').

The spirit of the times spilt over into other areas of policy-making. In many countries, social welfare policies were advanced a further step in the direction of communal obligation rather than individual initiative. This was to turn out to be the last step along this road. It was taken moreover at a time when countries could no longer afford it. For much of what has been called 1968 did not actually happen in that year. It began a few years earlier and extended well into the 1970s. Thus the final trimmings of the edifice of the social state were added when the storms of an increasingly unsettled world economy began to threaten its central structures. The years of fulfilment were also years of increasing precariousness. Few countries managed to avoid measures of regulation and redistribution in those years which were not at least severely tested in the 1970s.

The fulfilment in question is that of the social democratic consensus. This is the ideology of the majority class, and like that class it took a century to build. The ingredients of the social democratic consensus are all related to social citizenship rights in a prosperous world. They are above all a strong but benevolent government in a democratic system tempered by corporatism, a managed but market-oriented economy exposed with a degree of cushioning to world trade and monetary arrangements, and a society of far-reaching solidarity by entitlements and progressive taxation as part of a general propensity for equality in generally liberal conditions. This sounds like quite a mouthful, but then it is the very essence of the social democratic consensus that it seeks reasonable balances. This is what makes it attractive. This is why it meets so many different interests. This is why the majority class likes it. This is why it is vulnerable.

For the period which we are entering in our analysis marks in fact the end of the social democratic century. Some naturally find this statement objectionable. 'I have asked myself time and again,' Willy Brandt said in his farewell speech to the German Social Democrats, 'which decades those contemporaries had in mind who thought that the social democratic century is over. Have they overlooked the two wars, fascism and Stalinism, the great economic crises and the new existential threats?'[13] This contemporary has certainly not overlooked the second Thirty Years' War. He would agree also that for the time being the social democratic model remains a humane and reasonable political perspective. It is harder to argue that this perspective has the future on its side. The point about the end of social democracy is not that the consensus of the majority class abruptly loses its meaning, let alone that parties which call themselves social democratic can no longer win elections (though many seem to find this more difficult in the 1980s than in the 1960s and 1970s). It is rather that a historical force has lost its momentum. This happens not because it has been pervasive and dominant throughout the century, but because after a century of struggle it has at last largely arrived. Great social forces die at the moment of victory. Their end is nigh when the future is no longer with them.

There was a time in the late 1960s when Harold Wilson tried to snatch from the Tories the claim of being the 'natural party of government'. Labour lost the election soon after, yet Wilson was right in a deeper sense. All governments of whatever persuasion tended to be social democratic for a while. They all subscribed to the consensus of the majority class on the beneficent role of government, the mixed economy and the social state. 1968 symbolizes the triumph of social democracy, but it also marks the beginning of the end. The rule of the majority class and of the eminently reasonable consensus of social democracy turned out to be unstable. They may be with us for some time to come; one might even hope that they will not be overwhelmed by the partisan and often fundamentalist ideologies of the 1980s; but the changes which happened after 1968 have altered the scenery and the subject matter of the modern social conflict.

6 · Crisis in the 1970s

A World Order Crumbles

Rarely in the twentieth century has it been possible to write or talk about social developments without reference to international constraints, effects and influences. The decades of the wars, of depression and the arrogance of power were intensely international. For most parts of the world, this has not changed after 1945. A number of countries, notably in East Central Europe and in East and South East Asia, found their internal developments brutally subjugated by an imperialist power. More recently, several Central American countries have had similar experiences. Many other territories in Africa and Asia emerged from colonial rule into statehood and had to struggle with the change in their external status as well as with internal development. Moreover, the Cold War had an impact on all concerned. It drew boundaries which made a difference within each bloc as well as between them. Yet it is possible to argue that social, economic and political developments within the OECD countries remained relatively undisturbed by external influences for a quarter of a century. More than that, they were actually helped by a stable world order. When this order began to crumble in the 1970s, the effect was felt everywhere. Today's world is a very different place from that of the post-war era.

The system of organized international relations was a part of the post-war miracle. Its emergence itself was surprising. Given the disillusionment with the League of Nations especially in the United States, given moreover the intense preoccupation of the allies with the war in 1944 and 1945, it is remarkable that planners and politicians found it within them to conceive and construct a deliberate set of international institutions. It is true that so far as the universal ambition of these institutions was concerned, it did not go much further than the United Nations Organization itself. George Kennan's famous 'long telegram' from Moscow in 1946 bears witness to the unreadiness of Stalin to be tied to rules of economic co-operation. It shows above all that big countries are always liable to see the international system as an instrument of their more narrowly defined interest. For similar reasons, even the remaining supporters of a world order had difficulty agreeing on an International Trade Organization. But in fact if not in name systems of co-operation in monetary matters, trade and development were set up, and for two and a half decades they worked fairly well. Given the enormous economic superiority of the nations which participated in the IMF, the GATT and the World Bank, stable money, free trade and considered aid may even be said to have benefited the non-members of these organizations.

Within a relatively stable international system, regional co-operation flourished also. It did not come about without its own aches and pains, and in some cases, as with the Accord of Cartagena of Andean countries or even the Association of South East Asian Nations, it remained rudimentary. The European Community tells by comparison a story of success, although it was constructed on the debris of the European Defence Community and the hollow shells of several earlier attempts at integration. In the fields of trade, areas of research, aid to development, aspects of social policy (which include the common agricultural policy) the European Community has become the first lasting example of the joint exercise of sovereignty by initially six, later nine, then ten, and twelve nations. The Community began with the Coal and Steel Community in 1952. In 1958 the European Economic Community and the European Atomic Energy Community were added. In 1967 the three were merged into the European Communities. Two years later they reached a turning point in their affairs. The first great project, a common market, was about to be completed at least in law. The next project on which the Community decided to embark (at the summit conference of The Hague in December 1969) was its enlargement by the accession of Britain and others. This too was accomplished; but it left the question of the substance of

119

cooperation open. This was to be extended by the third project, the creation of an economic and monetary union within a decade. After thorough preparation, ambitious decisions were taken in the spring of 1971. They lasted a few weeks. When the world system began to crumble, the calendar of the European Community was the first to be upset, though it was by no means the only casualty.

The key date is 15 August 1971. On that day, President Nixon and his Treasury Secretary John Connally unilaterally gave notice to the trade and monetary systems of the post-war period.[1] They suspended the convertibility of the dollar into gold, imposed a surtax on imports, and above all gave as the reason for their actions the right of the United States of America to put its own interest before any responsibility for others. The world's strongest power – and therefore the guarantor of the international system – declared that it saw itself as no different from anyone else. These announcements had a history which did not make them altogether surprising to those immediately affected. They also had consequences which led to a negotiated settlement of some of the grievances. But the Bretton Woods monetary system has never recovered from the replacement of the dollar as the stable standard for others by floating rates, and the GATT trade system has been under pressure ever since.

Retelling the story is not to allocate blame. Enough of that was done in the tense months after 15 August 1971, from the initial exchanges at a special meeting of GATT in Geneva to the Smithsonian Agreement in Washington in December. The disputes left all participants scarred but not much wiser. The important point here is that the removal of what had clearly become the illusion of the international order has left everybody quite openly exposed to the winds of a cruder exercise of power. Sometimes these winds seemed to abate, but before long they picked up again and on several occasions they turned into unpredictable hurricanes. The Yom Kippur War of October 1973 and the attendant first oil shock was one example. Inflation in the OECD world is not so easily dated, but its net effect on the rest was no less severe than that of the two great oil price increases. These in turn are directly related to half a decade of loans to the Third World which are at the basis of the debt problem of the 1980s. In 1971, there were some who advocated currency floating as a market prescription. At last money would represent the underlying worth of an economy. Today, few if any would maintain this position. Floating has contributed to the separation of exchange rates, and of money more generally, from real economic growth; it is one of the factors in the emergence of the casino capitalism of the 1980s.

It is not easy to offer a summary description of the international system at the end of the 1980s, though whatever colours one uses to paint the picture it cannot be pretty. The organized world system is crumbling. For many years, the Soviet Union has blocked developments; more recently, this negative attitude has been rivalled by the United States. America has left UNESCO, discontinued negotiations of a Law of the Seas agreement, ignored judgments of the International Court, downgraded its representation at many international bodies, withheld funds from the United Nations, threatened GATT if it does not tackle matters of American interest, kept the World Bank on a short leash and generally expressed its dissatisfaction with the institutions which it created after the war. There may be reasons in every case, but the world is affected more by the results. They are, in a word, a return from Kant to Hobbes; power rather than the law determines what happens between nations. There is a tendency for everyone to fend for himself. Alliances, including the North Atlantic Treaty Organization and the European Community, find themselves weakened. The developing countries sink deeper into their quagmire; several have become net exporters of capital to the rich. World peace depends entirely on the two superpowers and their leaders.

The implications for political and economic developments are considerable. The first of them is that no one in the world is able any longer to conduct a defence or economic policy as if everything else can be kept equal. Unilateralism has ceased to be viable, unless a country wants to opt for living in defenceless poverty outside the real world of interacting others. In this interdependent relationship few things can be held constant. Shock waves can have their origins in many places. One has to be alert to survive, and very streetwise to flourish. Protection is difficult; much of the time it will lead to decline. Since there is no organized system, it is hard even for the most powerful countries to influence the actual course of things. If one is interested in the politics of liberal reform, these are strong constraints. It is all the more important not to be overwhelmed by them.

It will be disappointing if questions of defence and détente are left out of the following discussion; yet even a general analysis of contemporary trends cannot deal with everything. Let me leave no doubt however about my belief that the combined threats of nuclear and biological warfare, which are not confined to the superpowers and are as much threats of technical or bureaucratic incompetence as of political malevolence, are the great risk to humankind. Within minutes, they can condemn everything said in this book to irrelevance. When I return once again to the idea of a world civil society at the end of this book, distant objectives will be formulated. For the foreseeable future, however, every step, however small, which contributes to bringing the threat to human survival under control is to be welcomed. It will be noted that every such step of necessity requires international action.

Turning to economic and political matters, there is little reason to believe that the tempered anarchy of the world will give way to any kind of order in the foreseeable future. (If it was true anarchy, it might have some of the textbook strengths of markets, but in fact this is tempered by streaks of apparent order such as currency controls, commodity agreements, subsidies for declining industries, mafia-type cartels; the result is hard to bear and harder to manage.) It is not as paradoxical as it sounds that internationalization becomes an economic and political imperative at a time at which the international system is weak: if one cannot rely on rules, one has to react to events and if possible forestall them.

Economic internationalization involves one risk above all. Given the obvious need for all actors on the scene to respond effectively to quickly changing circumstances, entitlement issues may fall by the wayside. As long as there is no genuine world order and thus no international law worthy of the name, international action tends to concentrate on provisions in any case. Even if the problem is clearly one of entitlements, as in the case of *apartheid* in South Africa, the instruments of the international community are largely economic and only indirectly political. At a time at which a volatile world economic condition impinges on political decisions everywhere, the tendency is bound to be even stronger to neglect questions of people's rights and instead try to make sure that the flow of provisions continues.

On a world scale, this must mean the systematic neglect of some of the underlying issues of development which are as much sociocultural and sociopolitical as they are socio-economic. Within the OECD countries, the effort of withstanding the on-slaught of the storms of the world economy detracts from domestic problems of citizenship. The 1970s mark both the climax and the beginning of decline of widespread interest in the social prerequisites of liberty.

Little has been said about the causes of the change in the world scene in the 1970s. The omission is important: it is not my intention to conjure up the world economy as a *diabolus ex machina* which has destroyed all that was otherwise well and good. Of course, international changes have something to do with what went before. Perhaps they too illustrate what must be called contradictions of modernity. Certain trends go over the top as it were. They continue to a point at which their cost is greater than the benefit derived from them. In the process of advancing them, measures have to be taken which defeat the ends for which they are designed. Yesterday's solutions become tomorrow's problems. There are, as one can see, many ways of expressing the dilemma, though it is better to point to real developments than to figures of analysis.

The Economic Growth Debate

The 1970s were among other things a time of enormous exaggeration. The exaggeration of gloom and doom. Not since *The Revolt of the Masses* and *The Decline of the West* in the late 1920s and early 1930s have so many books been written with titles like: *What's Wrong With the Modern World?*, *Ways Out of the Affluence Trap*, *Future Shock*, *The Decadence of the Modern World*, *The Rise and Decline of Nations*, *The Discontent of Modernity*, *The No-Growth Society*, *Can We Survive Our Future?*[2] Certain words recur in these books with a regularity which makes one want to engage, now that we can put the 1970s on the couch so to speak, in a spot of sociopsychoanalysis. The most significant is the word 'limit'. 'The idea of limit', says the German author of a book entitled *Limits of the Future*, 'has joined the circle of ideas which determine history.' Another author,

German also, sees the pathos of European history since the Renaissance in the demonstration of man's ability to overcome limits, but today 'mankind has encountered limits of which at least in the two preceding centuries it did not know or want to know'.[3] Arguably, no one book has reflected and determined the mood of the 1970s as well as the first report to the Club of Rome by Dennis Meadows and others, *Limits to Growth*.

When the Italian entrepreneur and humanist Aurelio Peccei first assembled a group of distinguished businessmen, scholars and politicians in Rome in 1968, his interest was in the common denominator of a whole set of seemingly disparate facts emerging from below the surface of visible events. Peccei himself lists (in his account written in 1976, thus with a degree of hindsight) a whole catalogue of such facts – population growth and social injustice, unemployment and the energy crisis, monetary disruption and protectionism, illiteracy and alienation, terrorism and corruption, and so on and so forth – in order to make the case: 'This baffling intractable tangle of difficulties is what the Club of Rome calls the *problématique*.' The solution of the *problématique*, or rather the despairing answer offered by the Club of Rome in the Meadows Report, was simple, unconvincing and influential: 'If the present growth trends in world population, industrialization, pollution, food production, and resource depletion continue unchanged, the limits to growth on this planet will be reached sometime within the next hundred years.'[4]

The Meadows Report was first published in 1972. To call it unconvincing is not to detract from the issues it raises. The Club of Rome itself soon realized that the global figures which it used made little specific sense anywhere; a Second Report by Mihajlo Mesarovic and Eduard Pestel disaggregated its data. Both groups of authors underestimated the world capacity for food production. There was never the slightest reference to the possibility of hunger in the midst of plenty, that is to entitlements. (The Club of Rome shared the quantitative obsession with those against whom it intended to argue.) Fifteen years later, we have a better understanding of the complexities of available resources. Savings, new methods, alternatives have come to the foreground. Pollution has entered the agenda of action everywhere, in part as a result of the publicity which the Club of Rome gained. The growth of world population continues unabated, although new forms of death in Africa and elsewhere make one both shiver and wonder about the future.

The weakness of the Report to the Club of Rome is in its very idea of limits. Extrapolation is not a very plausible way of looking into the distant future, and the claim that problems will grow exponentially rather than in a linear fashion may shock simple souls but contributes little to solutions. Thinking in terms of limits betrays a one-track mind. One can go forward, stop dead, and reverse gear. Many think in these terms. Habit confines imagination. The recommendation to go on as before whatever the obstacles and the advocacy of a reversal of trends are the most likely in any situation, and especially when one is faced with a new set of problems. This is what actually happened in the 1970s and to some extent in the 1980s too. Some were whistling the old tunes of growth in the dark; some were calling to undo everything that had been done in the 1960s. Neither of these had very good advice to give. In fact, history progresses differently, like the knight in chess perhaps, sideways and forward, or by a change of themes, or by new instruments of attack which make yesterday's limits appear as irrelevant as the Maginot Line in an age of aerial warfare.

This is not to say that it is enough to sit back and let things work themselves out (though I share the doubts in human planning and the preference for markets which have informed modern liberal thinking). It is not to say either that nothing of consequence happened in the 1970s. On the contrary, the experience of the 1970s marked a turning point in modern social development. It is early days to be certain just how important a turning point it was. I tend to think that it was as important as the transition from the liberal to the social-democratic century a hundred years ago. But contemporaries always have a tendency to claim secular significance for the ephemeral; the frisson of living in important times is hard to resist for intellectuals. 1789 (so to speak) saw the dramatic inauguration of the principle of citizenship; 1889 (so to speak), the year of the publication of the *Fabian Essays* and of the formation of the trade unions of the unskilled in Britain, marks the incipient organized class struggle which was to lead to its institutionalization and much later to the creation of a majority class; there is no name yet for the new departures of 1989.

Economic growth has much to do with the change. When the

Club of Rome predicted limits to economic growth, this may have seemed unduly gloomy to many. Only a year later, however, the oil shock produced memorable pictures. The shortage of petrol left motorways empty; electricity was rationed for many homes; industries seemed in jeopardy. This was temporary, to be sure, and partly symbolic, but the symbol represented unexpected possibilities. In the 1970s, most countries have experienced at least one year of 'negative growth'; average growth rates were much lower in the OECD world in general than they had been in preceding decades;[5] coping with the new condition became the major preoccupation of politics everywhere. Politicians did not find it easy. Many failed to get re-elected.

Economists were bewildered, at least for a while. Then some of them came up with theories that are worth recalling, if only because they form the background of the thinking of the 1980s and 1990s. These theories were intended to explain the new difficulties of growth and help show a way out of the quandary. The simplest of them was not a theory at all, but the invocation of 'long cycles' which are presented as a kind of law of nature. Walt Rostow listed, with explicit reference to the Russian economist Kondratieff who had invented these cycles, several downward 'trend periods' in the last 200 years: 1790–1815, 1848–1873, 1896–1920, 1936–1951. Some of these look a little surprising, depending on the country which one has in mind. However, Rostow's point is that no one should be surprised about another such period beginning in 1972. It will run its course and end in another upswing twenty-five years later. By the year 2000, 'high and steady rates of growth will have been reconciled with price stability'.[6]

Some were not satisfied with such unexplained regularities. Albert Hirschman spoke with characteristic irony and scepticism of cycles of 'disappointment' which are the human response to impersonal contradictions, and which are hard to avoid although they must not be allowed to discourage reasonable action.[7] Mancur Olson went further. In explaining the most characteristic economic phenomenon of the 1970s, stagflation, he introduced a 'logic of collective action' which is all but inescapable. The longer societies and economies are allowed to develop undisturbed by internal or external shocks, the more likely they are to become rigid, incapable of adjustment and innovation. Cartels of special interest groups hold down entrepreneurial initiative. The whole system runs aground. How does it get going again? Olson has been much attacked for his conclusions, though these follow quite plausibly from his analysis. He quotes Jefferson: 'Every now and again the tree of progress has to be fed with the blood of patriots.' Only wars and revolutions can break up the stagnation of economies and reverse the decline of nations.[8]

The core of the economic growth debate of the 1970s was less dramatic though equally remarkable. It had two main character-istics. One was that the debate vacillated in a rather confusing way between the question of whether continued economic growth was viable, and the totally different question of whether it was desirable. The other characteristic was a curious propensity to offer non-economic solutions for economic problems. The first of these was most evident in the controversy between Ed Mishan and Wilfred Beckerman. Mishan published his *Cost of Economic Growth* as early as 1967, and later added *The Economic Growth Debate*, Beckerman responded with *In Defence of Economic Growth* in 1974. Mishan clearly never liked growth, or any other part of the modern world. 'The private automobile is, surely, one of the greatest, if not *the* greatest, disasters that ever befell the human race.'[9] Such romantic preferences cast doubt on his vicious attacks on the 'growthmen' around. Beckerman in return takes the moderate, social democratic line. The cost of non-growth is greater than that of growth; there is much still to be done to increase welfare for all; and, of course, 'increasing total incomes is a necessary condition also for increasing the equality of income distribution'.

It is all the more interesting that Beckerman too says: 'In the richer countries of the world there *is* more cause for misgiving as to the desirability of fast economic growth than perhaps at any time in the past.' He is therefore not averse to seeking measures of welfare which include factors other than gross domestic product and real income. It is indeed one of the lasting consequences of the debate of the 1970s that the language of public discourse has changed. The OECD itself, once the hotseat of growthmanship, has encouraged the application of social indicators as well as straight economic measures. Politicians and even governments have come to talk of 'balanced growth' or 'qualitative growth' to indicate their conviction that it is not enough to proceed along the well-trodden path of the 1950s and 1960s.

Not all have followed those economists who have gone a step further and advocated fundamental changes in values. Ed Mishan was just one of them. Tibor Scitovsky (*The Joyless Economy*) distinguished between the pleasures of novelty and the comforts of certainty, and played down the importance of the standard of living for either. Fred Hirsch (*Social Limits to Growth*) advocated a 'new social ethic' which takes people's mind off the striving for provisions which they cannot attain because from a certain point onwards growth defeats its own ends. Fritz Schumacher (*Small Is Beautiful*) put his trust in the development of 'new loyalties' within more humane units of economic activity than the giganto-mania of the growth period had brought about. The idiosyncratic elements in these and other proposals for new values is unmistakable. Perhaps one should note above all that, in the views of these representatives of an ordinarily hard-nosed discipline of social science, the crisis of the 1970s called for something quite different from the normal prescriptions of economic policy.

In the late 1980s, some of those who have lived to see the day may not be too happy about being reminded of what they wrote in the 1970s. The growthmen were temporarily replaced by the gloom merchants, though the conjuncture of the latter was short. Having passed through their misty patch one is, however, faced with a new perspective on provisions. It says first of all that from being the universal solution growth has become the problem. It is no longer a matter of course. The 1980s have been a decade of quite uneven economic performance, with good years and bad, relatively successful and relatively poor economic performers. While there is always a Hudson Institute about which promises the skies, official and unofficial economists have become cautious in their predictions. The precariousness of growth adds further to the importance of the world economy for all actors.

Kondratieff cycles are not exactly a useful instrument of policy; historical inevitability never is. But there is a widespread sense that some of the successes of past decades are responsible for the failures, or at any rate the difficulties, of today. From another point of view, social citizenship rights appear as non-wage labour costs (and taxes) and are seen as reducing international competitiveness. Economies of scale used to be thought of exclusively as economies of a larger scale, until the cost of bigness to investment and to flexibility came to be recognized. Some elements of the corporatism which arose from the democratic class struggle came to threaten both growth and employment by impeding adjustment processes.

Choices had to be made by governments and by citizens. Some decided to opt out and turn green. They had to be able to afford the luxury, for such it was, capricious and rather short-lived. Others tried to revive the spirit of economic growth in its crudest quantitative form. They tried to get rich quick. The theory and practice of economic policy responded by turning to the supply side, to stimuli for entrepreneurs, incentives for employees and subsidies for technology. One begins to see how the politics of the 1980s emerged from the quandaries of the 1970s, a subject about which more will be said presently. It will then become apparent too that the destructive aspect of this change is more evident than its constructive counterpart. For change to come about, many social democratic institutions had to be dismantled, but the society arising from the ashes is as yet nebulous and of uncertain duration.

A State of Uncertainty

It is not easy to put one's finger on the real consequences of the reforms which I have associated with a date of somewhat misleading exactness, 1968. Many of them were talked about as much as implemented, though by changing language the road was paved for changes in values. Some of the measures adopted in a reformist spirit merely added final touches to the edifice of the social state. In a number of cases, they actually turned out to be the straw that broke the camel's back, as when in Germany statutory sick pay for employees was extended to the first three days of illness which had earlier been exempted; thus a sensible system became wide open for abuse and unaffordably expensive.[10] But if one wants to quantify the reforms of the time, one fact stands out. It is the enormous increase in the number of public servants during that period. The revolution of 1968 (if that is what it was) was a revolution of the public service.

This is true in more ways than one, but in the first instance it describes the lasting effect of the reforms of the 1960s and early 1970s. In 1984, 4.6 million Germans were directly or indirectly employed in the public service; another 300,000 were in analogous employment and 1.2 million received public service pensions. If one adds family members, one reaches the figure of at least 15 million people in a population of fewer than 60 million. This figure has not changed much from the mid-1970s, but in the preceding decade, from 1965 to 1975, it had increased by more than 35 per cent. Moreover, the bulk of the increase concerned so-called higher public servants with special benefits and entitlements whose number doubled within that decade.

The German case is in some ways exceptional. (Although the Swedish Institute for Opinion Research calculated before the Swedish elections of 1985 that 54 per cent of all voters received their income from government, 28 per cent as public employees and 26 per cent who are dependent on transfer incomes.) In Germany, teachers and railwaymen and telephone engineers and airline pilots are all public servants, or in a strictly analogous employment status. However, if one includes, in Britain and elsewhere, those in local government jobs, in the health service, in schools and elsewhere whose employment conditions involve near-total job security, de facto indexing of incomes and special privileges in illness and old age, the figures are not so dissimilar. In the United States, the picture is clearly different; but in the rest of the OECD world, one-quarter of all people were in public service types of employment by the mid-1970s, with many having acquired that status in the preceding decade.

The reasons for this process are easy to see. Depending on one's taste, they can be described in more or less cynical terms. Some of the reforming energies of the late 1960s issued from the products of a rapidly expanding system of higher education. They needed jobs. At the same time, they pressed for reform against what they saw as societies dominated by private economic interest. To them, public was beautiful. Thus their jobs had to be in the public realm. In fact, a whole generation of graduates managed to slide with great ease into planning and teaching, supervising and administering jobs in the public service. The fact that after them the same door was closed by the double lock of the end of expansion and the occupation of existing posts by relatively young incumbents has much to do with the politics of the 1980s.

Less cynically, there is the obvious fact that many of the reforms of the time involved more government or para-governmental activity. They had to be administered. A more subtle set of partly unintended consequences has to do with democratization. The slogan covers a multitude of things, but paradoxically most lead to bureaucratization rather than people power. Democratization means committee meetings, and committee meetings are not only time-consuming but also involve paperwork. Democratization means the creation of instances of appeal for every decision and by the same token more red tape. Democratization means the substitution of elaborate and explicit reasons for personalized judgement; such routinization requires forms and archives and administrators. Advocates of unconstrained communication and fully argued decisions on values may believe that they are replacing unquestioned authority by the participation of all in everything, but in the first instance they subject all to the subtle torture of bureaucracy.

One other reason for the expansion of the public service during the years of reform is relevant. What one might call the public-service mentality has a great deal to do with the preferences and beliefs of the majority class. Even in societies in which the majority do not hang on the drip of government for their survival (as they do in Sweden), the values of security and orderly progression, of assured though not very burdensome work and a calculable impersonality of relations of authority have tended to become the preferred values of people in many walks of life. Once again, irony is inappropriate. The public-service life may not be exciting or inspiring, it may not give much scope to innovation and to unusual careers, but it is a remarkable social construction which satisfies many aspirations.

It is also another instance of the contradictions of modernity. Max Weber acted them out in the ambivalence of his concept of rationality. The rational exercise of power overcomes the dilettantism and arbitrariness of earlier patterns of rule, but if taken to its extreme it also accounts for the threat of a cage of bondage in which all initiative and individualism is stifled. The abstract metaphor has quite specific applications, especially if we consider the welfare state, or social state. It documents what has been called the cost of good intentions, and this cost is high. The welfare state is the embodiment of social citizenship rights. In order to achieve the objective of a full status of citizenship for all, formal entitlements, incomes transfers, and programmes of

131

health care, education etc. are necessary. The resulting package has to be financed, and it has to be administered. So far, there is nothing surprising or problematic. But there comes the point at which the machinery of the social state defeats its objective.

On the expenditure side, modern social policies involve almost open-ended commitments. There can never be enough education, or medical care. The latter in particular exceeds all realistic cost horizons when medical technology becomes more and more intricate and expensive, and demographic and social factors conspire to increase needs. On the income side, there are problems even apart from a growing desire of many not to increase government spending further. If the proportion of retired people rises, education is extended, and a significant number are out of work, the remaining employees and companies have to be taxed beyond the limits of efficiency and in some cases endurance. Curious paradoxes arise. While people's real incomes increase, their transfer incomes do too. They are no longer basic entitlements of citizenship but a part of the provisions which members of the majority class expect. In the process, quite a few discover that they are getting back as much as they are paying in; taxes return as entitlements to the pockets from which they were taken in the first place.

These statements are incomplete. One must add: minus the cost of administering the process. There is a friction cost of the circulation of entitlement moneys, and its name is bureaucracy. Bureaucracy is the greatest contradiction of the social state. It means that those who should care for others, like nurses and teachers, get submerged in paperwork. It also means that the recipients of services, instead of being able to claim simple and comprehensible rights, have to go through humiliating processes of filling in forms, having their means tested, queuing, and haggling about pennies from this pot or that. As a result of a bureaucratization which seemed and at one point was inevitable, essentially individual problems are generalized, formalized, turned into impersonal cases in a filing system. The incongruity of the result leads to frustration and anger. Many people fail to use their entitlements; they cannot be bothered, they do not know about them, they do not want to know or be bothered. Injustice results from a system of justice.

These are overstatements, to be sure, and they are not a call for

132

dismantling the social state. But they are intended to underline the discovery of the 1970s that past trends cannot simply go on. In any case, the discovery has not been confined to the political right. When Johano Strasser wrote his book *Limits to the Social State?* he replied in the affirmative to his own question mark, but pleaded for more rather than less social welfare. The manner in which the familiar social state defines social problems (he argued) in fact creates new social problems. Old people in poverty, marginalized foreign workers, young addicts, those afflicted by 'civilization diseases' including psychological disturbances, accident victims are all in need and yet there is no effective way of helping them. Strasser will not abandon the belief of the traditional left in the benevolent state altogether, but he wonders about ways to increase people's 'self-determination and responsible participation' and therefore advocates more self-help, the strengthening of community networks, a new solidarity.[11]

The solutions are debatable, but the problem is clear. One of the crises of the 1970s was that of government. It was in fact a crisis of Big Government. The social state is only one example of how big government came about in democratic societies. Public expenditure is another illustration. In many OECD countries, the share of gross national product disposed by government rose to 50 per cent and more in the 1970s. The public-service mentality came to be founded not only in employment patterns but in the economic role of the state. Keynesianism, or what went under this name, swept the globe. Everywhere, and in every respect, governments claimed and were expected to deal with all issues, from recessions to disasters, and from the smallest village to the world at large.

As expectations rose to the skies, disappointments lurked just around the corner. The 1970s were also the time of *Democracy in Crisis* (to quote the title of a conference report by the Trilateral Commission of American, Japanese and European leaders in 1975).[12] It would not be difficult to add a list of political scientists who contributed to the governability debate of the 1970s to that of economists and the growth debate. Moreover, in one respect at least, the two arguments are related. If democracy for the majority class becomes a competition of political entrepreneurs for votes, and if success in this competition is dependent on the ability to deliver at least some of the promised goods, then increasing provisions are a necessary condition of the functioning of the game. Democracy, in other words, is a positive-sum game which is at risk once the economic sums no longer add up.

I have tried to show that the economic theory of democracy is not only seriously lacking at the best of times, but also inapplicable in most political cultures. Nevertheless, economic circumstances clearly affect questions of governability, and perhaps even legitimacy. The British author James Alt has looked at opinion research data over time. He found that it is perfectly possible for people to live with incompatible views of the immediate and the remote and believe that they themselves are doing quite well, although the country is going through a bad patch. In normal times, it is quite amusing to be personally content and politically worried. But in the 1970s these normal times came to an end. Suddenly, people saw their personal well-being linked to that of the country, and both were seen to be in decline. At the time, inflation was the most obvious example of government weakness. The result, according to Alt, 'was not a politics of protest, but a politics of quiet disillusion'. People no longer expected government to deliver. They reduced their expectations.[13] Big government was not so much dismantled as deserted by the citizens.

In cultures which are prone to use heavier language, this kind of observation has led some to claim that democratic (or capitalist, or modern) societies are passing through a 'crisis of legitimacy'.[14] This is a burdened and burdensome phrase which I have avoided for that reason, but also on substantive grounds. A crisis of legitimacy is presumably a state of affairs in which doubt in political institutions threatens their very survival. There was a crisis of legitimacy in the Weimar Republic in the early 1930s. There probably was one in the French Fourth Republic in the late 1950s, though its exact complexion is more doubtful than the creation of the Fifth Republic in 1959 suggests. In the 1970s, the Vietnam War and Watergate led to widespread doubts in the institutions of the presidency in the United States, but the constitutional crisis passed. In any case, there is little sign of similar dramatic events occurring in all democratic countries in the near future. Thus speaking of a crisis of legitimacy is as misleading as the forecast of unspecified disasters by the Club of

Rome. There are new problems and there will be changes. Past trends cannot simply continue. Government in the 1990s will be different from government in the 1970s. But this is much more likely to happen by stealth than by drama.

That is why it is so difficult to give the process a name. The nightwatchman's state of the nineteenth century failed to cope with the requirements of expanding citizenship rights. In fact, there never was quite such a state, least of all in Germany where the socialist leader Lassalle coined the phrase with polemical intent. However, gradually, governments took on more tasks which required more taxes and more public servants. From being a nightwatchman who looks after law and order while the citizens – or is it the bourgeois? – sleep, the state became more like a nanny who never lets go of the citizens' – or is it the subjects'? – hands. This involved what Michel Crozier and others have called an 'overloading' of government functions.[15] It was never likely that this kind of big government could cope, let alone cope and maintain the constitution of liberty. In fact, the social democratic state did better than one would have predicted, corporatism and all. But in recent years, it has run into all the issues discussed in this chapter, from a harsher international climate to doubts about economic growth, and from a troubled social state to quandaries of participation.

For some, the answer is simple, at least in words. It is: less government. But even those who advocate such a reversal do not practise it when they have the chance. Supply-side economic policy for example is a curiously interventionist approach, especially if it involves systematic support for big science and technology with or without a defence component. Those others who take Johano Strasser's prescriptions all the way to an alternative life style removed from traditional politics also contribute little; they tend to leave the powers that be to their own deserts which are those of the life chances of the majority. For the moment, then, uncertainty is the name of the state. In one way or another, big government will continue for some time, though centres of activity outside government will grow in importance and the tone-setting as well as the refereeing functions of government will come to the fore. After the nightwatchman and the nanny it is not easy to tell what the state is going to be: an animator who makes people feel good? a travel guide who claims to be in charge but from whom one can also run away from time to time? or perhaps a player-manager who is a part of the game but also responsible for the distribution of roles and the spirit of the team?

Post-Industrial Society?

For most of this book, I have preferred analysis in terms of the structures of society and politics to speculation about rather less tangible matters such as values. The preference is not unfounded. In the world of values, almost anything goes and assertions are as easily made as they are hard to substantiate, let alone to refute. But the closer one gets to the present, the harder it is to resist attention to what people think and feel and therefore might do. Many structures have not yet crystallized, so that one has to look at them in an earlier aggregate state. The notion of 'post-industrial society' has a lot to do with this amorphous state of affairs.

It is of course not entirely intangible. At the beginning of the 1970s, changes in patterns of employment were already advanced in the OECD world. Agricultural employment had dwindled, notably during the post-war decades; manufacturing employment, after rising rapidly in that period, had reached or even passed its peak; expansion occurred very largely in the areas of distribution and services. (Once again, patterns varied from country to country.) In most OECD countries, the 1970s added a dramatic twist to this change. Where possible (as in Japan, Italy, France) there was a further significant drop in agricultural employment, which by 1980 was below 10 per cent in most, and below 5 per cent in many OECD countries. At the same time, the proportion of those employed in manufacturing began to decline, rapidly in some cases as in Germany (from 50 to 44 per cent in the 1970s) or in Britain (from 34 to 27 per cent). This meant that the modern service economies grew. By 1980, more than 50 per cent of all employment in the OECD world was provided in the admittedly ragbag category of services, that is not in either primary or secondary occupations. The trend has continued since.

In a technical sense, this trend alone justifies speaking of a 'post-industrial society'. If industry means manufacturing and a society is characterized by dominant areas of employment, then industrial societies have been replaced by service societies. The majority class is also a service class. But of course this is not what 'postist' language means. It is intended to convey the idea that there was a change in values which accompanied that in employment patterns. Several descriptions of this change have been offered, and they are not necessarily compatible.

Daniel Bell, who coined the term 'post-industrial society', was initially much interested in the shifts in employment. As modern societies moved away from the production of goods, new driving forces of progress came to the fore. They were above all knowledge and information. Moreover, these forces and their scientific base had moved beyond mere trial and error to codification. This in turn meant that scientists and technologists had become an established and indispensable social group; they mark, as Bell put it, 'the advent of a new principle of stratification'. Their world is actually a very deliberate world. 'Planning provides a specific locus of decision, as against the more impersonal and dispersed role of the market.' As one rereads Bell's book, one is struck by its tone, which is very much that of an industrial society, albeit one which has progressed beyond manufacturing to information-led economic growth.

While published in 1973, *The Coming of Post-Industrial Society* is also a book of the 1960s. (Some might say of the 1980s, when the information society was discovered as a possible engine of new economic growth.) It was born out of a certain obsession with the year 2000 which actually never advanced beyond the extrapolation of earlier trends. Bell, who is one of the most sensitive and brilliant social analysts, realized this. In 1976 he added to the earlier study a very different book, *The Cultural Contradictions of Capitalism*. Here he argued that while social structure might be characterized by the 'techno-economic order', Western culture had gone in a very different direction. The Protestant ethic of saving, hard work and deferred gratification, which had determined centuries of capitalist economic growth, had at last succumbed to a culture of immediate enjoyment. Not production but distribution, not making but selling dominates life, and selling emphasizes prodigality. While the economy continues to be based on efficiency and rationality, the culture is dominated by a loose sense of enjoyment; it has 'become primarily hedonistic, concerned with play, fun, display, and pleasure'.[16]

Ten years later, one is tempted to take such observations much further. If saving was the classical engine of growth, it has been replaced by credit. The casino capitalism of the 1980s is debt-fuelled. One mortgages the future rather than using the accumulated wealth of the past. Even the stock exchange trades 'futures' and 'options'. While deferred gratification meant that one was working now in order to enjoy oneself later, the new mood is one of enjoyment now and (perhaps) work later. This is moreover more than a mere mood, let alone a fashion. Without increasingly elaborate credit arrangements neither individual lives nor total economies could be sustained. The new extrapolators once again see catastrophes at the end of this road. They are likely to be wrong, rather like their predecessors of the Club of Rome. But there are clear signs of a change in cultural attitudes.

The hedonistic turn of the Protestant ethic is however not the change commonly associated with the notion of 'post-industrialism'. Rather, it is Ronald Inglehart's *Silent Revolution*, which of course also took place in the 1970s. Inglehart likes to relate his conclusions to the *problématique* of the Club of Rome and the theories of Daniel Bell; but in essence he simply claims that there is a slow yet inexorable shift in Western societies from 'materialist' to 'postmaterialist' values. 'The values of Western publics have been shifting from an overwhelming emphasis on material well-being and physical security toward greater emphasis on the quality of life.' There are variations among countries as well as between different groups within countries. One phenomenon stands out however. While the old working class has become 'embourgeoisified' and has moved to the right politically, a new left of young middle-class people has become a social and political force for 'postmaterialist' values. This is probably due to the prosperity and peace of Aron's world, and it is a value pattern which is spreading and may well become dominant in the foreseeable future.

This (apart from 'Aron's world') is Inglehart's contention. One may doubt whether his opinion research data actually bear it out. One has to remind oneself that the key concepts of 'materialism' and 'postmaterialism' merely summarize six survey questions each. In Inglehart's interpretation, 'materialism' includes the preference for law and order as well as economic stability, which certainly begs the left–right question, and 'postmaterialism' includes not only the love of beauty but also free speech and the wish to have more say in government. Furthermore, in all the countries studied – nine member states of the European Community and the United States – 'materialist' values far outstrip 'non-materialist' ones. Fighting inflation was the dominant 'value' everywhere in 1973 except in Denmark, where it was outstripped by the need to maintain order, and in Luxembourg where economic growth came first. Economic growth came second on average, though the Italians in the sample thought that fighting crime was very important, and the French longed above all for a 'less impersonal society'. A postindustrial society?

Inglehart's thesis is that a new trend has begun. 'After a prolonged period of almost uninterrupted economic growth, the principal axis of political cleavage began to shift from economic issues to life-style issues, entailing a shift in the constituency most interested in obtaining change.' His evidence is at best inconclusive. When he reports repeated surveys in 1970, 1973 and 1976, it emerges that in a number of countries people were less 'materialist' in 1973 (presumably before the oil shock) than in 1976. In other words, one is talking of fickle values which are subject to ephemeral influences.[17] Perhaps the 'postmaterialist' mood is not so much a new trend as a characteristic of the 1970s. It could be a symptom of the crisis of that decade rather than a sign of new directions.

The 1970s were a confused time in the OECD world. For some, it represents the very fulfilment which I have associated with the glorious thirty years after the war, that is citizenship rights and reasonable prosperity. Some indeed remember the 1970s as a time of great progress, especially in entitlements. Activists of the women's movement certainly have reason to think so. Others had less satisfactory experiences. Real wages were eaten up by inflation; jobs were harder to come by. As the decade went on, this was notably the case for the children of 1968. Their 'post-materialism' was born of desperation as much as preference, though they were also instrumental in activating social movements for environmental protection, the rights of minorities, and disarmament.

Politicians found it hard to cope with the 1970s. In Germany, the reformer Willy Brandt gave way to the *macher* or operator Helmut Schmidt, whose Social Democratic Party slipped away from him at the end of the decade. In France, Giscard d'Estaing tried in vain to reach across the centre to the left and slipped in public opinion until he lost the election of 1981. In Britain, after Wilson's surprising defeat of 1970, Edward Heath suffered the same fate in 1974 ('Who governs Britain?'), and Wilson's successor James Callaghan again after the 'winter of discontent' in 1979. In the United States, two incumbent presidents lost elections in 1976 and 1980, after Nixon's resignation had put the country in turmoil in 1973. There is a special story behind every one of these events, and yet those in power could often be heard to say in the 1970s that in such difficult times it was almost impossible to be re-elected because one was bound to disappoint too many. The 1980s present a very different picture indeed.

To repeat, it is early days to tell just how important a turning point the crisis of the 1970s represents. Perhaps it is necessary also to move some distance away from apparent precision. Neither 1 January 1970 nor 31 December 1979 is very significant in this connection. What is important is that decades of economic growth and social progress ended in a period of fuzziness. The advances of the past had built up problems which defied proven methods of coping. External and internal factors combined to create a worrisome predicament. Some thought that the end was nigh. Had the 1970s been closer to the end of the century, they might well have given rise to a new chiliasm. Many felt that it was time to stop and think. If a certain irony in this discussion of values is unmistakable, this is not to say that the subject is without reality. Values were challenged, and also changed when both economic growth and social progress came under pressure. A significant group advocated a reversal of trends. For the first time in modern history, innovative thought about politics and society came from the right rather than the left.[18] A lot of confused thought also issued from all sides of the political spectrum. The conclusions which one draws from such observations are of necessity somewhat personal. I shall assume that there is no way back to the sweet reality of social democracy, although in the absence of plausible alternatives what is left of it may be an acceptable second-best for the time being. Much less is there a way back to the harsh dreams of the day before yesterday, to social Darwinism and its cost which after all informed the last century of change. The way forward requires a new definition as well as assertion of citizenship, life chances and liberty.

7 · Conflict After Class

Out of Work

Stagflation was the bane of the 1970s, but the 1980s saw the much more disconcerting phenomenon of unemployment despite growth spread to many advanced countries. Unemployment had actually risen in the 1970s. At the time, however, it seemed merely the normal concomitant of a slowdown in economic activity. Consequently the number of unemployed declined when OECD economies began to recover from the crises of the 1970s. But the decline was smaller than expected, and soon it stopped altogether. In the good economic years of the 1980s, unemployment was rising and in any case stayed high. The fears of governments that one million unemployed (in countries with fifty or sixty million inhabitants) would surely topple them, were soon forgotten. Modest but significant rates of economic growth even distracted the majority from taking much note of the figure crossing the two-million line. An unemployment rate of 10 per cent has become almost normal.

This is not true in the United States. A good part of the following story is distinctly European. It will therefore be necessary to supplement it by taking into account the American experience of job creation and relatively low unemployment. In a comprehensive analysis, the Japanese story of underemployment in large companies and the plight of the retired would also have to be added. Like the rest of this book, the discussion of work has a Western cultural bias and applies primarily to the European, North American and Oceanian parts of the OECD world.

High unemployment in the midst of economic growth raises

questions of economic development, of the history of work, and of citizenship. They will all be considered because the story of work is critical for recent twists of the modern social conflict. But first I must recognize the doubts of those who wonder whether we really are in the midst of economic growth in the 1980s. Much of the boom preceding the crash of the autumn of 1987 was financial. The stock exchanges of Wall Street and the City of London continued to beat all records. The amounts of money earned and placed, if not invested, exceeded the imagination, let alone the experience of earlier periods. But this was 'casino capitalism' (as Susan Strange has called it), a game of luck and perhaps flair rather than the result of thrift and hard work. Distinguished analysts on both sides of the Atlantic, like Felix Rohatyn or Peter Jay, saw the economies of the West 'on the brink' long before the stock market seemed to confirm their suspicions; in early 1987, a book about the 'great depression of 1990' became a bestseller in the United States.[1] Underneath the futures and options and other elements of the great money game, there is of course the real economy. A stock market crash does not necessarily herald a recession. Yet it gives pause that the real economy is largely debt-fuelled. The hedonistic ethic has come to full fruition. Sneaking doubts accompany the new-found wealth of many.

Still, when all is said and done, the 1980s are a phase of significant economic growth. Gnp or gdp figures tell us too much about things which we do not care about and too little about those which matter, but they are still a useful approximation; and gdp in the OECD countries has grown in the 1980s. Published figures are actually deceptively low because they are usually percentages of a total which is four times as big as its equivalent was in 1950. If one retranslates growth rates into the additional goods and services produced in a given year, some of the 1980s exceed many of the 1950s and 1960s. In Britain, this is true in any case because the thirty years after the war were not so glorious; but even in Germany, 1984, 1985 and 1986 were years of higher absolute growth than most years between 1950 and 1970.

Yet such growth has done little to unemployment. To some extent it may even be said to have been built on unemployment. There are two ways of increasing productivity. One is to produce more with the same number of hands, the other is to produce as much with fewer hands. In the 1980s, the latter method has prevailed. Governments bent on competitiveness have made it possible for employers to reduce their labour force to its indispensable minimum. Leaner companies have produced as much or more. There are striking German figures about the relationship between gdp and the quantity of work per capita (measured in terms of the total hours worked).[2] Until the late 1950s, both increased, though even at that time gdp growth was faster than that of the quantity of work. Since then however the two curves have veered in opposite directions. While gdp grew from 100 in 1950 to 400 in 1986, the quantity of work per capita first increased to about 110 and then declined to 66 during the same period. Vastly increased provisions resulted from significantly less human effort.

Extrapolations from such observations have long been made. Politicians and economists have become wary of them. The notion in particular that technical developments make human labour superfluous, while repeated regularly in the last two hundred years, has fewer official supporters today than at the time of the automation debate of the 1950s. Yet those who think that they have seen it all before should be careful. Changes in the nature of work have been profound, and they have affected individual lives as well as social structures. Today, work is no longer the obvious solution to social problems, but a part of the problem itself.

Work is the hidden agenda of the industrial world which it might be instructive to bring to light in another book. (This has of course been done before.)[3] One would then encounter a paradox. Modern societies are work societies, built around the work ethic and occupational roles, but they also seem to be driven by the vision and the apparently increasingly realistic perspective of a world without work. Jobs are the entry tickets to the world of provisions. They determine people's incomes, including those from transfers, their social standing, their self-esteem and the way in which they organize their lives. Long hours of hard work on the other hand are regarded as an intolerable burden; for centuries, and most particularly in the industrial societies, the privileged class which many watched with awe or envy was a leisure class of people who did not have to work.

The paradox played itself out in many ways and with surprising effects. In the work society, people's social lives can be summarized under four main headings. There is the early phase of life before people can be employed; there is the time of the day, the week and the year when employed people do not actually work; and there is the twilight phase of life when people are retired from employment. A century ago, these three facets of life were all related to the fourth, work. Childhood was preparation for work by learning skills and absorbing values; spare time was recreation from and for work; retirement was the reward for a lifetime of work. Today, all three have acquired their own significance. They have grown in scope, and they are often defined as quite separate. The world of education espouses and defends its own values; some authors have argued that it has come to dominate modern societies at the expense of work. Spare time has given rise to a whole new set of industries; many people draw as much satisfaction and even recognition from their leisure pursuits as from their work. Retirement has become a *troisième age*, a third life which for many lasts twenty years and more, and which has generated proper structures, including 'grey panthers' to represent them in the political arena.

Unexpected things have happened to work in the process. Worried neoconservatives join forces with bewildered socialists in extolling the virtues of hard work when neither have enough employment to offer to all. They are really talking about social and political control, for which no other mechanism than the discipline of employment has yet been found. In fact, from being a burden, work has become a privilege. Few would describe today's upper-status groups as a leisure class; they are a class of 'workaholics' instead. A good many of its members are always complaining about not knowing the difference between week-days and Sundays, and not having a holiday for years; but in fact such complaints are another form of conspicuous consumption, of displaying the new wealth of work.

A little game of figures illustrates the process well. In a typical OECD society today, 20 per cent of all people are below the age at which they can enter the labour market; another 20 per cent are retired. Of the rest, 10 per cent spend their time in educational institutions. (Some of these estimates are on the low side.) Of the remaining 50 per cent, some are not seeking gainful employment, and others are for one reason or another incapable of it; the estimate is not implausible that both groups together comprise

144

about 15 per cent. Another 10 per cent may be unemployed. This leaves 25 per cent of the population. These 25 per cent spend about half the days of the year at work, and on these days, their jobs demand their presence for about half their waking hours.[4] Are we really still living in a work society?

We are, and the proof of the fact is the fate of the unemployed. They are the one group in the calculus which does not fit. It is all right to be a student, a pensioner, an accountant on a trip around the world and even a visiting scholar on a sabbatical; it is objectionable to some though pleasing to others to be a house-wife; it is sad but unavoidable to be physically or mentally handicapped and unable to work; but to be unemployed is not all right. It destroys people's self-esteem, upsets the routine of their lives, and makes them dependent on the dole. It defines them out and thereby creates a new entitlement issue.

The case made here is that unemployment in the 1980s differs in some important respects from earlier versions of the phenomen-on. People have long worried about losing work. Often, they were the victims of seasons, or of the whims of employers. In the late nineteenth century, systematic economic reasons for unemploy-ment were first recognized.[5] Full employment became an issue of social and political reform. It was declared desirable and measures were taken to bring it about. Notwithstanding some of the entitlement language used in the process, these measures were all based on the assumption that healthy economic growth would provide full employment, and vice versa. From early claims for the regularization of casual labour through budgetary demand stimulation and public works projects to the compre-hensive planning of 'full employment in a free society' (all of which were associated with the names of Beveridge and Keynes at least in Britain) there was never any doubt that unemployment was not only undignified but wasteful, and that macroeconomic expansion was an indispensable part of the answer to the problem. In the 1980s, this no longer seems to be so clear. There are signs of a certain dissociation of economic growth and employment. A policy of full employment would therefore have to be different in kind.

This is not to say that there are not enough jobs to go around. It is to say however that the distribution of work has itself become a problem, and also that there are probably not enough jobs at a

145

level of pay which most would associate with a decent standard of living. The proximate causes for this development may be technical. The process of inventing labour-saving devices has continued for many decades. The deeper reasons for what appears to be a shortage of jobs are however social. New inventions are applied for reasons of cost and reliability, and these in turn have to do with the defence of real wages by organized labour, sometimes helped by legislation, and the unpredictability of what people are going to do next. If we dig even deeper, we come back to the modern history of work.

This is clearly a success story. The ability to produce more with less work creates many opportunities. Since 1870, the total product in today's OECD societies may well have increased by a factor of ten, but the average hours worked per person per year have been halved.[6] A new balance of heteronomous work and autonomous activity can be found which supersedes the more thoughtless patterns of the industrial work society. The quality of work itself can be improved. Inevitable elements of super- and subordination in the world of work can be mitigated by representation and participation. While some are addicted to work, others can develop and live out their talents in the many hours and days which they do not have to spend at their workplace. Altogether, there is more scope for activity both within and outside the world of work.[7] But this is not true for all. The fact that more can be produced with less human input means that work can become scarce. This in turn means that under certain conditions some can be defined out of the marketplace of labour.

What are these conditions? Postulating a natural rate of unemployment of 6 or more per cent helps little, even if the word 'natural' is interpreted to refer to the rate which cannot be reduced without risk of increasing inflation. In recent years, much has been made of the segmentation of labour markets into two or even many relatively insulated parts with peculiar skill requirements and access routes. The existence of such barriers helps us understand why there is not one perfect labour market, and why therefore certain groups are the first to go out and the last to come in when conjunctural fluctuations occur, but it does not by itself explain persistent unemployment. The flexibility of real wages, or its absence, does offer such an explanation. If wages are truly sticky, and it is not possible to create jobs at much lower levels of pay than those which are customary for established jobs, then unemployment is in a narrow monetary sense cheaper than employment.

However, other factors have to be added. One is that unemployment leaves many of the core functions of the economy unaffected. Agriculture has long been a high-productivity but low-employment sector. Industry in the sense of the secondary sector of manufacturing production now follows suit. Industrial output increases while industrial employment declines. Those who are left in secondary employment probably have fairly safe jobs; certainly they are well-paid. But what of the rest?

There is first of all a necessary tertiary sector of activities which are needed to keep primary and secondary production going. Traditional administrative and distributive employment has grown, and probably had to grow in order to serve complex tastes and demands. Certain other activities, notably in relation to the organization of income transfers, or social citizenship rights, have been added. In all these fields, productivity is a more complicated notion than in agriculture or industry; their extension tends to drag productivity figures down, but this has little meaning. Primary, secondary and traditional tertiary activities comprise what one might call the core economy. It can be maintained with significantly less than full employment.

If one wants full employment, one therefore has to create peripheral or dispensable jobs. The notion is obviously problematic. Who is to say that a job is not strictly necessary? Personal service occupations were once numerous; they then all but disappeared; more recently, they have returned as organized service jobs, like cleaning firms, or companies providing 'meals on wheels', or even shoe-shine shops. But it is noticeable that they do not exist everywhere to the same extent. If one were to draw up a schedule of jobs needed to maintain a modern economy, one would not have to include them. Other examples are more complicated still. It has been suggested that the 'information society' has generated more information than anybody can possibly use, and jobs of a considerable level of skill with it. Stories of strictly superfluous public-service jobs abound; one need but think of the illustration of Parkinson's Law by the inverse relation between the number of employees and the number of ships in the British Navy. Many have wondered

147

whether the conjuncture of management consultancy firms adds much to management, let alone to production. Thus a whole host of jobs have sprung up which in good times contribute to the prosperity of those who have them, but which are dispensable in bad times. Indeed, some of them are the first to go where competitiveness is taken seriously.

It may nevertheless be a good thing to have such jobs, though I shall turn to their social cost presently. The interests of the majority class are probably split in this regard. On the one hand, its members will jealously guard 'true' jobs or those which have all their perquisites, on the other hand they do not like the untidiness of unemployment. In any case, a new boundary begins to emerge between those who have safe, well-paid and apparently purposeful employment and those who do not. Persistent unemployment in countries with sticky real wages and a fairly short-sighted majority class is one of its symptoms, though the dividing line runs probably through the lower half of the employed rather than between them and the unemployed.

The entitlement issues created by such developments are serious and far from simple. Jobs as a key to life chances in the work society were for a long time not merely the entry ticket to the world of provisions but also a condition for the entitlements of citizenship. Suffrage for example depended on paying taxes, and later on being a member of certain professions. Social citizenship rights were tied closely to employment, notably by the use of the insurance principle for welfare entitlements. In defining citizenship, I have argued that the status is not the result of a commercial contract, nor is it marketable. The separation of citizenship from occupation was therefore progress, much as those who control the world of work may wish to make it undone. However, the entitlement party proceeded to make its own mistake when it sought to establish a right to work. This is either an empty phrase or a misuse of the word 'right'. It may be desirable to find work for everyone, and politicians may wish to make a commitment to that effect, but no judge can force employers to hire unemployed people. Moreover, employment for its own sake is a recipe for economic inefficiency. In terms of liberty, it is more important to establish the right not to work, so that governments cannot force people into a dependence which they want to escape.

Nevertheless, long-term and persistent unemployment raises

entitlement issues.[8] As long as access to markets and thereby to provisions depends on employment, unemployment means by implication that access is denied. This is true even if unemployment pay is such that people are able to survive. In Europe, a debate has begun about the progressive dissociation of work and citizenship: there are those who regard liberation from employment as a necessary step in the progress of emancipation. In the United States even radical authors take the opposite view and argue that work, including the relationships of power and dependence which it involves, is a prerequisite of civilization.[9] The debate takes up ancient themes and it is topical precisely because of the changes in the world of work to which I have alluded. It is, however, of little relevance to the unemployed, or to the foreseeable conflicts in the OECD societies.

A Matter of Definition (1): The Underclass

The story of the new social problem is not yet complete; in particular, its American aspect is missing. There is, to be sure, persistent unemployment in the United States as well. Moreover, economists have adjusted their assumptions about probably unavoidable unemployment upwards to 6 or 7 per cent. But in the United States, millions of new jobs have been created, and no one uses or even understands the notion of a scarcity of work. The reason is not just the pervasiveness of the work ethic and its rhetoric in American life; it has to do above all with one of the conditions which I stipulated for unemployment and the scarcity of work, that is the (downward) flexibility of real wages. American real wages have in fact declined. As a result, people find employment, but many remain poor. Persistent poverty is the American equivalent to persistent unemployment in Europe.

The decline in real wage levels in the United States began in the mid-1970s. At that time, a long-term trend was broken. Average incomes for men in full-time employment had been rising steadily since the 1950s, but in the ten years following 1973 they declined by 10 per cent. (Average incomes for employed women remained steady or rose slightly.) During the same period, the percentage of those below the official poverty line, which had declined steadily since the 1940s, rose from 11 to 14 per cent.[10]

This does not primarily reflect an actual decline in the incomes of those employed in the same jobs in 1973 and 1983; rather, it is the result of the fact that relatively well-paid jobs disappeared and new ones were created at a much lower level of pay. If one takes into account the disappearance of perks with the jobs – of health care support and job security – the change is even more drastic.

The overall result of this process is bound to be depressing. If large numbers of people have to expect declining incomes in the coming decade, they are not likely to feel very buoyant about life. (Frank Levy has calculated that for the first time since statistics were compiled, the average forty-year-old has to look forward to a 14 per cent decline in real income during the next ten years of his life.) But of course the overall picture conceals specific trends. Some are doing very well, and expect to continue to do so. Significant numbers find themselves at the margin. They have good times and bad ones. If 'decasualization', that is the permanent employment of hitherto casual labour, was one of Beveridge's prescriptions against unemployment before the First World War, one observes a certain 'recasualization' today. This is not always involuntary, but it leaves a sense of jeopardy. Again, the employment position spills over, in the United States, into economic status more generally. Large numbers of people move in and out of poverty in terms of the official poverty line. Many of them have work; they are the 'working poor'. One can look at them in two ways. Their hold on full participation in the life of society is clearly tenuous; at the same time, they have not irretrievably lost their citizenship rights. They have not only memories of better days, but at least some of the skills to work their way out of destitution.

This is not so clear for the group below them, the underclass. The American 'ghetto' underclass is much studied and even more widely invoked in debate; yet there remains some doubt whether it is a construct or a reality. There is no industrial society without a residual group of drifters, scroungers and unemployables. In large cities, they are clearly in evidence. But those who are down and out in Paris and London are not an underclass. For an underclass to come about, there have to be systematic processes of recruitment, of definition and of behaviour. In American cities, these appear to exist. Descriptions vary in detail, but focus on many of the same characteristics of 'minority groups living in the poorest areas of our large cities, characterized by low attachment to the labour force, drug and alcohol abuse, out-of-wedlock births, long-term welfare dependency, and, among men at least, a tendency toward criminal behaviour'.[11] In other words, one is talking about a group in which social pathologies cumulate to create a long-term condition. The absence of skills and un-employment, residence in particular areas, dependence on wel-fare support are its characteristics. Many members of the under-class belong to minorities and live in incomplete families. They tend to engage in aberrant behaviour.

Several authors have tried to calculate the size of the under-class. This of course is very much a matter of definition. Richard Nathan has looked at the 100 largest central cities of the United States. His most stringent definition includes only poor, black or Hispanic people living in concentrated poverty areas; they still amount to 8.7 per cent of the city population, or over four million people. Most estimates vary between 1 and 5 per cent of the total population, though some are much higher.[12] Indeed, if one includes all who suffer from a cumulation of disadvantage which cannot be reached by macro-policies, whether social or eco-nomic, 5 per cent is likely to be a low rather than a high estimate.

However, such deductions from census tracts and other statisti-cal information are bound to be unsatisfactory. If the term 'underclass' is to make any sense, it has to describe an identifiable category of social position and behaviour. Nathan in fact speaks of a 'hardened residual group that is difficult to reach and relate to'. The person most often quoted on this question is the sociologist William Julius Wilson.[13] He has argued that as a result in part of the civil rights movement and in part of favourable economic conditions, many members of minorities have moved out of the inner cities of America. By doing so, they have removed a crucial link between inclusion and exclusion; with them, the 'role models' for the less skilled and motivated were gone. Those who were left behind found themselves in a state of 'social isolation'. Soon, a 'concentration effect' set in which emphasized and hardened the boundary between the 'ghetto' and the rest. Instead of being at the lower end of an escalator, or at least dragging along in the rear of the marching column, the underclass found itself disconnected and in a hardening cycle of deprivation.

151

In Europe, less attention has been paid to the underclass so far, with the exception of Britain, where the phenomenon most nearly approximates the American experience. Yet even in Britain the process of decoupling described by Wilson is much less advanced. Occasional and anecdotal evidence suggests that there is much energy, skill and motivation in the deprived areas of inner cities, and that opportunity is a greater problem than any 'concentration effect'. Elsewhere in Europe the physical concentration which is a part of the definition of the underclass is rare, and certainly much less extensive than in the 100 largest American cities. Even the long-term unemployed are more often scattered and dispersed which may add to their dismay but makes it less plausible to describe them as a class.

This question arises for the American underclass as well. Ever since the term gained wider currency (as a result of a series of articles by Ken Auletta in the *New Yorker* in 1982), it has been used without much thought about precision of language. Recently, Richard Nathan has tried to remedy this deficiency. Reluctantly, he says, he has come to the conclusion 'that the word *underclass* reflects a real and new condition in the society with which we must come to terms. It is a condition properly described by the term *class*.'[14] The reason why Nathan may be right is that it appears that the social category described as an underclass is separated from the rest by what amount to entitlement barriers. Official, normal policies do not seem to reach these people. When the economy picks up, they are still left behind. There may be schools in their areas, but children do not attend; in due course, the schools are closed. Even jobs of sorts may be available, but they are not taken up. Some may not call this a barrier of entitlement; the poor have always been blamed for their fate by the official society. In fact however, a definition is made, a line is drawn which leaves some outside.

This is not to say that nothing can be done about the underclass. Few things are as characteristic of the United States as to try out solutions as soon as a problem is discovered. One other American trait is the emphasis on work, and so it is not surprising that most remedies emphasize the need to coax or shove the members of the underclass somehow or other into the world of work. Wilson tells us however that workfare of whatever style often fails with this group; the 'concentration effect' is too strong. It has got to be broken. Community development agencies of many kinds have been successful at least at the margin. (Americans are not discouraged if they reach only 25 or even 10 per cent of a problem group.) I have suggested on occasion that a company be founded, to be called Charisma Ltd. (or Inc. – for the company limits and incorporates charisma at the same time). Charisma Ltd. would encourage individuals who are able to inspire others at the local level. They may be teachers or doctors or managers of housing estates, but their main talent is that they can reach and relate to those who are inaccessible to most. There may be other methods, but their common denominator is that they are not simply extensions of macro-processes. Neither the new unemployment nor the new poverty will be swept away by economic growth. Additional and in the widest sense political action is needed which is a sure sign of the presence of an entitlement rather than a provisions problem.

Such action may not be taken. Without wishing to compound the confusions surrounding the use of the term 'class' in this connection, one other observation is apposite. It cannot be assumed as a matter of course that the majority class has an interest in breaking the cycle of deprivation of those who have dropped into an underclass position. On the contrary, in precarious times, the majority may well have an interest in actively defining some out and keeping them out to protect the position of those who are in. Certainly, the institutions and organizations of the majority do not help. Educational institutions are very useful for those who make it; indeed documented skills are the single most effective entry ticket into the modern, often high-tech economy; but those who lack access or motivation or staying power will be totally out. Many of them are today at least functionally illiterate and all but unemployable. Trade unions make public statements deploring unemployment and poverty; the memory of a past lingers on in which employment and a decent standard of living were directly correlated with economic growth; but in fact unions do little for the underclass. In some countries, the unemployed automatically lose their union membership. Public opinion surveys regularly show unemployment at the top of the list of people's concerns, and no one likes poverty, but when it comes to elections, parties which promise another dollar or pound or mark in the pockets of those who are in, are more likely to win than those who demand sacrifices of redistribution in order to help those who are out.

The majority class protects its interests as other ruling classes have done before. The difference is one of dimension. Marx thought that bourgeois society was unique in that for the first time the suppressed class – the class of the future – would comprise the overwhelming majority of the people who would organize and topple the ruling minority. In one sense, the opposite has happened. The overwhelming majority of the people have found a reasonably cosy existence. In any case, they have discovered life chances which their parents and grandparents barely dreamed of. But they are not sure that the good times will last. They begin to draw boundaries which leave some out in the cold. Like earlier dominant classes they have all kinds of reasons for drawing such lines, and they are prepared to let those in who accept and adopt their values. Also, they argue with conviction if not very convincingly that boundaries of class should not exist. They want them removed; but they are not prepared to do what it takes to remove them. Lack of imagination on the part of a class which lives in the provisions world and therefore does not recognize the entitlement claims of others is coupled with vested interest in preserving one's own position. Things are not quite as bad yet, but the signs of persistent unemployment and hard poverty could be ominous.

A Matter of Definition (2): Citizens and Separatists

It was not liberal fuzziness when in describing the American underclass I glossed over questions of race and ethnicity; it was rather the importance of the issue which warrants a separate discussion. As the majority class draws lines of belonging, it draws them not just horizontally but also laterally. Some lose their social citizenship rights, but others are denied civil rights altogether. This process has deep roots. It is painful at the best of times. In introducing citizenship earlier in this essay I have hinted at the problem. In the 1980s there are signs of it being aggravated by a new spirit of protectionism which spreads like wildfire and not only creates much human misery but also gives rise to forms of violence which defy traditional methods of coping.

154

The phenomenon is not yet well understood either, and I therefore confine myself to a few tentative comments. The American underclass is not just a characteristic of the black community. In so far as rural poverty has similar consequences, it is on the contrary predominantly white. Hispanics account for a considerable part of the urban poor. But the 'ghetto' is largely black. The collapse of the traditional family and the predominance of female-headed households are more pronounced among black Americans than among others. It leads to the apparent inability or unwillingness of many to adopt the values of the surrounding society. The difference is underlined by the fact that those blacks who have been able to take the middle-class fork of the social road in the great process of bifurcation which followed the civil rights push of the 1960s have remained outsiders in important respects. They have become mayors and executives and owners of villas and yachts, but a deep cultural boundary has remained. It is not often talked about, and perhaps there is not much to be gained by talking about it.[15] Obviously, civil rights are one thing, and full participation is another. It takes a long time for people's basic attitudes to adapt to new conditions. For the moment however the fact remains that when analysts refer to 'social pathologies' and their cumulation, being black is regarded as one of the disadvantages.

The British experience of immigration from former colonies is much more recent and different in many respects. For one thing, Asians and West Indians came voluntarily rather than being brought as slaves. (In the United States, West Indians seem to have a slight edge on other blacks.) Yet in Britain too the incipient underclass is characterized by a cumulation of social pathologies of which race is often one. Moreover, the majority class is drawing subtle and not-so-subtle boundaries. This is not least true for the traditional labour movement and it applies to housing estates as it does to membership in clubs and associations and even to the position of members in trade unions and the Labour Party. There is clearly no need for 'rivers of blood' to flow, but the charms of the 'multiracial society' are lost on the majority which is more concerned about drawing boundaries than about openness.

For the progress of citizenship, this is a setback. It calls for the re-assertion of civil rights. This must include affirmative action

155

which helps bridge long-standing differences by formal aids to participation. However while such familiar prescriptions have lost none of their appropriateness and urgency, they seem to miss an important new point. More and more people (it appears) do not want to live in a multiracial or even a multicultural society. Furthermore, this applies not only to cosy majorities but to the affected minorities as well. They demand their own niche if not their own region or country. Separate but equal was a slogan much scorned by liberals in the 1960s; in the 1980s it has become very topical, and often separateness is stressed more than equality. There is a clamour for homogeneity which rejects all attempts to build civilized societies by having civil societies first and cultural differences within them second.

The resulting conflicts are subtle in some places and glaring in others, but they are almost ubiquitous. It may seem quaint to distant observers when an elected mayor in the Flemish part of Belgium is deposed by government because he speaks only French, but it is not funny. The Swiss had to accept in the end the separation of a canton of Jura from the old canton of Berne. In California, a referendum has gone in favour of English as the only official language, but it is obvious that many Californians will continue to speak Spanish and that they will probably win another day. (The probability that activist minorities win in the end is part of the story.) The Irish civil war has a long history, but has taken a turn for the worse in recent years, one which makes the prospect of power-sharing most unlikely. Basque demands for autonomy are accompanied by the sound of explosions and gunfire. There is hardly a country in the OECD world which does not encounter strong demands for the recognition of separateness by some group or other. Among new nations outside the OECD world such demands are even more violent, and there are stirrings of ethnic self-assertion in the countries of really existing socialism as well.

The rediscovery of ethnicity was a step forward in the process of civilization. It meant an incipient understanding that common citizenship rights are not in conflict with cultural distinctions but on the contrary give them new scope. But the happy harmony did not last. In many places, difference came to be used as a weapon against citizenship. The weapon was often strengthened by what has come to be called fundamentalism, which means that belonging to a group is given an aura of extraordinary, often quasi-religious significance. Even in Israel, which has as one of its *raisons d'être* the promise to provide a home for all Jews who want to come, Jewishness has come to be debated in terms of an orthodoxy which excludes reformers. (The apparent impossibility of creating a multicultural Jewish–Arab state of Israel poses one of the more frightening problems of the world today.) From 'Buy British' to *La France aux Français* and the rediscovery of *Mitteleuropa* in Germany, nationalist fundamentalism is gaining ground. Membership is not conceived as a matter of rights which can be extended, but of unchanging, ascriptive features which must be preserved against contamination by strangers.

The free-floating fundamentalism of cultural despair has a similar effect. The reaction against the gigantomania of the 1950s and 1960s, and against the assumption that economies of scale are invariably economies of a larger scale, was understandable. 'Small is beautiful' seemed quite a nice slogan of the 1970s.[16] In its name, however, people have turned away not only from unnecessary bigness, but also from the strengths of an international community on its way to a world civil society, and even from the citizenship rights guaranteed by the nation-state. A new search for authenticity fuels the romantic politics of 'real' rather than 'formal' relations, of legitimacy by the warm feeling of permanent discourse rather than by law and the institutions which it inspires.

Such observations call to mind the issue of modernity and ligatures. In some ways the modern world may seem a cold place which opens up opportunities by breaking ties without which it is hard to live. But I am not suggesting that the examples given, and others which will readily come to the reader's mind, have one common cause or call for one common remedy. All I am suggesting is that many of them have one aspect in common which is directly relevant for the modern social conflict about citizenship and life chances. They are an attack on the civilizing forces of citizenship in the name of minority rights or cultural, religious, ethnic autonomy. What is more, the very people who should know better because they fought for citizenship in the past are at least partly to blame for the success of this attack. A 'wet' liberalism has developed which abandons the great gains of a common floor of civil rights and entitlements for all in order to accommodate the separatism of minorities. Minority rights are first misunderstood and then transformed into minority rule. In the end, this attitude even offers little resistance to the fundament-alism of activists, so that noisy minorities can claim the support of silent majorities.

This is a big step backwards in the history of civil society, and it is costly. The cost is in the first instance one of conflicts which defy solution. None of the experiences of organization, insti-tutionalization and regulation which have brought about the democratic class struggle are applicable to active minorities which either demand separation or try to impose their funda-mentalist creed on the rest. It is no accident that acts of terrorism and threats of civil war accompany the process, and that both, if they do not get worse without hope of containment, tend to come in irrational waves which it seems impossible to break.

The deeper cost is in terms of life chances, and of progress towards a world civil society. Clearly, this objective can be achieved only if and when it is understood that citizenship for all does not make everyone alike. Citizenship is not a levelling but an enabling process. I have tried to show that it makes socio-economic inequalities bearable because it contains them within a common house of entitlements. (And, if it fails to do so, change can be demanded in the name of the principle of citizenship.) Similarly, citizenship makes cultural diversity bearable. The right to be different may well be one of the basic rights of membership in a society, but it implies that one foregoes methods of persuasion which put the principle of common citizenship in jeopardy. Contemporary experience shows that this is easier said than done. Separatists have other priorities than civil libertarians. They want a Catholic Ireland or a Basque state first and only much later civil liberties for Irish Catholics and for Basques wherever they live. Separatists, fundamentalists and romantics want homogeneity, but liberals need heterogeneity, because it is the only way to universal citizenship. The choice is stark and reminds one of Karl Popper's plea for the open society: we can return to the tribe, but if we wish to remain human, we must move forward to the civil society.

The Risks of Anomy

Conflicts have to be seen to be real. It makes little sense to impute deep cleavages to social structures if no apparent social and political clashes arise from them. It is therefore clear that in contemporary OECD societies there is no class conflict in the classical sense of the term. Most observers cannot detect political battles between social groups which are divided by generalized barriers of power and entitlement. There are remnants of the old conflict. The majority class continues its skirmishes about redistribution. In some parts, the language of class conflict is still employed, and as one looks at the North–South divide in Italy, or the South–North divide in Britain, one appreciates the reasons. But, even in these countries, class in the old sense is not the dominant basis of conflict, and whatever new lines of division and antagonism are about to emerge, so far do not lead to organized struggles between new haves and new have-nots.

There are reasons why this should be so. The size and the weight of the heavy hand of the majority is one. It is hard for anyone to take on a dominant majority class, and harder still for those who are defined out. The individualization of social conflict in open societies is another reason. Perhaps solidary action in organized groups is at all times a second-best method for promoting one's interests. The cost in energy and emotion is high, and it takes a long time to get anywhere. Wherever possible, people will try to make headway by their own efforts. In the United States, this has long been the dominant mode of conflict. Today, the same is true in most countries. Individual mobility takes the place of the class struggle.

In so far as people act in organized groups, these are more likely to be special interest groups, or social movements, than class parties. Such segmentation has been explained by social changes. Once citizenship rights are almost general, disparities of realms of life take the place of generalized demands for civil, political or social rights. People fight for the recognition of comparable worth for women, or against pollution, or even for disarmament, but they do so from a common basis of citizenship. In that sense, social movements are formed strictly within the bounds of civil society. Even civil disobedience makes sense only if a firm framework of civil rights – and the obligation to obey the law – can be assumed.

Yet the question remains: why do the long-term unemployed and the persistently poor not join forces and march on their capital cities to demand their full share of citizenship? Why is there not at least an unemployment party or a poverty party? And if this is asking too much, why does the underclass not go on a rampage to break up the furniture of the house which the majority class built for itself?

From time to time it does. All of us carry with us images of events which hurt even years later. When the 1985 European cup football match in the Heysel Stadium in Brussels erupted into violence and murder, long-standing fans of the game were tempted to turn away. Lord Scarman's humane and suggestive report on 'the Brixton disorders' of 1981 cannot wipe out the television pictures of angry faces, stones and firebombs thrown at the police, of looting and disarray. In America, riots and police violence have a long tradition; even so, the 1984 bombing of militant squatters from a helicopter in Philadelphia sticks in the memory. The sight of police with helmets and shields battling away against demonstrators has become almost a regular feature of the evening news. Middle-class terrorists with fancy organizational names like *Rote Armee Fraktion* or *Brigate Rosse* have taken businessmen and politicians hostage until their corpses are left in the boot of an abandoned car. This is not even to mention the everyday violence of muggings and robberies and killings in the cities. It is hardly surprising that Barbara Tuchman found many readers when she held up the 'distant mirror' of the fourteenth to the late twentieth century. 'Plague, war, taxes, brigandage, bad government, insurrection, and schism in the Church' were then the 'strange and great perils and adversities'.[17] The list could easily be modernized to read: AIDS, war, taxes, terrorism, bad governments, riots, and two hostile nuclear superpowers.

One other thought comes to mind. In the *Communist Manifesto*, Marx and Engels comment almost by way of an aside on what they call the *Lumpenproletariat*. This 'social scum' (as some have translated the word) is, as Marx and Engels say rather unkindly, 'the passive rotting away of the old society'. It is not the stuff from which revolutions are made. Although its members may be drawn into the revolutionary whirlpool in the end, their condition really makes them a reserve army for reactionary activities. Theodor Geiger took up the subject in the early 1930s. The lowest stratum is 'socioeconomically without a place'. Its mentality is one not of organized defence of interest, but of 'rabid rebelliousness'. 'Communism and National Socialism have a much easier time in these quarters than the *realpolitik* of social democracy and unions.' 'There is, as we know, a sediment of the working population who do not find a place in employment, have lost the ability for a steady life, and therefore hire themselves out without asking in whose interest they use their fists, clubs and knuckles.'[18]

Yet all this does not account for the social conflict of the 1980s. It is like putting one and one together and discovering that it does not add up to four. There is a great deal of what might be called situational conflict, disconnected acts of public violence which achieve little apart from the aches of the participants and the fears of the bystanders. But even those who go on a rampage are often not members of the underclass. In fact, the underclass, whether North American or European, is neither violent nor even opposed to the official society. If persistent poor or unemployed vote at all, their preferences do not differ much from the rest. (Even in the 1930s for which Geiger wrote, they did not. It was not the unemployed who voted Hitler to power, though their fate may have had something to do with the hysterics of the middle class.) As one author put it, the underclass 'is alienated and populist but not radical'.[19] It is split a hundred ways so that most of its members look for their own personal ways out. It does not care much either way about most issues of current concern. It is lethargic.

But it is alienated. The condition is as important as the sentiment. The crucial fact about the underclass and the persistently unemployed is that they have no stake in society. In a very serious sense, society does not need them. Many in the majority class wish that they would simply go away; and if they did their absence would barely be noticed. Those who are in this position know it. Society to them is above all distant. It is symbolized by nothing so much as the police and the courts, and to a lesser extent by the offices and officials of the state. The separation of people from the official society is rarely as total as such statements make it sound. For many, individual social mobility continues to be a viable alternative to aggression and resentment. They have been and will continue to be in and out of the underclass, as it were. On the other hand, the sense of not having a stake in society seems to have spread beyond the groups for which it is founded in unemployment and poverty. Young people in particular have a tendency to borrow their values from the social fringe even if they have work and could find a place within the majority. There is a curious convergence of the culture of the underclass and the counter-culture of the middle class; it is, so to speak, 'in' to be out. Not caring about the norms and values of the official society has become a widespread habit.

This habit is arguably the most telling feature of the OECD societies in the last decades of the twentieth century. It has a name, anomy. Societies seem to be infinitely imaginative in the ways in which they·give expression to their tensions and antagonisms. Street battles and violent strikes, elections and wage negotiations, collective and individual mobility are all manifestations of the same underlying forces. Today, a further variant has been added. Conflicts appear not as battle lines drawn in a revolutionary war, or even as a democratic class struggle, but as anomy.

The notion is sufficiently important to dwell on it. I have used the old English word, 'anomy', which the Oxford Dictionary calls 'obsolete' while referring to the helpful definition given by William Lambarde in 1591 according to which it means 'bringing disorder, doubt and uncertainty over all'.[20] In modern social science, it has been credited to Emile Durkheim who used *anomie* to describe the suspension of the effectiveness of social norms by economic or political crises. As a result people become disconnected to the point of regarding suicide as the only way out. Robert Merton has added his own twist to our understanding of 'anomie' by defining it as a 'breakdown in the cultural structure' which occurs when people are unable by virtue of their social position to comply with the values of their society.[21] If the young are told to put patience and hard work into their careers, but the obvious way to make money is to speculate in the markets of futures and options, or foreign exchange, anomy results.

One can turn the concept into a description of a peculiar feature of modern societies. It is often claimed that the incidence of crimes of violence ('serious crimes') has grown in recent times. The evidence is sketchy and inconclusive. Crimes against property and drug-related crimes have clearly become more frequent; homicides (and suicides) have always fluctuated in frequency and do so today; the number of serious crimes (assault, robbery with violence, rape) has doubled in some countries between the 1950s and the 1980s but not changed much in others. Yet there is a more important point which is not the incidence of violations of norms but the inability of societies to deal with them. In the normative world of the 1980s certain 'no-go areas' have emerged. In part they are what the name says, that is areas to which the forces of the law actually do not go. The police will deny this, but in fact there are parts of inner cities as well as subway trains and stations which are 'in bounds' so that whatever happens in them is not likely to be sanctioned. Sometimes one wonders whether some schools and even universities have not become 'no-go areas' with respect to the enforcement of prevailing norms as well.

The symbolic 'no-go areas' of our societies are even more serious. They have to do with the way in which the law is applied, or rather not applied. What has been called 'the acquittal of the guilty' has become a familiar phenomenon in contemporary society.[22] People are known to have broken the law; they even confess to it; but it is also known that they go unpunished. More important still, they themselves know when they commit their deeds that they will go unpunished. The young present a particularly telling problem in this connection. For decades, the trend of social mores was to hold 'society' responsible for their actions and therefore let them get away with murder; in these same decades, about one-half of all traditional crimes and an even higher percentage of crimes of violence have been committed by people under twenty-one years of age. The normative 'no-go area' of youth is probably the most significant of all, for it exempts those who are supposed to learn from the norms which hold society together.

Anomy from this point of view describes a state of affairs in which breaches of norms go unpunished. In part this is an underclass phenomenon. The 'missing' fathers of America's unwed mothers raise questions which need to be answered. Also, Amartya Sen is not always right that the law stands between availability and entitlement; some of those who have no entitlements simply take what is available, and the forces of the law find it hard to deal with them. In large part, anomy describes a much more general condition. It includes child abuse and rape during marriage as well as tax evasion and other forms of economic crime. People have no stake in society and therefore do not feel bound by its rules. But this is only one side of the picture. The other is that society's confidence in its rules has declined; rules are not enforced.

Here as elsewhere in this book I do not want to destroy a case by overstating it. Norms have always been violated, and all societies have found it difficult to enforce their norms. A certain amount of transgression of norms may even be healthy; after all, one way of immobilizing the economy is by 'working to rule', and the same would be true for society in general. Yet I wonder whether the most recent form of the social conflict is not that the social contract itself is at issue. By that I do not mean the more subtle extensions of the social contract to elaborate citizenship rights, though these too are important. I mean the elementary articles of the social contract which are about law and order. Liberals do not like these words which are often used to kill the spirit of the laws by their letters. However, this is precisely the issue which draws the argument about the modern social conflict together.

Many remnants of earlier conflict are still present in the contemporary world. They include versions of the class struggle of old. No comparable new conflict has emerged. The relationship between the majority class and the underclass is not one which can or will give rise to organized conflicts like those between bourgeoisie and working class. But it raises a question which has serious ramifications. A society which appears to accept the continued existence of a group which has no real stake in it has put itself in jeopardy. Like the statement that society's confidence in its rules has declined, this is abstract language. What it means is that the majority class is no longer confident of its own position. It draws boundaries where there should be none and it wavers when it comes to enforcing its rules.

This may be a passing phase. There are countries to which many of the statements of this chapter do not apply, like Sweden or Switzerland, or Japan for that matter. The differences between those to which these statements apply have been emphasized throughout. But in the United States of America and Western Europe the signs of uncertainty are unmistakable. I have given this section the heading 'The Risks of Anomy'. Some of them are obvious. 'Bringing disorder, doubt and uncertainty over all' is bad enough. But the greater risk is another one. Anomy cannot last. It is an invitation to usurpers to impose a false sense of order. What liberals so dislike about the advocates of 'law and order' is precisely what they provoke by their own lack of a clear sense of institutions. The risk of anomy is tyranny in whatever guise.

8 · A New Social Contract

Who Wants Change?

Social democracy is nice, but it is stifling as well. One cannot
easily think of a more benevolent political consensus than that
around democratic government for the defence of social citizenship rights, coupled with a sense of reasonable co-operation
between groups in each country and between countries in the
world at large. Moreover, when the protagonists of this view
come under threat, one will find them on the side of the defenders
of freedom and justice. Such social democrats have all kinds of
political names, Labour right and Alliance and 'wet' Tory in
Britain, Social Democrat, Christian Democrat and Free Democrat
in Germany, the entire *pentapartito* of the coalition partners of
Christian Democrats and Socialists in Italy, and a large part of the
two political blocs in France and in the United States. It is more
difficult to name those who do not belong.

Indeed why should anyone not be a social democrat? Because
there is another side to the pretty picture. Its main name is
bureaucracy. This Weberian nightmare appears in many guises.
As I have noted, one of them is corporatism. Political scientists
have described it in great detail, and have recently moved on from
corporatism to neocorporatism; either way, it involves government by arrangement and thus a curious denial of leadership as
well as democracy. Another guise of bureaucracy is the old
welfare state. This is the elaborate transfer of resources not only
from A to B but also from A to A with forms to fill in and queues
outside the offices of welfare on the way. High taxation is one of
the instruments of bureaucracy; it is in fact its lifeline. Without

166

taxation no administration. In one way or another, all social democratic roads end up with big government, though perhaps it would be more correct to say, with weak government and strong bureaucracies. Even the heroes of the social democratic world tend to be super-bureaucrats rather than leaders with an innovative sense of direction; Max Weber's strictly formal notion of leadership has come into its own.

This almost reverses the question: why should anyone be a social democrat? The answer is that social democracy represents the interests of the majority class. They may have become a little shaky of late as the majority class began to lose heart, but they are still widespread and weighty. The interests of the majority class will dominate the politics of the OECD world for some time to come. Meteorologists joke that the safest prediction they can make about tomorrow's weather is that it will be much like today's. Political pundits could do worse than follow their example. There will be adjustments to the social democratic position – interesting adjustments which betray the perception of new pressures and demands by the majority – and there will be shocks to its claim to dominance, but on the whole it will prevail. This is not a gloomy prediction. It may make the politics of the next decade a little boring, but after the excitements of this turbulent century worse things could happen. (The only real victims of such boredom are political analysts and theorists for whom unfortunately few will shed tears.) Progressives will continue to be puzzled by their inability to think up a truly new programme, and the new right will find that its alleged radicalism does not get them nearly as far away from social democracy as they had hoped. Yet there are problems, and there are pressures for change. In this final chapter in which I shall try to take the analysis into the 1990s, the problems and pressures, and some possible answers, are the issue.

This is evidently a speculative exercise, but not entirely so. In line with the style of this essay the first question to ask is not what it would be nice to do but who actually has an interest in breaking the mould of social democracy, and why. This takes us to two new political forces of the 1980s, Thatcherism and the Greens.

Both terms use one instance to describe a larger force. There is not just the politics of Mrs Thatcher, but Reaganomics and the programme of the 'Market Count' Lambsdorff and of M. Chirac and others. The emphasis on economics is significant. We are concerned here with the ultimate provisions party. Its success in Britain may be particularly surprising; it is the result of a rare conjunction of personal leadership, party loyalty even where it goes against the grain of many old Conservatives, and an electoral system which translates minorities of just over 40 per cent into massive parliamentary majorities. Whatever the historical explanation, Thatcherism is an evocative description of one programme of radical change.

Its central objective is to offer a great quantity and variety of choices in a world of corporatist rigidity. These choices are in large part economic. Some of the advocates of Thatcherism seem to echo the famous exhortation by Minister Guizot under Louis Philippe in France: *Enrichissez-vous, messieurs!* Enrich yourselves, gentlemen, and ladies as well! Money that is quickly made is rewarded by social honours, in some cases just in time before the house of cards collapses. The irony has quite a few examples to go on. Who now speaks of Sir Freddie Laker? Several colleges have quietly taken the plaques off buildings donated by Ivan Boesky because they are embarrassed by the name. At the same time, 'casino capitalism' has created enormous wealth. Susan Strange feels gloomy about it to the point of apocalypse when she imagines the New Year's Eve party on 31 December 1999, at which 'only those financial gamblers that still survive in the great office blocks towering over the city centres of the capitalist world will be raising their glasses'.[1] But then this could be a traditional – social democratic – objection to new ways of getting on, for of course those who have enriched themselves in the 1980s are *nouveaux riches*, upstarts and parvenus.

The new departure in economic mood has found a surprising number of intellectual advocates. None of them has the breadth and depth of Schumpeter whose theories of innovation by entrepreneurship are being revived in the 1980s. Schumpeter himself had become doubtful about his belief in 'the innovations made from time to time by the relatively small number of exceptionally energetic business men' who apply scientific knowledge, develop new forms of organization, conquer new markets and generally do unfamiliar things.[2] As Weber anticipated the destiny of bureaucracy, so did Schumpeter that of what he called 'socialism', and when one considers the counterrevolution of Thatcherism, one should beware of allowing one swallow to predict a new summer. But 'supply-side economics', if it is about anything, is about stimulating initiative, and so is the 'Laffer curve' which tells us that from a certain point onwards taxes are counter-productive. Much of the new technology fad has the same objective; Daniel Bell's belief in the 'scientific-technical estate' has found many vulgarizers. All this is embedded in a wider creed which either advocates or states a 'reversal of trends'. There is no necessary connection between intellectual neoconservatism and Thatcherism, but both are radical departures from received wisdom which certainly use the name 'conservative' in vain. Their alliance is therefore no accident.

To understand the success of this radical 'conservatism' it is important to see that the provisions explosion did not remain confined to a few 'chain-smoking young men' whose 'eyes are fixed on computer screens flickering with changing prices'. Not only are there quite a few of them, hundreds of thousands rather than thousands, but there is also some spin-off for those who look at the screens of control rooms of industry or even of warehouses and customer service counters and travel agencies. The interest is extended further by the fact that the new choices of Thatcherism do not remain confined to money. Old monopolies are broken; rigid systems are deregulated; state enterprises are sold to the public; special interest groups are de-cartelized; the power of trade unions is curtailed. Choice in education becomes an issue. Public services, including the health service, are exposed to the winds of competition. No other politician has gone quite so far in all these respects as Mrs Thatcher in Britain, though perhaps Mr Reagan found a more receptive and less social democratic public in the first place. Also, there are cultural variants of Thatcherism, all the way to Bettino Craxi's Italian or David Lange's New Zealand 'socialism'.

Who supports this kind of change? The majority class does not, though some of its members may be attracted by some of the new policies. The great school demonstrations in France drew millions, and there are examples of a similar interest elsewhere. Hundreds of thousands have bought shares of privatized enterprises. Many people are pleased to be pushed about less by impenetrable organizations or anonymous bureaucracies.

Beyond such statements, however, it is difficult to identify a specific group which found the world of social democracy so stifling that it wanted radical change. The word 'yuppies' is used to describe young urban (or upwardly mobile) professionals who are said to have wanted more scope for initiative. For some, this is undoubtedly true. It is evident also that there was more hidden entrepreneurial spirit in the bureaucratized societies of the OECD world than one would have thought in the 1960s and 1970s. But while it may be possible to identify groups which are all but immune to Thatcherism – the deprived, and also the public-service groups which I described earlier – its appeal is diffuse. It is the conjunction of a set of ideas, a leader, and an undefined discontent in the minds of many.

This raises the question of whether Thatcherism will last. Is it an episode or a new social force? This may be the wrong way round to put the question. There are episodes which have lasting effects, and Thatcherism is probably one of them. In Britain, it will not be forgotten for a long time to come. It has broken the mould of a peculiar combination of what the English call 'class' and corporatism. In the United States, the Thatcherism of the Reagan administration has reminded many of traditional American values. (Contrary to the claims of Mrs Thatcher, these are not the traditional values of Victorian or any other England.)[3] The new consensus on a social policy based on individual effort which Democrats misleadingly like to call 'a new social contract' demonstrates in fact a revival of the American dream.[4] In countries like France and Germany the picture is much less clear. But everywhere it would seem that the extreme emphasis on provisions is in fact going to highlight entitlement issues. It will become increasingly clear that more choices as they are understood by Thatcherism are of necessity more choices for a minority. The only question is whether the old majority will re-assert itself and another episode of social democracy will be ushered in, or whether a new liberal radicalism will emerge which accepts the gains of a greater diversity of provisions and more scope for those who are enterprising, but concentrates the attention of politics on entitlements.

If Thatcherism is a peculiarly British phenomenon, then the Greens are uniquely German. Green parties have sprung up in many European countries, and the 'Rainbow Group' in the

European Parliament worries many of the more established political groups. But in most cases the Greens are merely the translation of a social movement into a political organization. The social movement responds to one of the disparities in people's social position, the threats to the environment of life. Since these threats affect everybody, a 'party' to represent them is an obvious contradiction in terms. This does not make the party any less real or even necessary, but it means that in the end majority decisions will have to be taken to alleviate the damage done by thoughtless production and consumption. It is hard to shift the majority class, and it may take organizations and practices which are regarded as a nuisance by most to do so; but ultimately there is no reason why environmental control should not become a part of the agenda of social democracy, as has already happened in many places.

The German Greens, however, combine ecology with two other sets of interests. They have become an umbrella for alienated minorities, and they assemble those who would like to dissect the entire 'system' of the majority class. The former include important social movements like feminists as well as fringe groups like paedophiles. Their coalition is uneasy, and the probability must be high that feminists will not be content with advocating their case through one small political party, whereas paedophiles will become an embarrassment to this party (as similar groups have become to the British Labour Party where they came to represent the so-called 'Loony Left' especially in London). There remains what the Greens themselves call the 'fundamentalist' wing which can be described almost as a party to end all parties. The thrust of its views is an attempt to dissolve all firm and fixed structures of power in the society at large and thus also in the Green party itself. Every trick in the book of 'basis democracy' is used to achieve the immediate objective. Office holders have to rotate at regular intervals; in any case they are mandated by assemblies open to all members; such assemblies take place frequently and become family occasions – babies, pets and all.

For a while in the 1980s, the combination of ecology, minorities and democratization found significant popular support in Germany, especially in university towns in which the Greens polled 20 per cent and more. There may be a connection beyond the obvious middle-class, not to say 'academic' character of the whole project. A generation of products of the expanding universities of the 1960s and 1970s found jobs in the public service which was expanding at a similar rate. But a next generation found this avenue blocked. With the curbs of public expenditure in the 1970s, the growth of the public service stopped abruptly. At the same time, many current public-service jobs were occupied by relatively young people who would not vacate them for another twenty years or more. The blockage meant frustration and alienation. I have not discussed the unemployment of academics specifically. Arguably, it has a very different effect from general unemployment and produces activists.[5] It also produces 'eternal students' who hang around universities for many years as well as people whose 'alternative life styles' are in fact a version of severe poverty, and Greens.

The condition does not last. A next generation either does not go up to universities at all or does not aspire to public-service jobs. This is not the only reason why the Green party is intrinsically unstable. Some of its members are better served by larger parties in which they are likely to be absorbed. Others need social movements outside parliament rather than parliamentary political parties. And fundamentalists will run into the 'iron law of oligarchy'. They should have read Robert Michels before they set up a party. Organization has certain prerequisites and consequences which no one has yet been able to defy. The Greens are much more clearly an episode than Thatcherism. This is not to say that they are an episode without consequence. Whether as a political party or not, they clearly have changed the agenda of politics in several countries. They have also added at least a touch of 'postmaterialist' values to political thinking.[6] Indeed, this may yet turn out to be their most lasting effect.

The picture which emerges then is one of a dominant social democratic mood represented by many different political parties, and episodic attempts to break out of the great consensus either by innovation and entrepreneurship, or by fundamental democracy and alternative life styles. I am not going to produce a *deus ex machina* to relieve the familiar and slightly depressing picture. This book would not have been written were it not for the hope and the hunch that there can be a radical liberal alternative. The rest of this chapter will be devoted to exploring some of the ideas which are relevant to it. But so far as the class of the future is concerned – the constellation of interests which will sustain the desire for change – all that can be said for the moment is that the current position is unstable. The majority class has lost confidence and has become protectionist in every sense of the word. Social democracy has come close to the end of its tether. The electorate has become volatile. Most political persuasions are shallow and liable to be influenced by compelling individuals or unforeseen events. This is a risky state of affairs, but also an opportunity.

A Liberal Agenda

John Maynard Keynes had an appealing way of defining his liberalism in a minor key. 'If one is born a political animal, it is most uncomfortable not to belong to a political party; cold and lonely and futile it is.' He could not see himself as a Conservative; 'I should not be amused or excited or edified'. The Labour Party was in some respects better; but when it came to class, Keynes saw himself 'on the side of the educated bourgeoisie' and in any case he worried about 'the party which hates existing institutions and believes that great good will result merely from overthrowing them'. So what is there left? 'I incline to believe that the Liberal Party is still the best instrument of future progress – if only it had strong leadership and the right programme.' I have not spoken much about liberalism in this essay, though the advancement of liberty is its ultimate objective. Had I done so, I would have described it in similar terms, although of course Keynes wrote about very different parties in 1925, or even in 1938 when he said in a letter: 'The Liberal Party is the centre of gravity and ought to be the focus of a new alignment of the progressive forces.'[7]

The difference is nowhere more evident than in the programme. Keynes suggests (in 1925) five headings for the liberal agenda: 'peace questions' (pacifism), 'questions of government' (more government, but devolved to 'corporations'), 'sex questions' (emancipation of women), 'drug questions' (how to combat addiction), and 'economic questions' ('deliberately . . . controlling and directing economic forces in the interests of social justice and social stability'). Questions of gender apart, Keynes's 'New Liberalism' may not sound very liberal today. It certainly has a strong flavour of what I have called 'social

173

democracy' including even its moralizing posture. But perhaps this merely goes to show that liberalism, as one author put it, 'is the political theory of modernity'.[8] It follows the passages of modern times, insisting only on the need for progress in the interest of extending the life chances of individuals to as many as possible.

A liberal agenda for the 1990s follows from the analysis of social conflict and political change in this essay. It has four main headings: historical questions, entitlement questions, institutional questions and international questions. The first three will be set out in this section, whereas the last will be the subject of a separate section on the 'world civil society'.

The first prerequisite of any radical and progressive political agenda today is to accept the lessons of the past, and notably of the 1970s and 1980s. This is not as paradoxical as it sounds. It has much to do with the notion of strategic change which will be made explicit in the final section of this chapter (and with the help of Keynes). It means in essence that a policy which sets out to dismantle all that exists is not likely to get very far, and will certainly fail to advance the real life chances of living human beings. The attempt to pretend that one can start building the world from scratch is also childish. It disqualifies people from the political process.

The lesson of the 1970s is that unilateralism cannot work. It was never a very wise prescription, and it was certainly contrary to the internationalism of liberals. But, since the 1970s, unilateral action notably in the fields of defence and economic policy has become self-defeating. The statement needs to be qualified for some very small or very distant countries, though they too, by acting unilaterally, merely emphasize their lack of independence. If New Zealand leaves its defence pacts, it becomes in part a satellite and in part a playball of larger powers, and the same is true for any country which tries to opt out of the world economy, however chaotic the latter may seem. Wise small countries, like Switzerland, have known this for a long time, and have on the whole managed to strike a useful balance between autonomy, including neutrality, and the acceptance of interdependence.

I have, reluctantly but unambiguously, refrained from discussing matters of defence in this book and will not change this self-denying ordinance now. Accepting the world economy – which is the other major challenge to unilateralism – means forswearing all attempts to go it alone. Even if one is not hysterical about protectionism and recognizes that it exists in many guises, it is undeniable today that the attempt to close economic borders has at best very short-term benefits, but is bound to lead to considerable malefits soon. This is widely recognized. It is often not seen so clearly that domestic policies based on the assumption of all economic things being equal and remaining that way are doomed. The winds of international economic relations blow into every nook and cranny of domestic policy. They certainly affect whatever is done to redistribute wealth, organize transfers and reform the welfare state.

This is not to plead for a fatalistic acceptance of the world economy as it is. On the contrary, international economic relations raise some of the most important issues of policy today. But no one who opts out will be a part of the settlement of these issues, and in the meantime it is crucial not to confuse one's desired blueprints for change with the current reality.

A similar point can be made about the lessons of the 1980s. They have to do with the consequential political episodes of Thatcherism and the Greens, and notably with the former. Recognition of new values and new needs for ecological understanding is important. But it is even more important to accept the gains in life chances which can be made, and to some extent have been made by the new emphasis on provisions. Opening up the barren world of bureaucracy is one of the major tasks of liberal policy. The encouragement of innovation and entrepreneurship is as much a part of it as the replacement of corporatist structures by individual participation and an effective interplay of democracy and leadership. It would be wrong to say that Thatcherism has achieved this objective, let alone achieved it in ways of which liberals can approve; but then the right things rarely happen in the right way. Accepting the 1980s means above all that there is no way back to the cosy days of social democracy. There is only a way forward to new liberty.

This way poses entitlement questions above all. While accepting the provisions spurt of recent years, the liberal agenda is in the first instance about citizenship. This is in part a classical subject of liberal politics. Sex and gender questions are still not resolved. Civil rights are always under threat. Human rights need active defence everywhere. Liberals must be found in the vanguard of these movements. The new entitlement questions are however above all social. They have to do with the tendency to define people out of the social universe of the majority, with persistent unemployment, inner-city blight, regional disparities and the underclass. These are not subjects which old-style benevolent social democrats will tackle, nor do the prescriptions of new conservatives resolve them. On the contrary, they may be said to have aggravated them by concentrating on one side of life chances only.

Working out the details of a liberal policy of basic common entitlements for all citizens is the most important single pro-grammatic task ahead. The principles should be clear, at least to readers of this essay. Let us take unemployment. Given the apparently increasing scarcity of work (in the sense in which I have defined it in the last chapter), and given further the continuing significance of work as a key to income, self-esteem and the organization of life, full employment continues to be a desirable objective. The labour market can achieve it only at a price, the American price of poverty as it were. Countries which do not want to go down this route, have to find ways of redistributing work. This can be done in part by shortening working hours. In part it requires more flexible working con-ditions, diverse forms of contract, reductions of overtime.[9] All these measures and others like them are painful for the haves of the work society, but they are necessary to hold society together.

To be sure, redistribution of work is only the beginning of a liberal approach to what I have called the problem of work. At one end, the question of community service arises. It may be necessary for everyone to pay a time tax (as it were) as well as an income or sales tax. At the other end, the extension of 'free' time beyond employment offers new opportunities of activity. Re-thinking the place of education in people's lives is one obvious challenge in this context. During working lives, much can still be done to instil the sense of autonomous activity into the conditions of heteronomous labour. But the basis of all this is work for all. To repeat an important point, this is not in order to implement a fictitious 'right to work' which merely camouflages a desire for discipline. Even more than in Keynes's time, full employment is a 'short-term objective'. But under given social conditions, it is a prerequisite of a society of citizens which helps make entitlements real.

A similar case can be made for poverty, and more particularly for preventing the formation of an underclass. I have discussed the difficulty of breaking the cycle of deprivation, especially if ethnic or racial discrimination is added to poverty and other disadvantages. General policies are not sufficient to help people out of this condition; community development activities and even the charisma of individuals are often indispensable. But certain general measures are needed. They include educational opportunities. In my view, they should also include a basic income guarantee for all. This need not be a guarantee for an income which is competitive with normal wages or makes by itself a reasonably comfortable life possible. But it should be an entitlement which is not subject to the pressures of political fashion. The simpler its construction is the better; this is why I would still favour a negative income tax system which dispenses with bureaucratic complications.[10]

Behind such suggestions there is the notion of a welfare state which has been turned into a social state by being based on the principle of common citizenship rights for all. This was of course William Beveridge's radical idea when he proposed his famous plan in 1942. All citizens were to receive 'benefits up to subsistence level, as of right and without means tests, so that individuals may build freely upon it'.[11] Beveridge made much of the other side of these benefits, the insurance method ('benefit in return for contributions, rather than free allowances from the State is what the people of Britain desire'), but he saw quite clearly the significance of the principle of universality (and incidentally, of the non-proportionality of contributions and benefits) for social cohesion and solidarity. Today, it is necessary to reassert this principle. Means tests have crept back in, and the notion of 'deserving' as against 'undeserving poor' emphasizes the intention of the majority class to define out rather than in. For reasons of cost as well as taste, social services will have to be composed of a common floor and individual contributions to raise the standard. But the common floor is more than a manner of speaking. It is the assertion of citizenship against a new onslaught of privilege.

The third set of issues on the liberal agenda sounds more

nebulous; I have called it 'institutional questions'. In fact, it goes
to the heart of liberal attitudes to the rule of law and social order.
On a few occasions, I have referred to 'wet' liberalism. The word
has come to refer to a political posture which is prepared to
relativize principles to the point of making them indistinct.[12]
'Wet' liberals would be those who always find an excuse why
things which are in principle unacceptable should nevertheless
be allowed to happen. This is in part simply a frame of mind, or
even a manner of speech as it is likely to develop among people
who have got used to civilized discourse and who do not expect
others to violate an implicit code of rules of behaviour. 'Wet'
people are nice, 'dry' people are not. In part however I am
referring to an explicit attitude to norms which has much to do
with the 'no-go areas' of anomy. Criminal justice reform has done
a great deal to make the police, the courts and the prisons more
humane. But it has also overshot the mark where it has tended to
impute all aberrant behaviour to 'society' until in the end it is no
longer the criminal but his victim who is guilty. Some 'no-go
areas' like youth, or the acquittal of the guilty, are actually the
result of reforms which were intended to humanize the law and
ended with the dissipation of institutions. Analogous developments have occurred wherever codes of conduct have been
weakened to the point of making it impossible to enforce norms.
For some, the word 'liberal' has come to be synonymous with a
lax attitude to rules and norms generally.

No greater mistake could be made in the name of liberty. For
one thing, institutional laxity does not work. Those who assume
that we are or even should be living in the sweet world of
Rousseau's Emile, from whose vocabulary 'the very words obey
and command will be excluded, still more those of duty and
obligation', are more likely to find themselves in the nasty and
brutish world of Hobbes's war of all against all where people live
in 'continual fear' and there is of course 'no society'. If we do not
hold on to institutions, we have little else to sustain us. More than
that, institutions are the only instrument for enhancing life
chances for all. One could conceive of a few enriching themselves
with provisions in a pre-institutional world, though the great
seventeenth- and eighteenth-century authors have all shown that
even the wealth of the few cannot last without the institution of
property, and thus civil government. Certainly, the civilizing

force of entitlements requires that attention is paid to norms and sanctions and the instances which establish and uphold them.

Such institutional liberalism has practical consequences. I have avoided loose talk about a crisis of legitimacy in contemporary societies because there are few signs of it and those who make the claim have to go to great lengths to find the evidence which they so dearly want to explain. (Keynes had nice things to say about the 'Party of Catastrophe'.[13]) But what signs of anomy there are call for a clearer understanding of institutions. This requires an end to the proliferation of rules and norms which has become characteristic of all bureaucratic modern societies. One hesitates to make this point which is promised by so many parliamentary candidates who then proceed, a year after their election, to pride themselves on the number of laws which have been enacted with their help; but the point is still valid. The next task is one of institution-building. This means the reconstruction of institutions from their objectives and intentions. Laws effect little without the spirit of the laws. This requires what has come to be called 'discourse', rational debate and reasoned argument. Quite possibly, such discourse will of itself lead to a sorting process and thereby to greater concentration. Underlying all laws and institutions there is the core of rules of the social game which we call constitution.

One of the most useful impulses to liberal political thought has been provided in recent years by those who worry about the 'constitutional contract'. They are mostly political economists who recognize that 'institutions do indeed matter' and seek to 'assist individuals, as citizens who ultimately control their own social order, in their continuing search for those rules of the political game that will best serve their purposes, whatever these might be'.[14] Perhaps 'constitutional political economists' like James Buchanan have a tendency to assume one blueprint of rules which is removed not only from the vagaries of politics but also from those of history. I have indicated when the subject was first raised that the social contract is itself the subject of history. Its contents are not the same in our time as they were for Keynes in 1925, or indeed for John Locke in 1690 when his *Treatise on Civil Government* appeared. A new social contract embodies entitlements of citizenship as well as the limitations on power implied by that status. But it is still a version of the constitution of liberty, that is of institutions which deserve the most passionate defence by liberals.

Notes For an Address to Young People

As the argument of this essay draws to a close, something is still missing. After all, unless they are activists, real people in real life situations cannot live by a political agenda. They ask for a statement of the values by which they should be guided. Freedom in the most elementary sense is such a value. It is the simple desire not to be fenced in. Those who love freedom want to break every cage of bondage whether it is that of bureaucracy, of an unbearable human situation, or of a prison camp. But politics, including liberal politics, tempers this simple desire. I have just argued that it recognizes institutions and I have called for their defence. This is hardly a thesis which is likely to kindle the enthusiasm of the young. In fact, it is difficult to kindle such enthusiasm today. I have thought from time to time about what I would say if I was asked to give an address to young people leaving school or college. The following remarks are notes for such an address, not the address itself.

For, to be trite, there are no easy answers. In the 1940s, the answer would have been obvious: fight for freedom and defend with tooth and nail what you have gained! The world at large and the lives of individuals were indissolubly intermeshed and everyone would have understood. In the 1950s it would not have been difficult to say: work hard and you will be rewarded! There were careers to be seen to, and the early pleasures of having a refrigerator, a car, a home. In the 1960s the focus would have shifted: material well-being is fine, but there are other matters to worry about! The Vietnam War, social reform, democratic participation were all on the list for a rousing address. (I confess that I enjoyed my campaign speeches in the 1960s and would not have varied them much for a commencement address.) In the 1970s things got more tangled: fasten seat belts, there are turbulences about! Such advice would hardly capture the imagination of college graduates. In fact the 1970s were the time of (delicious) gloom and doom talk, about the coming environmental collapse,

180

or nuclear disaster, or limits to economic growth. It was actually quite a good time for addresses to young people.

But the 1980s are not. People are fed up with the gloom of the last decade. Not that any of the problems have been resolved, but as politicians of the left discovered to their dismay, after a while people cease to listen. The occasional drama apart, like a 'Band Aid' pop concert for the starving of Ethiopia, they want to turn to other, better things. These are not easy to find. An American presidential hopeful told his audience that he was in favour of upward social mobility. He sounded curiously like a man of the 1950s, although he clearly had the 1980s in mind and wanted to be upbeat.

In fact, the two apparently attractive ways of life on offer to young people in the 1980s, while different in all other respects, have one feature in common; they are both addictions. One is the addiction to money. We have already encountered the 'chain-smoking young men' in the 'towering office-blocks that dominate all the great cities of the world'. It is surprising that a woman author should have confined her portrait of 'casino capitalism' to young men. In fact, many young women too have found a job somewhere in the new universe of financial services, and are working twelve hours a day. On the dawn commuter train they read the financial daily, and on the dusk train home they carry a briefcase full of analyses. Young men and young women alike expect to make the salary of a professor in their first year after university, and twice that within a couple of years. Occasionally they play; but then they tackle tennis or jogging as hard as they tackle their work. They believe in what they are doing, and so they invest their own money along with that of others. If a better opportunity arises, they change employers, just as they help merge and demerge companies, make old names disappear and new ones come up. Their role models are the great success stories whose names are Trump or Hanson or Goldsmith, and many lesser ones known to a few. They want to make millions, not so much because they need them in order to buy or do things they want, but because they are after success, and money is their only yardstick. They are in fact the entrepreneurs of the new wave of financial capitalism.

The category is quite large, though not all of them make a million dollars a year at the age of thirty-five. Like all upward paths, this one is littered with those who have fallen by the wayside. It may even be that almost all who are on the path have to expect a levelling-off of their success and a difficult transition to slow decline at an age at which their parents were still looking forward to one or two crucial advances in their careers. Indeed it may be that the chances of taking home winnings from the capitalist casino will never be as good again as they were before October 1987. Decline is hard to cope with for addicts. Life to them is like flying an aeroplane which has no brakes and must therefore accelerate when faced with danger. One gets a sense of precariousness as one thinks of the new moneymakers, even apart from the obvious mental and physical side-effects of addiction. But, again, personal risk will not deter young people to whom this might be addressed.

The other addiction is costly rather than lucrative. It is to opt out instead of getting on top. In some ways the two are related. The story is told of the funeral of a drug dealer in a large city on the American West Coast who was unusually successful. His cortège was more than a mile long and included many of his victims who had loved him for his wanton generosities which made them forget his wanton cruelty. (Probably the mothers had not forgotten.) He would buy all the ice cream in the vendors' vans of the town and let them distribute it free, paid for of course with the dollars which youngsters had stolen to buy second-rate crack and other drugs. The drug scene highlights the boundary between the addiction of success and that of failure: there are those who sell the stuff and make millions, and those who use it and need hundreds which they do not have. Both are incidentally breaking the norms without which a free society cannot survive.

The addiction of opting out does not have to be led by drugs. I have noted the curious convergence of the culture of the under-class and the so-called counter-culture of the middle class. Both are protests against the bureaucratized world of the majority class. Indeed, as we have seen, even casino capitalism is a version of the same attitude. Hostility to an immobile, boring reality and its stifling values and life styles is the common denominator of some of the preferred choices of the young. The trouble is that the alternatives are essentially negative. They combine wild styles of dress and hair with a preference for deafening noise, whether hard rock or disco sound, and with a search for ways to put a distance between themselves and the established world. But none of this leads anywhere. It is not supposed to lead anywhere of course; but it is a strange dead end.

This is true even for the milder forms of the addiction, though some who have succumbed intend to find alternative life styles. Paradoxical as it sounds, young people feel lost in the cage of bureaucratic bondage. They are looking for bonds. The social movements of the 1980s have often had two objectives side by side, the immediate one of preventing the deployment of missiles or of demanding equal rights for women, and the latent one of creating a climate of solidarity. Even the German Greens were, for many of their members, as much a family as a party, quarrels and all. It gives one a warm feeling to sit all night with dozens of others outside an American air base and talk about life and death, sweet lives of love and horrible deaths from nuclear burns and cancer.

My address to young people is clearly not progressing. Why appear to make fun of those who try to do something different? What is so attractive about the predictable life of an accountant who gets married and promoted and divorced and promoted and worried about his children and promoted and remarried and retired early because his company has been bought by a twenty-eight-year-old wizard and needs to be streamlined in order to become a successful profit centre in a larger corporate entity? One can see the poor man take to drink (since he does not dare worse) and thus offer little incentive to his children to follow in his steps.

The point is to find a life which is neither bureaucracy nor addiction. No, the point is not to 'find' it, but to make it. Young people have to do something which has meaning. Meaning has two aspects. What people do has to be fun, and it has to matter.

'Fun' is shorthand for a personal experience. There are more high-falutin' words to say the same thing. Some talk about self-realization and the like. I think it is fair enough if one enjoys what one is doing, and gets a good feeling about it every now and again. Ideally, this is one's work, that is the activity which fills normal days. No doubt the financial whizz-kids do get a good feeling. Success is fun. But success can be measured in many ways. A reasonable amount of money not only comes in handy but is a part of most success stories. Meeting interesting people is enjoyable. The act of work itself can bring satisfaction. A sense of accomplishment is also a sense of success. A job well done is something which almost everyone appreciates.

The point which I am trying to make is that fun is more important than a career. The two can be related of course; some enjoy the next star and stripe on their uniform. But something has gone wrong with the career vision of life. It begins with mother's pride about early signs of talent; the next step is to do well at school, even very well in order to get into a good college or university. There again the point is to do well by examination standards; if one does, a job is waiting in some reputable organization where one can advance at regular intervals . . . One can see that this has lost its attraction for many. It has incidentally taken much of the fun out of education which should be about skills and knowledge and creativity and free thinking rather than careers. More generally, it has made people yawn before they have even started their lives. (It has also made them older than they need to be to do things.) My plea is to introduce some enjoyment much earlier.

This is not a plea for the children of the rich only. I am probably advising the children of the majority class, though underclass children too need more than just a job which they themselves do not take seriously. It is a plea for breaking out of the straitjacket of career thinking and using other standards of success. Fun is one half of it, but the other is that what one does must matter. Fun is a personal sense of enjoyment, but what matters is decided as much by others. It connects one's work with the values of others. It defines what is important and what not. It distinguishes addictions from activities.

Once again, there is no intention of exaggerated high-mindedness. Many things can matter, including a well-made dress which pleases others, a carefully worked-out travel plan for retired people who want to see the world on a limited budget, a film about the plight of Afghan refugees in Pakistan. The film has two aspects which are special. One is that it is a form of artistic expression. It may require special and comparatively rare skills, but I have heard young people use the word 'creative' for a whole lot of things which are accessible to most. Bringing about something new which is not necessarily unique or original but which one has produced with one's own hands or mind is for many an element of what matters.

184

The other point about the film is that it has to do with refugees. I do not want to invoke a world of do-gooders, but many things that matter are in one way or another connected with justice, or rather with remedying injustice in the world. Some will want to fight it, set up organizations, take part in demonstrations, write and sell pamphlets, and all this is fine. Others will want to do something about it, light the proverbial little candle rather than curse the darkness, and a lot of little candles have to be lit to give everyone a chance to see. Work which in some direct or indirect way improves the lot of other people – whether jobs, voluntary work, spare-time activity, whatever – matters in a special way.

It also has meaning. A great deal of legerdemain is done with meaning these days. Clever entrepreneurs of meaning have cashed in on people's desire to find ligatures in a disconnected world. They have set up church-like organizations which ease consciences, mostly on television, for a not-so-small fee. Like clever salespeople they make people feel grateful for being able to give money for something which they had not known they wanted at all. The 'return of the sacred' is both deeply, even desperately serious and a temptation for quick fixes which cannot work. It is not always easy to tell how one distinguishes between the real and the phoney in this respect. Even the patina of institutions with a long history is no guarantee against deceit. I suppose the important point is to be sceptical, but not to allow one's scepticism to become cynical. We do not know the answer to many questions; no human being does. There are thus likely to be answers which transcend our everyday experience. It is even possible that some have more to say about them than others. But no human being is infallible. No one therefore has a total claim to our lives.

One remedy against the temptation of false sanctity is to do things. I suppose this sums up the advice for the 1980s and 1990s: for heaven's sake, do something! Do something that has meaning because you enjoy it and it is important for others. There is a lot to do in this imperfect world.

As people give their lives meaning, they will discover that this requires a framework. The address to young people need not be a political address, but it makes political assumptions. One cannot do things which are fun and which matter if one is caught in the cycle of deprivation, or if one lives in an environment in which some person or agency has arrogated the power to push people around. Even the choices before young people today presuppose free societies. They may be more concerned about what to choose, and there is no need to blame them for their preferences. I have not argued anywhere that political participation is a value in itself, or even an obligation associated with citizenship. The view of politics underlying this essay, and explained in some detail with the help of Max Weber, is not one of a society of activists and of permanent political debate, but one of alert citizens who are ready to defend the institutions of liberty and sensitive to violations of their principles. At the same time, some have to take an interest in guarding, working and developing these institutions. If more people took an interest, it would not do any harm. For the politics of liberty is never a luxury.

World Civil Society

Of all the things which need to be done, the most difficult, intractable, and important concern the Third World. The incipient underclass in the inner cities of the United States and possibly Britain is a minor and insulated problem compared to poverty and injustice on a world scale. Still, the two problems have features in common. On a world scale too, the growth of some has left others behind, although the proportions are sadly reversed. Whereas in the OECD societies, a majority is doing relatively well and only a minority is defined out, the OECD world itself constitutes but a minority of mankind. The overwhelming majority of all humans are poor and deprived. Another similarity concerns the limited success of macro-policies. Just as economic and social policies made in capital cities do not reach the underclass, so the grand designs of international institutions fail to have a sustained effect for the better in Africa, Asia and Latin America. This is not to decry such policies and organizations with easy generalities. They are clearly necessary and must remain in the picture. But the colours of the picture and thereby its total effect are made in another way. They are made by many thousands of individuals who do something to get things moving in the localities in which people live. Most of these individuals are from the countries which now undergo often traumatic change.

Some come from the developed countries. Theirs is extremely worthwhile work, and while it may not be fun in any ordinary sense to truck water to a refugee camp on the Cambodian border or reassemble generators in the famine-stricken areas of the Sudan, it certainly matters.

Simple humanity may be a good enough reason to do these things, but they have a wider significance. I have argued on several occasions that civil societies cannot be maintained unless they are seen as steps on the way to a world civil society. This is a Kantian argument. In some of his occasional papers the great philosopher was a little less austere than in the *Critiques*, though no less persuasive. I have a special liking for a paper first published in 1784 and translated as 'Idea for a Universal History With Cosmopolitan Intent.'[15] One critical argument of this paper has been used in an earlier chapter to usher in conflict. In the Fourth Proposition (there are nine) Kant suggests that 'the means employed by Nature to bring about the development of all the capacities of men is their antagonism in society, so far as this is, in the end, the cause of a lawful order among men.' He then introduces the notion of man's 'unsociable sociability' which serves as a spur to leaving Arcadia and giving life a greater value than that of the sheep tended there. 'Thanks be to Nature, then, for the incompatibility, for heartless competitive vanity, for the insatiable desire to possess and to rule!' Conflict is the source of progress towards civilization and eventually the world civil society.

Kant's argument is straightforward and plausible (though Karl Popper, who otherwise belongs in a Kantian tradition, might not approve of all its steps). Given people's free will, they cannot be said to pursue an explicit common purpose; in fact we see contradiction, even chaos. Yet there may be a hidden 'intent' in the chaos, some clue to what it all adds up to. Let us see then whether we can find it. All natural capacities of creatures are destined to be fully developed. Man's (and woman's: Kant is fortunate in being able to use the German, *Mensch*) distinctive natural capacity is reason, but this will be fully developed only in the species and not in any one individual. Such development will moreover be the work of men and women in society. (This raises the paradox of progress: how can we justify 'that the earlier generations seem to perform their laborious tasks only for the sake of the later ones'?) The method of development is conflict, 'antagonism' (as we have seen), which leads Kant to the Fifth Proposition: 'The greatest problem for the human species, the solution of which Nature compels man to seek, is the achievement of a universal civil society which administers law among men.' Human unsociableness drives history forward but also requires the constraints of constitutions, a social contract. This will be the last human task to be achieved, if it is ever completely attained. The road to it is painful. It leads through revolutions within societies, and through wars between them. But in the end one world authority is as necessary as central authority is in particular societies, for war, and even constant readiness for war, 'stunt the full development of human nature'. Given the initial assumptions one must therefore regard history as the realization of a hidden plan of Nature to 'bring forth a perfect constitution of internal as well as external political relations as the only condition in which the capacities of mankind can be fully developed'.

Kant is nothing if not self-critical. He wonders (in the final, Ninth Proposition) whether it is not strange to the point of absurdity to conceive of history in terms of assumed rational ends, and he adds that none of his ideas will streamline the course of history or indeed make deliberate action unnecessary. (For him, philosophy has always been about how we might think of things in view of the fact that we do not really know how they are.) Nevertheless it is hard to fall in with his enlightened optimism two centuries later. Things may not work out that way, and mankind may yet destroy itself, or at any rate continue in a state of stunted development. However, this does not invalidate the moral case. If we want to extend our life chances, we need the constitution of liberty to do so. We need civil societies in the classical sense of the term. Civil societies are worth defending; after all, citizenship first entered the scene as a value for which young Athenians gave their lives. But as long as it has to be defended by armament and warfare, its development is stunted and incomplete. It is stunted and incomplete also as long as it is a privilege for the few whereas most of mankind struggles to stay alive. The moral case for a world civil society is hard to deny.

As one would expect, the practical consequences of this position are more problematic. A moral case for a certain order of things can easily turn into unjustifiable imperialism. Pericles was quite right to praise the openness of Athens while not demanding that Sparta change its ways, except of course for abstaining from attack. This is indeed the immediate point. The next step towards a World Civil Society is the recognition of universal rights of all men and women by the creation of a body of international law. The rudiments which exist are pathetically limited and weak. In most cases, they are pseudo-law, legal-sounding texts to which no sanctions are attached. Even court-like instances have been created whose sentences are never enforced. This may be a possible way forward; every avenue of promise must be tried. Regional arrangements like the European Communities have gone a step or two further, at least within the narrow remit of the treaties on which they are based. Whatever a world civil society may eventually look like, it will be one which, as Kant put it, 'administers law among men'. Freedom under law begins with the universal recognition of human rights. Fighting for such recognition is another task which matters.

On Strategic Change

It is tempting to finish a book on a high note, but I shall (almost) resist the temptation. Distant objectives are easily put into words; the question is how one gets there. In part this is a matter of first steps. A number of them have been mentioned as illustrations in passing, in this chapter as well as in earlier ones. But the question of method and style is more basic. It is one of approach, and of what some would call 'mindset'. How should one tackle problems if one wants to put into practice the line of analysis suggested in this essay?

The persons inhabiting what I have described as my pantheon have a number of things in common. They are all quite thoughtful and can expect to be regarded as men of the mind. Their experience of practical politics was usually short, lasting in most cases no more than a year. Wilhelm von Humboldt the minister is remembered for things which he did not do while he held ministerial office, like the foundation of the University of Berlin, and Alexis de Tocqueville the foreign minister is hardly remembered at all. Max Weber was merely a candidate for the Weimar National Assembly. Few now speak of William Beveridge's year as the member of parliament for Berwick-on-Tweed, or Raymond Aron's stint in the *cabinet* of André Malraux. Joseph Schumpeter was minister of finance for a few months in an uncongenial Austrian government. Maynard Keynes on the other hand remained, according to Schumpeter, 'impervious to the lure of the charmed circle of political office.'[16]. This did not prevent Baron Keynes of Tilton from speaking in the upper house of Britain's parliament, nor of course did it alter his self-perception as a natural peer of the leaders of the world on whom they would call to help them in times of crisis.

This is only the formal part of the story: wanting to influence those in power by working alongside them or addressing them in print. The more important part concerns substance, or at any rate the quality of advice. In the cases which I have in mind, it was simultaneously radical and conservative. More precisely still, radical specific advice was given in a general conservative framework. These men did not set out to change systems, but they (some of them at least) did change them. The debate is still continuing whether Keynes, by the argument of his *General Theory*, saved capitalism, destroyed it or perhaps saved it by destroying it. The debate is somewhat metaphysical. After all, what is capitalism? But it points to a sense of the need for change within a framework of institutions which is peculiar to a rare breed of authors and actors in the modern world.

This sense seems to take people as if driven by some compelling force to the boundary between economics and politics. The boundary has become a lively place with the recent revival of political economy and the eighteenth century more generally. Few writers are better guides across its byways than Albert Hirschman. His distinction between 'exit' and 'voice' points to two modes of human action which make abstract concepts like 'market failure' and 'government failure' manageable and real. When things do not work, people often have two options; they can go away and they can complain. The former, exit, is the typical economic option, the latter, voice, the political one. However, all the most interesting modes of action concern the 'conjunction of these two forces', their 'elusive optimal mix'.[17] Hirschman, like other advocates of strategic change, abhors Manicheans, whether they are Thatcherite exit-advocates or Green voice-activists. His plea for 'understood complexity' is a version of that conservatism which recognizes that so far as we know we have only one life to live and we had better accept its constraints and get on with things.[18]

Hirschman's choice of words is telling and perhaps a little unfortunate. He himself writes of the 'poor fellow' (a university president) who remarked that his book was written 'from below'. It is. Politics for Hirschman is 'voice', that is protest, rather than 'action' or 'change'. At least he appears to see the world from the point of view of its victims, the poor and downtrodden. Keynes cared about them as much as anyone but his vantage point was quite different. He was always looking for levers of action 'from above'. His instinct led him, whenever he was faced with a major problem, to find them in that precious corner in which entitlements and provisions meet. In his time, this meant in the first instance bringing the issue of provisions to the attention of politicians. Robert Skidelsky reminds us that this was the lasting effect of Keynes's first bestseller, *The Economic Consequences of the Peace*. 'It was a revolt of economics against politics.' This does not sound quite right. The point is not battle but conjunction. Skidelsky shows it when he goes on to speak of 'the new breed of economist-politician' in the 1920s 'who talked about the gold standard and the balance of trade as fluently as pre-war politicians had talked about the Two-Power standard and the balance of power.' 'The idea that the creation of opulence was the main task of rulers was born in 1919 though it came of age only after the Second World War.'[19]

The *Economic Consequences* made the point that the imposition of a simple, almost mechanical demand for reparations on Germany would destroy the economy which it is supposed to tax. This was only a prelude to Keynes's central thesis in the *General Theory* ten years later, which is that without effective demand there cannot be full employment and an effective use of economic resources. Effective demand, however, is not automatic; it may require government action, including redistribution. Keynes used strong language in the 'Concluding Notes' to his book: 'The outstanding faults of the economic society in which we live are its failure to provide for full employment and its arbitrary and inequitable distribution of wealth and incomes.'[20] More importantly, he recommended strong medicine. In the language of this essay, he suggested that entitlement structures have to be changed in order to increase provisions. The critical notion in Keynes's prescriptions for policy is that of 'effective demand'. It is not enough to rely on the supply side and the operation of the market alone; social and political changes have to be used to stimulate economic growth by enabling people to demand more.

I am not suggesting that his particular medicine is applicable today. In different times, it may well be necessary to stimulate growth in order to give entitlements substance. Keynes himself retained a glorious ambiguity about this matter which is perhaps a part of his particular conjunction of exit and voice, and makes it possible to wonder whether he would have been a demand-creator or a supply-sider today. I for one look forward to the second volume of Skidelsky's masterly biography of Keynes to learn more about this ambiguity. But the theme is clear. It recurs in Keynes's later writings as in the articles on 'How to Pay for the War' in 1940 in which he develops a plan 'which uses a time of general sacrifice, not as an excuse for postponing desirable reforms, but as an opportunity for moving further than we have hitherto towards reducing inequalities'.[21] Once again, Keynes is squaring circles: the war must be paid for, but consumption must not be damaged, and justice must be done. Squaring circles never really works. If one looks at the facts, Hirschman was right about the 'elusive optimal mix'. But if there is one utopian lapse which the liberal may be allowed, it is not to stop trying to stimulate the extension of entitlements and the growth of provisions by the same act.

Several examples of possible reforms to this end have been mentioned in this book; others could readily be added. At this point, they are no more than illustrations. In the poor countries of the world the key issue is how to combine economic development and citizenship. In some cases, the organization of co-operative ventures achieves the purpose. The more recent discovery of variants of privatization and the encouragement of small business may have similar effects. Clearly, a whole range of policies from profit-sharing to co-determination in the economies of the OECD world belong in this context. There may be even more strategic links between the rights of citizenship and the supply of provisions. A basic income guarantee for all could be one of them; so could the 'tax on time' of a general community service. In any case, community development schemes, in inner cities and elsewhere, often hit the intersection of people's rights and their economic needs. The time may also have come for another Keynes in the theory of economic policy, though of course no science policy, however well-funded and sophisticated, will 'produce' him.

Strategic change then is action taken by those who are placed to do so which is designed to raise people's life chances in a practical way. It assumes the arsenal of critical comments which Karl Popper offers about 'Utopian engineering' and all attempts of 'remodelling the "whole of society" in accordance with a definite plan or blueprint'.[22] At the same time, it is more than Popper's 'piecemeal social engineering'. Even apart from the unfortunate choice of words – which seem to imply a purely technical quality of political decisions – piecemeal engineering suggests a reactive rather than a constructive approach to action, and a slowness of change which is not acceptable to many. It is probably no accident that the term has been used above all by the great pragmatists who were concerned with method rather than purpose. Popper would be right to argue that this is a misunderstanding of his views. He not only speaks of 'the task of reforming society' but about the possibility 'that a series of piecemeal reforms might be inspired by one general tendency'. I have reason to believe that he would accept the notion of strategic change. But it is different from the concepts developed in *The Poverty of Historicism*. It involves a sense of direction as well as 'caution and preparedness for unavoidable surprises'. Moreover, the sense of direction is more than formal, and the methods of implementation are more than technical.

The direction of change was the major theme of this essay. There are times when strategic change requires more emphasis on provisions, and other times when it calls for greater entitlements. For the liberal, the most desirable changes aim at both. The critical points of the politics of liberty are those in which more people are brought in and more opportunities are offered at the same time. This is never a matter of course. It requires an awareness of unacceptable inequality even as taxes are lowered and incentives provided for the enterprising, but it also requires a consciousness of the need to keep choices open as privileges are broken in order to emancipate the deprived. The Martinez

Paradox is a challenge, not a destiny, and it has been resolved at great moments of modern history.

Revolutions are melancholy moments of history. Their extravagant promises have a high price and cannot be kept. But they are also an anchorage for human hopes. Even conservatives seek inspiration from revolutions once they have receded from immediate memories. What inspiration can guide strategic change? Many authors on social matters have been tempted to speculate about the desirable goal. Immanuel Kant's serious vision and the irony of its presentation are a model. Max Weber remained deeply gloomy throughout. Raymond Aron rarely allowed himself speculation, though on one occasion, as a part of the 'Hopes and Fears of the Century', he commended action rather than dreams to deal with 'the eternal problems of a just order'. Political economists are sometimes guided by a vision which puts them out of business. Neither Marx's 'communist society' nor Mill's 'stationary state' needs economists as advisers. Keynes adopted a version of this view. In considering possibilities for 'our grandchildren', he boldly stated 'that mankind is solving its economic problem' and will in due course be able to turn to better things. 'But beware! The time for all this is not yet.'[23]

There is much that is persuasive in such thoughts. Provisions are very imperfect life chances without entitlements, and life chances also include that less tangible element, ligatures. Even so they are chances, and our lives are what we make of them. Life is about activity and meaning for which both citizenship and the wealth of nations are merely a condition. When all is said and done, modern civil societies are not such a bad place to be, as long as we do not lose our zest for improvement.

Notes

1 For tracing the words 'modern' and 'modernity', I have benefited in particular from Hans Robert Jauss: 'Literarische Tradition und gegenwärtiges Bewusstsein der Modernität', in *Literaturgeschichte als Provo kation* (Suhrkamp: Frankfurt 1970). Jürgen Habermas also refers to Jauss in his book *Der philosophische Diskurs der Moderne* (Suhrkamp: Frankfurt 1985). The contributions by Jean Baechler and Walter Bühl to the issue of the *European Journal of Sociology* 'on the concept of modernity' (vol. IX, no. 2, 1968) are instructive both on this concept and on that of capitalism. On the whole subject, but specifically on the 'debate between the ancients and the moderns', see Robert K. Merton: *On the Shoulders of Giants* (2nd edn, Harcourt Brace: New York 1985). The discussion of Hakewill is on pp. 47–9.

2 A book to which some of the remarks in this passage allude is unfortunately not available in English; it is by Peter Koslowski, Robert Spaemann and Reinhard Loew (eds): *Moderne oder Postmoderne?* (Acta Humaniora VCH: Weinheim 1986). This book even includes a piece entitled 'After Postmodernity'.

3 I have in fact published eight mostly small books since that time. In order to avoid boring the reader with self-quotations from partly inaccessible sources, let me explain briefly how they relate to the present book. *A New World Order?* (University of Ghana Press: Accra 1979) was a series of lectures. The approach to international relations characteristic of the present book is foreshadowed there, including some of the remarks at the beginning of Chapter 6. *Life Chances* (Weidenfeld & Nicolson: London 1981) is a collection of papers. The concept of life chances is amended and I hope improved in the present book (see pp. 13ff.). The volume contains an essay on the demise of social democracy. *On Britain* (BBC Publications: London 1982) is a light-hearted book, but I have developed some of the points in the remarks on differences between countries here (see pp. 64ff.). *Die*

Chancen der Krise (DVA: Stuttgart 1983) was a straightforward political analysis which contains elements of the liberal agenda in Chapter 8 of the present volume. *Reisen nach innen und aussen* (DVA: Stuttgart 1984) is my first publication in which the 'underclass' figures. Otherwise it contains a number of rather autobiographical pieces. *Law and Order* (Stevens: London 1985) is based on the Hamlyn Lectures and shows this origin. Many elements of Chapters 5 to 8 of the present book are prefigured here, notably the distinction between a majority class and an underclass, the notion of social causes of individual violations of law, and the explanation of anomy. My contribution to the pamphlet *A Widening Atlantic? Domestic Change and Foreign Policy* (Council on Foreign Relations: New York 1986) makes some of the points about 1968, about the European Community and about US–European relations which are repeated in this book. Finally, the volume of papers *Fragmente eines neuen Liberalismus* (DVA: Stuttgart 1987) contains much of the framework of the present book, including the distinction between entitlements and provisions. In fact, many of the papers assembled in this German volume were originally written in English and have been published in a variety of places. I would like to think that the present book supersedes several of these earlier publications.

4   Giovanna Zincone: 'Cittadinanza', in G. Zaccaria (ed.): *Vocabolario del linguaggio politico* (Edizioni Lavoro: Rome 1987).

5   'Since the second Thirty Years' War from 1914 to 1945, the Europeans have come to relish some kind of comfortable insularity.' Thus Fritz Stern in an article entitled 'A Shift of Mood in Europe' in the *New York Times* of 2 September 1981.

Chapter 1: Revolutions of Modernity

1   Marx did not present his theory systematically in any one place. Also, as with so many of his more strictly social theories, he added little to it in his later years. Thus much of the material can be found in his earlier writings, in this case in *The Poverty of Philosophy* (1846), and the *Communist Manifesto* (1848), though there is also the famous Preface to the *Critique of Political Economy* of 1859.

2   Thus in both the *Paris Manuscripts* on economics and philosophy of 1844 and in *The Holy Family* of 1845 with obvious reference to Feuerbach and to Hegel.

3   Karl R. Popper: *The Poverty of Historicism* (2nd edn, Routledge & Kegan Paul: London 1960).

4   Evidence on the Nicaraguan economy is comparatively plentiful. I have relied above all on two research papers: Bill Gibson: *Stabilization Policy in Nicaragua* (WIDER Project on Stabilization and Adjustment Programs: United Nations University, July 1986); Francisco J. Mayorga: *The Economic Trajectory of Nicaragua 1980–1984: An Overview*

(Occasional Papers Series, No. 14, Latin American and Caribbean Center: Florida International University 1986). Perhaps the text understates the influence of the US and the 'Contra' war. One plausible assessment of the relative importance of external and internal factors is that by Gibson (p. 49): 'Stabilization policy in Nicaragua is now reduced to the question of how to allocate more resources in the midst of a reconstruction effort buffeted by deteriorating terms of trade and authentic internal conflict over the restructuring brought on by the revolution.'

5   Amartya Sen's original book is: *Poverty and Famines* (Clarendon Press: Oxford 1981). The 'later paper' referred to below is called 'Food, Economics and Entitlements' and has been published in several places, most accessibly perhaps in *Lloyds Bank Review* (April 1986). In 1986, the United Nations University institute WIDER in Helsinki organized a symposium on Sen's thesis with several further contributions. The proceedings are not published yet.

6   Robert F. Nozick: *Anarchy, State and Utopia* (Basic Books: New York 1974). Lawrence M. Mead: *Beyond Entitlement: The Social Obligations of Citizenship* (Free Press: New York 1986).

7   Fred Hirsch: *Social Limits to Growth* (Routledge & Kegan Paul: London 1977). For an extensive discussion see the contributions to Adrian Ellis and Krishan Kumar (eds): *Dilemmas of Liberal Democracies: Studies in Fred Hirsch's Limits to Growth* (Tavistock: London–New York 1983). The most important difference between Hirsch's concepts and the ones here proposed is that Hirsch regards 'positional goods' as either intrinsically or contingently immutable, whereas I argue that the interesting question is the relation between changes in entitlements and changes in provisions. Hirsch is most relevant to this analysis where he argues what economic growth cannot do.

8   In his article 'Mourir à Jonestown' (*European Journal of Sociology*, vol. xx, no. 2, 1979), Jean Baechler has analysed the outsize suicide wish of the leader and the anomic condition of the followers in ways deliberately reminiscent of Hitler and the last year of the war.

9   The quotations are all from Karl Marx and Frederick Engels: *The Communist Manifesto*, ed. Paul Sweezy (Modern Reader Paperbacks: New York–London 1964), and from Alexis de Tocqueville: *Democracy in America*, ed. J. P. Mayer (Doubleday: Garden City 1969).

Here are the original elements of the concoction in full:

'The bourgeoisie has played a most revolutionary role in history.' (Marx/Engels, p. 5)

'This whole book has been written under the impulse of a kind of religious dread inspired by contemplation of this irresistible revolution advancing century by century over every obstacle and even now going forward amid the ruins it has itself created.' (Tocqueville, p. 12)

'When royal power supported by aristocracies governed the nations of Europe in peace, society, despite all its wretchedness, enjoyed several types of happiness which are difficult to appreciate or conceive today.' (Tocqueville, p. 13)

'The bourgeoisie, wherever it has got the upper hand, has put an end to all feudal, patriarchal, idyllic relations. It has pitilessly torn asunder the motley feudal ties that bound man to his "natural superiors", and has left remaining no other bond between man and man than naked self-interest, than callous "cash payment". It has drowned the most heavenly ecstasies of religious fervour, of chivalrous enthusiasm, of philistine sentimentalism, in the icy water of egotistical calculation.' (Marx/Engels, pp. 5–6)

'But in abandoning our ancestors' social state and throwing their institutions, ideas, and mores pell-mell behind us, what have we put in their place?' (Tocqueville, p. 15)

'All fixed, fast-frozen relations, with their train of ancient and venerable prejudices and opinions, are swept away, all new-formed ones become antiquated before they can ossify. All that is solid melts into air, all that is holy is profaned, and man is at last compelled to face with sober senses his real conditions of life, and his relations with his kind.' (Marx/Engels, p. 7)

'Men of religion fight against freedom, and lovers of liberty attack religions; noble and generous spirits praise slavery, while low, servile minds preach independence; honest and enlightened citizens are the enemies of all progress, while men without patriotism or morals make themselves the apostles of civilization and enlightenment.' (Tocqueville, p. 17)

10 There are several recent books on capitalism (and democracy). One is Peter Berger: *The Capitalist Revolution: Fifty Propositions About Prosperity, Equality and Liberty* (Basic Books: New York 1986); the quoted definition is on p. 19. An opposing (anti-capitalist) view is taken by Samuel Bowles and Herbert Gintis: *Capitalism and Democracy: Property, Community and the Contradictions of Modern Social Thought* (Basic Books: New York 1986). I have learned most from the characteristically thoughtful essay by Robert L. Heilbroner: *The Nature and Logic of Capitalism* (W. W. Norton: New York–London 1985).

11 The relevant sections of the *Wealth of Nations* are the very first chapter of Book One, and Chapter I of Book Three 'Of the Natural Progress of Opulence'.

12 See David Hume: *A Treatise of Human Nature*, ed. L. A. Selby-Bigge (Clarendon Press: Oxford 1888), p. 475n.

Chapter 2: Citizenship and Social Class

1 Some of the important recent protagonists of this debate are of course John Rawls: *A Theory of Justice* (Harvard University Press: Cambridge

1971). Robert Nozick: *Anarchy, State and Utopia* (Basic Books: New York 1974). James Buchanan: *The Limits of Liberty* (University of Chicago Press: Chicago 1975). For the history of the concept of social contract I happily rely on J. W. Gough: *The Social Contract* (2nd edn, Clarendon Press: Oxford 1957).

2 One recurrent theme of this book is the debate with Jürgen Habermas, notably (though by no means only) with his *Theorie des kommunikativen Handelns* (Suhrkamp: Frankfurt 1985). The debate is complicated in that I share certain basic values with Habermas, including an appreciation of the rule of law and the need for a 'constitutional patriotism'. When it comes to German questions, we are clearly on one side. I do not share either the Hegelian roots or the Rousseauean hopes with Habermas, however. He too thinks in terms of systems and total change; and he dreams of the expansion of niches of 'unconstrained communication' to the whole of society. The reference here is therefore to Habermas, but the debate remains open.

3 Raymond Aron wrote a remarkable paper on the subject, 'Is Multinational Citizenship Possible?' (*Social Research*, vol. 41, no. 4, Winter 1974). He asks: 'How could a citizen possibly belong to several political entities at once?' His answer is that he cannot. Human rights are real only within the confines of (nation-)states. 'The Jews of my generation cannot forget how fragile these human rights become when they no longer correspond with citizenship rights.' The European Community does not alter this fact, for 'there are no such animals as "European citizens"'; it may even 'weaken people's sense of their citizenship'. This may sound surprising from one of the few Frenchmen of his generation who remained unimpressed by de Gaulle. It has a hard analytical core, however, in that citizenship and the law are inseparable, and the only law we know is national.

4 I have used the translation of Thucydides' *History of the Peloponnesian War* by Richard Crawley, revised by R. Feetham and published by the Encyclopaedia Britannica in its series of Great Books in 1952.

5 Robert M. MacIver: *The Modern State* (Oxford University Press: London 1926), p. 97.

6 The distinction is mine. Harry Eckstein, in his 'Civic Inclusion and Its Discontents' (*Daedalus*, Fall 1984), uses 'civic inclusion' for 'the processes by which segments of society previously excluded from membership (in Charles Tilly's sense) in political and socio-economic institutions are incorporated into these institutions as "citizens"'. See also Charles Tilly: *From Mobilization to Revolution* (Addison-Wesley: Reading, Mass. – Menlo Park, Calif. 1978).

7 In a letter to me, Giovanna Zincone has pointed out that modern citizenship is not transportable. Unlike medieval citizenship people do not carry it with them, but it is linked to the territory to which they belong (with limited international guarantees).

8 Lawrence M. Mead: *Beyond Entitlement: The Social Obligations of Citizenship* (Free Press: New York 1986).

9 To my knowledge, the best account of the history of the concept is Manfred Riedel's dictionary article 'Gesellschaft, bürgerliche', in *Geschichtliche Grundbegriffe*, ed. Otto Brunner, Werner Conze and Reinhart Koselleck (Klett: Stuttgart 1975). The extensive piece has, however, a distinctly German bias and is less satisfactory on the English term 'civil society'.

10 Published under this title (Cambridge University Press: Cambridge) in 1950, and later included in the volume *Class, Citizenship and Social Development* (Doubleday: Garden City NY 1965). The three lectures are short, so that I have not identified all page references.

11 The title of chapter I in Book Three of the *Inquiry Into the Nature and Causes of the Wealth of Nations*, from which the quotation is also taken.

12 Friedrich von Hayek: *The Constitution of Liberty* (University of Chicago Press: Chicago 1960), p. 46. Robert L. Heilbroner: *The Nature and Logic of Capitalism* (W. W. Norton: New York–London 1985), p. 45. Fred Hirsch: *Social Limits to Growth* (Routledge & Kegan Paul: London 1977), passim.

13 Friedrich von Hayek is delighted (op. cit.), Fred Hirsch angry (op. cit.), and the irony is that by Michael Young and Peter Wilmott: *The Symmetrical Family* (Routledge & Kegan Paul: London 1973), p. 167.

14 The notion of 'disparities of realms of life' was first held against class theory by authors of the Frankfurt School. See Jochen Bergmann, Gerhard Brandt, Klaus Körber, Ernst Theodor Mohl and Claus Offe: 'Herrschaft, Klassenverhältnis, Schichtung', in *Spätkapitalismus oder Industriegesellschaft*, Proceedings of the 16th German Sociological Congress (Enke: Stuttgart 1969). John Kenneth Galbraith's distinction between 'private wealth' and 'public squalor' (in *The Affluent Society*) is not dissimilar.

Chapter 3: Politics in Industrial Society

1 In this exercise I have benefited greatly from the collection of historical statistics by Peter Flora: *State, Economy and Society in Western Europe 1815–1975: A Data Handbook*, especially vol. I on 'The Growth of Mass Democracies and Welfare States' (Campus–Macmillan–St James's: Frankfurt–London–Chicago 1983).

2 An article on the fortieth anniversary of General George Marshall's Harvard speech which inaugurated the Marshall Plan (*Neue Zürcher Zeitung* No. 129, 6/7 June 1987) begins with the sentence: 'It rarely happens that economic events and decisions make history and are remembered.' Perhaps this is the case only when they are in fact not economic but political, not about provisions but about entitlements. The Marshall Plan changed the basis of economic activity, as do

currency reforms. The 'Black Friday' of 1929 and 19 October 1987 on Wall Street did too.

3 Keith Middlemas: *Politics in Industrial Society: The Experience of the British System Since 1911* (André Deutsch: London 1979).

4 Max Weber: *Gesammelte Politische Schriften*, 3rd enlarged edn, ed. J. Winckelmann (J. C. B. Mohr–Siebeck: Tübingen 1971). The text quoted was written in 1917.

5 Max Weber has written and lectured on political subjects throughout his life, but his publications in the months before and after the end of the First World War have a special intensity. Within weeks, the articles in the *Frankfurter Zeitung* about 'Politics and Government in the New Order of Germany' were turned into a booklet of 150 pages. During the 'revolutionary carnival' (as he called it) of 1918–19, Weber reluctantly abandoned his preference for constitutional monarchy in favour of a republic with a directly elected president; the result can be read in the articles about 'Germany's Future Form of Government'. In 1919, the famous lecture on 'Politics as a Vocation' followed the other on 'Science as a Vocation'; its published version would have taken several hours to deliver. All these pieces are included in the 1971 volume cited in note 4 above. The key quotation on the 'cage of bondage' and the questions which it raises is on pp. 332–3. I have translated the quotations from the German original myself.

6 All quotations in this paragraph and the subsequent one are from Seymour Martin Lipset: *Political Man: The Social Bases of Politics*, expanded edn (The Johns Hopkins University Press: Baltimore 1981). For the present paragraph see pp. 303, 309 and 310. For the subsequent paragraph see pp. 31 and 475. The critic mentioned there is Dankwart Rustow.

7 No British government since (and including) 1945 has had 50 per cent of the vote; Mrs Thatcher's 'landslide victories' of 1983 and 1987 were based on 43 per cent. In most countries, this figure would have been regarded as a defeat. The important question about Britain is therefore one of legitimacy: why does the electorate accept innovative minority rule as right?

8 John Goldthorpe, David Lockwood, Frank Bechhofer and Jennifer Platt: *The Affluent Worker: Political Attitudes and Behaviour* (Cambridge University Press: Cambridge 1968), esp. p. 73. For the 'establishment' see Anthony Sampson: *Anatomy of Britain* (Hodder & Stoughton: London 1962).

9 Martin J. Wiener: *English Culture and the Decline of the Industrial Spirit 1850–1980* (Cambridge University Press: Cambridge 1981).

10 Thorstein Veblen: *Imperial Germany and the Industrial Revolution* (1915, new edn, Viking Press: New York 1939). The quotes are on pp. 249ff.

11 In a paper entitled 'Some Questions About the Weimar Republic and

Possible Parallels to the Developed Democracies Today' (published in Peter Koslowski (ed.): *Individual Liberty and Democratic Decision-Making,* J. C. B. Mohr–Siebeck: Tübingen 1987) Olson argues that the collapse of Weimar can be explained in terms of his cartelization thesis. In order to sustain the argument, he has to interpret the revolution of 1918–19 away, which he does by pointing to cultural and institutional continuities. Olson acknowledges my doubts about his thesis in the paper.

12 Friedrich August von Hayek: *The Constitution of Liberty* (University of Chicago Press: Chicago 1960). Hayek does not formally define the concept, though he speaks of 'a constitution of liberty, a constitution that would protect the individual against all arbitrary coercion' (p. 182). I like his use of the word 'constitution' for the principles underlying laws and formal rules, but find his definition of liberty restrictive. Giovanni Sartori, in his eminently sensible and extraordinarily precise *Theory of Democracy Revisited* (Chatham House Publishers: Chatham NJ 1987) makes as good a case for retaining the word 'democracy' as can be made. I shall in fact use it from time to time as shorthand for the constitution of liberty, but prefer the latter.

Chapter 4: Temptations of Totalitarianism

1 This is quoted from the chapter on 'Working-Class Authoritarianism' in S. M. Lipset's *Political Man: The Social Bases of Politics,* expanded edn (The Johns Hopkins University Press: Baltimore 1981), p. 97. To save the face of others, Lipset concedes in this paper that the early working class may have displayed different patterns, but 'events since 1914 have gradually eroded these patterns'. One must be allowed to have some doubt about this benevolent assumption.

2 The quotations from Robert Michels are from the German original of his book: *Zur Soziologie des Parteiwesens in der modernen Demokratie,* reprint of the 2nd edn, ed. Werner Conze (A. Kröner: Stuttgart 1957), especially pp. 25 and 371. The thesis was first formulated in 1903 by M. Ostrogorski: *La Démocratie et l'organisation des partis politiques.* Georg Lukács is quoted from *History and Class Consciousness,* trans. Rodney Livingstone (Merlin Press: London 1971), p. 196.

3 Sombart wrote this before the First World War: *Das Proletariat: Bilder und Studien* (Rütten & Loening: Frankfurt/M. 1906), p. 86.

4 Emil Lederer and Jakob Marschak: 'Der neue Mittelstand', in *Grundriss der Sozialökonomik* ix/1 (J. C. B. Mohr–Siebeck: Tübingen 1926), p. 121. A similar thesis was subtly argued much later by David Lockwood: *The Blackcoated Worker* (Allen & Unwin: London 1958). For the opposing thesis see Theodor Geiger: *Die soziale Schichtung des deutschen Volkes* (F. Enke: Stuttgart 1932), esp. pp. 109ff.

5 Quoted from Karl Renner: *Wandlungen der modernen Gesellschaft*

(Verlag Wiener Volksbuchhandlung: Vienna 1953), pp. 199 and 211.

6 This is the much quoted definition by Carl Friedrich in Carl J. Friedrich and Zbigniew K. Brzezinski: *Totalitarian Dictatorship and Autocracy*, 2nd edn (Harvard University Press: Cambridge 1965), p. 21.

7 Leonard Schapiro: *Totalitarianism* (Praeger: New York–London 1972), p. 118. Hannah Arendt: *The Origins of Totalitarianism* (Harcourt Brace: New York 1951), p. 312. Franz Neumann: *The Democratic and the Authoritarian State* (Free Press: Glencoe, Ill. 1957), p. 245.

8 In Richard Crossman (ed.): *The God That Failed* (Bantam Books: New York–London 1965), p. 13. The theme recurs with the other authors in this volume.

9 Fritz Stern: 'National Socialism as Temptation', in *Dreams and Delusions: The Drama of German History* (A. Knopf: New York 1987), p. 148.

10 Some of these phrases are taken from S. M. Lipset's analysis of 'Fascism – Right, Left and Centre' in his *Political Man*, op. cit. Lipset's notion of an 'extremism of the middle' is probably unfortunate since it assigns a place to groups which according to his own analysis lack precisely a social location.

11 See note 8 above. The quotation is on p. 5.

12 Op. cit., p. 245.

13 The quote from Hannah Arendt is on p. 377 of the book mentioned in note 7. Franz Neumann: *Behemoth* (Octagon Books: New York 1963); see the 'remark about the name Behemoth' at the beginning of the book.

14 Karl R. Popper: *The Open Society and Its Enemies* (Princeton University Press: Princeton 1950), p. 195.

15 Herbert Spiro, in his article on 'Totalitarianism' in the *Encyclopedia of the Social Sciences*, expressed a similar view and added: 'If these expectations are borne out, then a third encyclopedia of the social sciences, like the first one, will not list "totalitarianism".' On that score I prefer to agree with Leonard Schapiro (op. cit., p. 124): 'We should be the poorer without it, if only because we should lack the reminder that there are stages in the history of nations, perhaps of every nation, when the fanaticism, the arrogance, the ruthlessness, the ambition and the hubris of one individual can plunge millions of men and women into madness, suffering, fear and destruction.'

16 Jeane Kirkpatrick: 'Dictatorships and Double Standards', *Commentary* (November 1979). It will be remembered that Ronald Reagan was elected President in November 1980.

17 In her article, Jeane Kirkpatrick dismisses totalitarianism by invoking a *deus* (or rather an *animal*) *ex machina*: 'From time to time a truly bestial ruler can come to power in either type of autocracy – Idi Amin, Papa Doc Duvalier, Joseph Stalin, Pol Pot are examples – but neither type regularly produces such moral monsters (though democracy regularly prevents their accession to power)' (p. 44). Was not Weimar Germany a 'democracy'? What about Hitler anyway?

18 The debate was carried on in many books and journals. In 1985 the journal *Transaction – Social Science and Modern Society* (vol. 22, no. 3, March–April 1985) published seven contributions under the heading 'Controversies: Kirkpatrick and Her Critics' which include a piece by Jeane Kirkpatrick and give a good impression of the subjects and of the temperature of the debate.
19 See Peter Wiles: 'Irreversibility: Theory and Practice', *The Washington Quarterly* (vol. 8, no. 1, 1985).
20 Phrases taken from pp. 37 and 38 of Jeane Kirkpatrick's article.

Chapter 5: Aron's World

1 Robert Colquhoun: *Raymond Aron*, vol. i: *The Philosopher in History*, vol. ii: *The Sociologist in Society* (Sage Publications: London 1986). The dates are 'awkward' (though the Sorbonne appointment in 1955 was certainly important), and so are the descriptions. Aron was never really a philosopher, and the word 'politics' should not be missing. The volumes of this biography are, however, very informative on Aron's writings. They should be read with Aron's own *Mémoires* and perhaps the long interviews of the *Spectateur Engagé*.
2 Walt W. Rostow: *The World Economy: History and Prospect* (University of Texas Press: Austin–London 1978), esp. ch. 5. See also the second volume of Peter Flora: *State, Economy and Society in Western Europe 1815–1975: A Data Handbook* (Campus–Macmillan–St James's: Frankfurt–London–Chicago 1987).
3 Peter L. Berger: *The Capitalist Revolution: Fifty Propositions About Prosperity, Equality and Liberty* (Basic Books: New York 1986), p. 44 and, in a slightly different formulation, p. 211. Berger is of course not an economist and has a sense of sociopolitical changes, but likes to opt for the economic answer.
4 See Lester Thurow: 'A Surge in Inequality', in *Scientific American*, vol. 256, no. 5 (May 1987), p. 30: 'Between 1969 and 1982 the people in the top 10 percent of the population [of the United States] raised their income share according to this set of data from 29 to 33 percent of total income, those between the 60th and 90th percentiles held even at 39 percent and the bottom 60 percent saw their share fall from 32 to 28 percent.'
5 Raymond Aron: *Eighteen Lectures on Industrial Society*, trans. M. K. Bottomore (Weidenfeld & Nicolson: London 1967). The 1955–6 lectures were in fact first published in book form (in French) in 1961. The main quotations on the following pages are on pp. 73, 111, 118, 123, 142, 175, 190, 204f. and 241f. In his 1965 *Essai sur les libertés* (translated as *An Essay on Freedom*), Aron makes a statement quoted by R. Colquhoun (vol. ii, p. 244) which shows his awareness of the problem discussed in the present book: 'The industrial society in which we live and which was foreseen by the thinkers of the last century is basically democratic,

in Tocqueville's sense of the elimination of hereditary aristocracies; it is normally, if not necessarily, democratic, in the sense that it excludes nobody from citizenship and tends to offer material well-being to all.'

6 The reference to Fourastié leads me to mention four books which have much to do with Aron's world, and indeed with the *Eighteen Lectures*. Colin Clark: *The Conditions of Economic Progress* (Macmillan: London 1940, 2nd edn 1951). Arthur Lewis: *Theory of Economic Growth* (Allen & Unwin: London 1955). Jean Fourastié: *Le Grand Espoir du XXe siècle* (Plon: Paris 1950). Walt W. Rostow: *The Stages of Economic Growth* (Cambridge University Press: Cambridge 1960).

7 In the (1971) Preface to the English edition of the *Eighteen Lectures* Aron actually writes: 'The idea that the Soviet and Western societies are gradually drawing closer together and are tending to converge towards a mixed form – an idea which critics in Moscow have attributed to me and have violently rejected – is at the most only a hypothesis. It is only with many reservations that I subscribe to it, as the careful reader of this book will see.' I do not subscribe to it at all, for one theme of the present book is a farewell to all variants of economic determinism.

8 S. M. Lipset: *Political Man: The Social Bases of Politics*, expanded edn (The Johns Hopkins University Press: Baltimore 1981), p. 230. The book by D. Anderson and P. Davidson was called *Ballots and the Democratic Class Struggle* (Stanford University Press: Stanford 1943), and uses the term loosely in the context of opinion research data.

9 Theodor Geiger: *Die Klassengesellschaft im Schmelztiegel* (Gustav Kiepenheuer: Köln–Hagen 1949), pp. 182ff. Soon after, several German authors would claim that either the 'levelled-in middle-class society' (Helmut Schelsky: 'Die Bedeutung des Schichtungsbegriffes für die Analyse der gegenwärtigen deutschen Gesellschaft', 1953), or indeed the 'classless society' (Siegfried Landshut: 'Die Gegenwart im Lichte der Marxschen Lehre', 1956) had been achieved in the West.

10 Joseph Schumpeter: *Capitalism, Socialism and Democracy* (2nd edn, Harper: New York 1942), p. 269. Kenneth Arrow: *Social Choice and Individual Values* (Wiley: New York 1951). The main author alluded to is of course Anthony Downs: *An Economic Theory of Democracy* (Harper: New York 1957).

11 This is quoted from the biography by Robert Colquhoun mentioned in note 1 above, vol. II, p. 342. The whole of Chapter 14 on 'May 1968' contains much relevant material. Apart from the *Mémoires*, Aron has left us with two documents of his attitude to 1968, his attempted analysis in *La Révolution Introuvable*, and the long conversation with two slightly bewildered children of 1968, *Le Spectateur Engagé*. I saw Aron fairly frequently both before and after 1968, and found that his mental processes almost stopped when they – or his interlocutors – led him to 1968. He never got over it and was thus much less relevant as an analyst of later events. Perhaps the events offended his unique French–Anglo-

Saxon blend of rationality and thereby pointed up the limits of a great liberal.

12 This need not be a bad thing. Robert Merton has reminded me of the concept of 'detached concern' which he developed in relation to the role of physicians. See his *Sociological Ambivalence and Other Essays* (Free Press–Macmillan: New York–London 1976), pp. 18ff.

13 Willy Brandt: *Die Abschiedsrede* (Siedler: Berlin 1987), p. 32. The subsequent appeal to 'labour, culture and science' – 'perhaps this is not exactly the centre, but it is the majority anytime' – carries little conviction. 'Culture and science' are not only not the majority, but are naturally divided in their political loyalties, and the vanishing proletariat is one of the reasons for the decline of the electoral fortunes of social democratic parties.

Chapter 6: Crisis in the 1970s

1 A good account of the events of 15 August 1971 and the consequences is given by Susan Strange in her account of 'International Monetary Relations' in Andrew Shonfield (ed.): *International Economic Relations in the Western World 1959–71*, vol. II (Oxford University Press: Oxford–London 1976). I should mention perhaps that as the European Commissioner responsible for foreign trade and foreign relations, I was directly involved in these events and actually led the EC delegation at the special GATT meeting of 25 August 1971.

2 The books of the 1920s are of course by José Ortega y Gasset and Oswald Spengler. Those of the 1970s are (in this sequence) by Michael Shanks, Peter Atteslander, Alvin Toffler, I. Robert Sinai, Mancur Olson, Peter Berger, G. R. Urban, Mancur Olson and Hans Landsberg.

3 Klaus Scholder: *Grenzen der Zukunft* (W. Kohlhammer: Stuttgart 1973), p. 83. Erhard Eppler: *Ende oder Wende* (W. Kohlhammer: Stuttgart 1975), p. 11.

4 The relevant books are: Aurelio Peccei: *The Human Quality* (Pergamon Press: Oxford 1975). D. H. Meadows and D. L. Meadows: *The Limits to Growth*, First Report to the Club of Rome (Universe Books: New York 1972). Mihajlo Mesarovic and Eduard Pestel: *Mankind at the Turning Point*, Second Report to the Club of Rome (Reader's Digest Press: New York 1974).

5 The change was dramatic and is worth documenting. By comparison to 1960–73, rates of growth of total output declined in 1973–83 from 4.17 to 2.04 in the United States, from 5.56 to 2.23 in France, from 4.43 to 1.64 in Germany, from 5.30 to 1.80 in Italy, from 10.43 to 3.70 in Japan. Only in Britain did they remain stable, and low: 2.28 v. 2.22. See Thelma Liesner: *Economic Statistics 1900–1983* (The Economist Publications: London 1985), Table 1, p. 127.

6 Walt W. Rostow: *The World Economy: History and Prospect* (University of Texas Press: Austin–London 1978).

7 Albert Hirschman: *Shifting Involvements: Private Interest and Public Action* (Princeton University Press: Princeton 1978), ch. 1.

8 Mancur Olson: *The Rise and Decline of Nations* (Yale University Press: New Haven 1982).

9 The quotes are from Ed Mishan: *The Economic Growth Debate* (Allen & Unwin: London 1977), and Wilfred Beckerman: *In Defence of Economic Growth* (Jonathan Cape: London 1974).

10 It could be argued that the unspoken rationale of some of the late additions to the social state in the early 1970s was to appease labour when the cost of adjustment to a harsher international climate first became evident. The bargain could only be made once, which explains in part the social climate of the 1980s.

11 Johano Strasser: *Grenzen des Sozialstaates?* (EVA: Köln–Frankfurt 1979), p. 113.

12 Michel Crozier, Samuel Huntington and Joji Watanake: *The Crisis of Democracy* (New York University Press: New York 1975).

13 James Alt: *The Politics of Economic Decline* (Cambridge University Press: Cambridge 1979). See in particular pp. 269ff.

14 See for example Jürgen Habermas: *Legitimationsprobleme im Spätkapitalismus* (Suhrkamp: Frankfurt 1973) and Claus Offe: *Strukturprobleme des kapitalistischen Staates* (Suhrkamp: Frankfurt 1972).

15 In *The Crisis of Democracy*, op. cit. Keith Middlemas made a telling statement to the same effect in his *Politics in Industrial Society: The Experience of the British System Since 1911* (André Deutsch: London 1979): 'Like an overloaded electrical circuit, the system began to blow more fuses than electricians could cope with in that dismal decade.'

16 Daniel Bell: *The Coming of Post-Industrial Society* (Basic Books: New York 1973) and *The Cultural Contradictions of Capitalism* (Basic Books: New York 1976), p. 70. It is hard to resist the comment that when Bell refers to a 'disjunction' of socioeconomic structure and culture, he is in fact talking about the disjunction of his books. Few if any social critics have been as sensitive to social change as Daniel Bell. His books are therefore landmarks of the post-war era. But they also betray the biases of their time. *Post-Industrial Society* belongs to the 1960s, *Cultural Contradictions* to the 1970s (and 'the return of the sacred' to the 1980s).

17 Ronald Inglehart: *The Silent Revolution: Changing Values and Political Styles Among Western Publics* (Princeton University Press: Princeton 1977). The quotes are on pp. 3 and 285. For the definitions see pp. 40–2. Table 2–6 summarizes 'goals of Western publics' (p. 49). Comparisons of 1970, 1973 and 1976 can be found in Table 4–1 (p. 104).

18 'Reversal of trends' is the favourite German phrase, and a whole literature has sprung up under the heading of *Tendenzwende* before the actual political *Wende* in 1982. American neoconservatism around journals like *Commentary* and *The Public Interest* similarly preceded the political change of 1980.

Notes

Chapter 7: Conflict After Class

1 Susan Strange: *Casino Capitalism* (Blackwell: Oxford 1986). Professor Strange too is gloomy: 'For when sheer luck begins to take over and to determine more and more of what happens to people, and skill, effort, initiative, determination and hard work count for less and less, then inevitably faith and confidence in the social and political system quickly fades' (p. 2). Felix Rohatyn: 'On the Brink', *New York Review of Books*, vol. xxxiv, no. 10 (11 June, 1987). Peter Jay made the point in several public speeches. The bestseller is by Ravi Batra: *The Great Depression of 1990* (Simon & Schuster: New York 1987). 19 October 1987 certainly had its Cassandras.

2 The figures have been gathered by Meinhard Miegel of the Institut für Wirtschafts- und Gesellschaftspolitik in Bonn and published in *Die Zeit*, 20 February 1987.

3 I have learned much from a big book and a short article on the subject, both of which originate from authors associated with the New School for Social Research. Hannah Arendt: *The Human Condition* (University of Chicago Press: Chicago 1958). Robert Heilbroner: *The Act of Work* (Library of Congress: Washington 1985).

4 Other games of figures supplement the picture, sometimes with surprising aspects. Take for example statistics of the number of hours worked by industrial workers per year. One would expect Japan to top the OECD league with 2156 hours, but not perhaps to find Germany at the bottom with 1708. Switzerland (1913) and the United States (1912) rank high, France (1771) and Britain (1778) low. See *Die Zeit*, 13 February 1987. (For slightly different figures, see the paper by Maddison quoted in note 6 below.) Jonathan Gershuny has turned the macro-story told here into a micro-story and calculated the number of hours of the day which people have 'saved' by modern developments of work. He has also speculated on the personal and social implications of such change, and on opportunities for giving the free time gained new meaning. See for example 'Lifestyle, Innovation and the Future of Work', in *The Royal Society of Arts Journal*, vol. cxxxv, no. 5371 (June 1987).

5 Cf. José Harris: *Unemployment and Politics: A Study in English Social Policy 1886–1914* (Oxford University Press: London 1972). Alexander Keyssar: *Out of Work: The First Century of Unemployment in Massachusetts* (Cambridge University Press: Cambridge 1986).

6 See Angus Maddison: 'Growth and Slowdown in Advanced Capitalist Economies: Techniques of Quantitative Assessment', in *The Journal of Economic Literature*, vol. xxv, no. 2 (June 1987), p. 686.

7 There are questions of language here which are more than that. Hannah Arendt (see note 3 above) distinguishes between 'labour' (to live), 'work' (to make things) and 'action'. Robert Heilbroner uses 'work' for all these. I have adapted Marx's distinction between (heteronomous)

'work' and (autonomous) 'activity' which is distantly related to Aristotle's 'practical' and 'theoretical life'.

8 The incidence of long-term unemployment is therefore an important test of the analysis suggested here. In Germany, the percentage of unemployed who were out of work for less than a year (and were therefore entitled to 'unemployment pay' rather than 'unemployment assistance' or 'social assistance') has declined from 57 per cent in 1981 to 50 per cent in 1983 and further to 38 per cent in 1986. In other words, in 1986, 62 per cent of the (2.2 million) unemployed were persistently unemployed.

9 For the European position see the contributions to Thomas Schmid (ed.): *Befreiung von falscher Arbeit* (2nd edn, Wagenbach: Berlin 1986). The 'American' position quoted here is R. Heilbroner's (see note 3 above), esp. pp. 22ff.

10 Figures are available from Bureau of Census publications. I have relied here on an unpublished article by Professor Frank Levy of the University of Maryland on 'Poverty and Economic Growth'. See also his book on *Dollars and Dreams: The Changing American Income Distribution* (Russell Sage – Basic Books: New York 1987).

11 This definition is by Mary Jo Bane and Paul Jargowsky in a paper on 'Urban Poverty: Basic Questions' written for the National Academy of Sciences (and as yet unpublished).

12 See Richard P. Nathan: 'Will the Underclass Always Be with Us?' in *Transaction: Social Science and Modern Society*, vol. 24, no. 3 (March–April 1987). Robert Reischauer, Senior Fellow of the Brookings Institution, writes in an unpublished article on 'America's Underclass: Four Unanswered Questions': 'If the underclass is defined to be the population that is poor, lacks skills or an education, and has a limited attachment to the labour force, it could represent as much as 6 percent of the nation's population or 43 percent of the nation's poor. If one subtracts from this group those who are not Black or Hispanic and those who do not live in a large city, the size of the underclass shrinks to 1.2 percent of the population or 8.7 percent of the nation's poor.'

13 There are a number of articles by William Julius Wilson, including 'Cycles of Deprivation and the Underclass Debate', in *Social Services Review*, vol. 59, no. 4 (1985), and the unpublished conference paper 'Social Policy and Minority Groups: What Might Have Been and What Might We See in the Future' (1986) from which I have here quoted. At the time of writing, Wilson's book *The Truly Disadvantaged: Inner City Woes and Public Policy* (University of Chicago Press: Chicago 1987) was not yet published.

14 In the article cited in note 12 above. It proves little that Robert Nathan adds to this statement a reference to the definition of class by 'sociologist Ralf Dahrendorf, in his *Class and Class Conflict in Industrial Society*'. Ken Auletta's articles have been published as a book: *The Underclass* (Random House: New York 1982).

15 When it is talked about, the terms are often wrong. In view of the irresponsibly easy 'genetics' of authors like Adolph Jensen or Hans Eysenck, it is a pleasure to read the piece by Christopher Jencks on 'Genes and Crime' in the *New York Review of Books*, vol. xxxiv, no. 2 (12 February 1987). However, Jencks also notes: 'We are not, I think, any closer to understanding why cultures differ from one another, or why they change over time, than we were thirty years ago.'

16 Fritz Schumacher: *Small Is Beautiful* (Blond & Briggs: London 1973). This book is as much about 'intermediate technologies' for developing countries as it is about decentralization in the First World.

17 Barbara Tuchman: *A Distant Mirror: The Calamitous 14th Century* (Knopf: New York 1978).

18 Theodor Geiger: *Die soziale Schichtung des deutschen Volkes* (F. Enke: Stuttgart 1932), pp. 97 and 111.

19 Lawrence M. Mead: *Beyond Entitlement: The Social Obligations of Citizenship* (Free Press: New York 1986), p. 22.

20 Lambarde's definition is quoted from the Oxford Dictionary on 'anomy'. On Lambarde, the spelling of the word (*anomie* or *anomy*) and the whole history of the concept, there is now the informative book by Marco Orrú: *Anomie: History and Meanings* (Allen & Unwin: Boston 1987).

21 These are references to Émile Durkheim: *Suicide* (Free Press: Glencoe, Ill. 1951) and the essays on 'Social Structure and Anomie' and 'Continuities in the Theory of Social Structure and Anomie' in Robert K. Merton: *Social Theory and Social Structure* (rev. edn, Free Press: Glencoe, Ill. 1957).

22 Michael Zander: 'What Is the Evidence on Law and Order?', *New Society*, vol. 50, no. 897 (13 December 1979), p. 593. Zander claims that in Britain alone 10,000 such cases are known to occur each year.

Chapter 8: A New Social Contract

1 Susan Strange: *Casino Capitalism* (Basil Blackwell: Oxford 1986), p. 193. The quotation on 'chain-smoking youngsters' a little later in the text is on p. 1.

2 I have taken this quotation from John Maynard Keynes's discussion of Schumpeter in his *Treatise on Money* (Cambridge University Press: Cambridge 1971), vol. 2, p. 85, which is interesting because in this respect Keynes 'unreservedly accepts' Schumpeter's view.

3 Mrs Thatcher may not have read Martin Wiener's book: *English Culture and the Decline of the Industrial Spirit 1850–1980* (Cambridge University Press: Cambridge 1981). In any case, it is striking that as an advocate of her own policies, she goes down better in the United States than in Britain. She appeals to an American tradition which has something to do with why people left Britain three centuries ago and looked for open frontiers across the seas.

4 A report to Governor Cuomo of New York in 1987 was entitled 'A New Social Contract: Re-Thinking the Nature and Purpose of Public Assistance'. However, this 'social contract' is usually related to 'workfare' (see for example 'Re-Writing the Social Contract for America's Have-Nots', *New York Times*, 12 April 1987), and is in my sense a private rather than a social contract.

5 This was the case in the 1920s too. See Theodor Geiger: *Die soziale Schichtung des deutschen Volkes* (F. Enke: Stuttgart 1932), pp. 100–1 on the *Intellektuellenproletariat*.

6 It may be no more than an accident that Ronald Inglehart refers to Charles Reich's *Greening of America* in discussing the 'post-materialist outlook' in *The Silent Revolution* (Princeton University Press: Princeton 1977), p. 64. In any case, Inglehart's book offers much material that is relevant to this discussion.

7 The earlier quotations are from 'Am I a Liberal?' in *Essays in Persuasion*, vol. ix of the *Collected Writings* (Macmillan: London 1972), pp. 296 and 299. There also the five headings of a liberal agenda (p. 301). The last quotation is from a letter to Sir Archibald Sinclair on 4 April 1938, reprinted in vol. xxviii of the *Collected Writings* (Macmillan: London 1982), p. 107.

8 John Gray: *Liberalism* (University of Minnesota Press: Minneapolis 1986), p. 82.

9 Here I had in mind the Report by a High-Level Group of Experts to the Secretary-General of OECD on *Labour Market Flexibility* (OECD: Paris 1986).

10 Basic income guarantees have been discussed, adopted, rejected and discussed again since Daniel P. Moynihan published his book *The Politics of a Guaranteed Income* (Random House: New York 1973). A very useful discussion of the subject and the literature (in German) can be found in Klaus-Uwe Gerhardt and Arndt Weber: 'Garantiertes Mindesteinkommen', in Thomas Schmid (ed.): *Befreiung von falscher Arbeit* (2nd edn, Klaus Wagenbach: Berlin 1986).

11 *Social Insurance and Allied Services: Report by Sir William Beveridge* (HMSO: London 1942), p. 11. See chapters 16 and 17 in José Harris: *William Beveridge: A Biography* (Clarendon Press: Oxford 1977).

12 'Wet' is of course Mrs Thatcher's description of her enemies in the Conservative Party, the Disraeli Tories who advocate 'one nation'. The Oxford Dictionary does not recognize the word, except perhaps in connection with 'wet Quakers' (or 'Mormons') who are 'not very strict in the observance of their sect'. I notice that Keynes (in the letter quoted in note 7 above) speaks of 'watery Labour men'.

13 In connection with his definition of a Liberal, see note 7 above.

14 Quoted from James Buchanan: 'The Constitution of Economic Policy', *The American Economic Review*, vol. 77, no. 3 (June 1987). Buchanan lists his own *Limits of Liberty* as well as the joint works with Geoffrey

Brennan (*The Reason of Rules*) and Gordon Tullock (*The Calculus of Consent*) in the context.

15 Actually, this is Carl Friedrich's translation of the 'Idee zu einer allgemeinen Geschichte in weltbürgerlicher Absicht' in the volume edited by him: *The Philosophy of Kant: Immanuel Kant's Moral and Political Writings* (New York 1949). I have used two other translations (and sometimes confounded them). One is by H. B. Nisbet, 'Idea for a Universal History with a Cosmopolitan Purpose', in Hans Reiss (ed.): *Kant's Political Writings* (Cambridge University Press: Cambridge 1970); the other by Lewis White Beck, 'Idea for a Universal History from a Cosmopolitan Point of View', in Ernst Behler (ed.): *Immanuel Kant: Philosophical Writings* (Continuum: New York 1986).

16 Schumpeter on Keynes is quoted from the obituary 'John Maynard Keynes 1883–1946', *American Economic Review*, vol. xxxvi, no. 4 (September 1946).

17 Albert O. Hirschman: *Exit, Voice and Loyalty: Responses to Decline in Firms, Organizations and States* (Harvard University Press: Cambridge–London 1970), esp. p. 19 and ch. 9.

18 See 'Around Exit, Voice and Loyalty' in Albert O. Hirschman: *Essays in Trespassing: Economics to Politics and Beyond* (Cambridge University Press: Cambridge 1981), esp. pp. 265 and (for the following point) 223.

19 Robert Skidelsky: *John Maynard Keynes*, vol. i (Viking Penguin: New York 1986), p. 399. Keynes's other recent biographer, whose book I have also found useful, makes the point about the conservative revolutionary even in the title. Cf. Charles H. Hession: *John Maynard Keynes: A Personal Biography of the Man Who Revolutionized Capitalism and the Way We Live* (Macmillan: New York–London 1984).

20 *The General Theory of Employment, Interest and Money*, vol. vii of the *Collected Works* (Macmillan: London 1973), p. 372.

21 Thus in vol. ix of the *Collected Works*, the *Essays in Persuasion* (Macmillan: London 1972), p. 373.

22 See Karl Popper: *The Poverty of Historicism* (Routledge & Kegan Paul: London 1957), esp. pp. 64–70 on 'Piecemeal versus Utopian Engineering'.

23 J. M. Keynes: op. cit., 1972, p. 331.

Index

Index